THE HOT
EMPIRE OF CHILE

Bilingual Press/Editorial Bilingüe

General Editor
Gary D. Keller

Managing Editor
Karen S. Van Hooft

Associate Editors
Barbara H. Firoozye
Thea S. Kuticka

Assistant Editor
Linda St. George Thurston

Editorial Consultant
Ted Woestendiek

Address:
Bilingual Press
Hispanic Research Center
Arizona State University
P.O. Box 872702
Tempe, Arizona 85287-2702
(480) 965-3867

THE HOT EMPIRE OF CHILE

Kent Ian Paterson

Bilingual Press/Editorial Bilingüe
Tempe, Arizona

ISBN 0-927534-91-6

Library of Congress Cataloging-in-Publication Data

Paterson, Kent Ian.
    The hot empire of chile / Kent Ian Patterson.
       p.   cm.
    Includes index.
    ISBN 0-927534-91-6 (alk. paper)
    1. Hot pepper industry.   2. Hot pepper industry—New Mexico.   I. Title.

  HD9235.P46 P38 2000
   338.1'7384—dc21

                                                00-037857

PRINTED IN THE UNITED STATES OF AMERICA

Cover and interior design by John Wincek, Aerocraft Charter Art Services

Photo Credits
The photos in this volume appear courtesy of the following sources and photographers:

Text pages
Glen Elliott: p. 9

Ken Hjelmstad: pp. 64, 75, 82, 97, 119, 184, 187, 209

Rose Palmisano: pp. 51, 52, 157, 212

Rio Grande Historical Collections/New Mexico State University Library: pp. 20, 31, 63, 86, 110

Sin Fronteras Organizing Project/Border Agricultural Workers Center, El Paso, Texas: pp. 55, 143, 144, 147, 148, 160, 173, 197

Color insert (following p. 118)
Ken Hjelmstad: p. 2, top; p. 4, top and bottom

Rio Grande Historical Collections/New Mexico State University Library: p. 1, top; p. 2, bottom

Sin Fronteras Organizing Project/Border Agricultural Workers Center, El Paso, Texas: p. 1, bottom; p. 3, top and bottom

Contents

Foreword

I certainly never set out to write a book about chile peppers. Like most New Mexicans, natives or longtime transplants, I took chile for granted, devouring it daily as part of my culinary routine. But back in 1985, in between college and graduate school and without a steady job, I pursued the insane notion of making a living as a freelance journalist. At the urging of a colleague and close friend, Jessamyn Young, the two of us embarked on an investigation of pesticide use in New Mexico. It was a time when union leader César Chávez was forcing the issue of farmworker poisonings onto the national environmental agenda.

With the support of Roger Morris and the Santa Fe-based New Mexico Project for Investigative Reporting, Young and I soon found ourselves in Hatch, New Mexico, the self-proclaimed "chile capital of the world," and then in the tiny offices of the then-fledgling Sin Fronteras Organizing Project/Border Agricultural Workers Union in El Paso, Texas. Subsequent travels on the chile trail took me thousands of miles from the roadside *ristra* stands of northern New Mexico to the first jalapeño cannery in Xalapa, Veracruz, well into southern Mexico. What resulted from these encounters was a long-term series of radio stories and print pieces not only about pesticides, but about the larger world of the New Mexico chile industry as well. Much of the information contained in this book was gleaned from news reports and documentaries I produced over the years for KUNM-FM in Albuquerque, New Mexico, and other public radio stations and networks. Special acknowledgment must be given to KUNM's venerable news director, Marcos Martínez, for maintaining an interest in the complex elements of this story long after most editors probably would have decided it was old hat. A very special thank you also goes out to Wayne Muller and Bread for the Journey of Santa Fe for providing some timely travel funds when money got tight.

Of course, mention must be made of the countless activists, scholars, farmers, farmworkers, processors, and others—the hundreds of them—who shared their time, talents, and thoughts with me. In this regard, I am forever indebted to Carlos Marentes, Raúl Medina, Pam Roy, Dennis Valdés, Carlos Vásquez, and Craig Newbill. Kudos to Norma Paterson for assisting with some tricky translations, and praise to the librarians and staff at Rio Grande Special Collections at New Mexico State University for facilitating the search of old, often dusty archives. To my parents, Antoinette and Ian Paterson, tons of credit for stressing the value and importance of education and questioning the powers that be. Timeless inspirations later came from Karina.

Much of the original material contained in this book was collected from 1985 to 1993, a time when the New Mexico chile industry was undergoing a historic boom and the state's first farmworker movement in decades was raising cain in the fields. Certain sections were revised, added, and updated some time later, when the combination of man-made and natural forces, i.e., the North American Free Trade Agreement and the pepper weevil, set off a historic decline of the New Mexico chile empire. As a result, it is my belief that this book represents a look at an important New Mexican economic and cultural institution during what were perhaps its most critical years. Finally, thanks to Gary Keller and the editors at Arizona State University's Bilingual Press for having the courage to publish a book that New Mexican publishing houses found too "hot" to handle. This book is dedicated to Laura Ixchel and Julia Zintil. May they live to see a world truly without borders.

Kent Ian Paterson
ALBUQUERQUE, NEW MEXICO

LAS FRONTERAS DE NUEVO MÉXICO Y CHIHUAHUA

THE BORDERLANDS OF NEW MEXICO AND CHIHUAHUA

© *Las Fronteras* (Columbus, NM), April-May 1993.

Introduction

NEW MEXICO AND THE INTERNATIONAL JUNGLE OF CHILE

Down a shortcut valley road between Las Cruces, New Mexico, and the old village of Mesilla are the incubation chambers of the hottest business in the contemporary world. Christened the Fabián García Science Center of New Mexico State University, this is the place where the latest varieties of the capsicum, or chile pepper, are bred.

Some regard this leafy, pod-bearing fruit, which flowers here in a dazzling variety of shapes and colors, as a wonder plant—a superhero of the horticultural world—that can entice the bite of a mouse, tempt the tongue of a wily coyote, send a grouchy bear roaring off into the thickets, and make many a macho man shed a tear.

Rich in both vitamin A and vitamin C, chile is the pizzazz in everything from salsas to spices to self-defense sprays. Not always pungent, it is used as a coloring in cosmetics and pill capsules. Discovered to be a good meat preservative, chile can make that frozen pork, chicken, or beef casserole a tasty treat after cold storage. Heatless chile,

or paprika, is a good natural color substitute in salad dressings, tomato sauce, condiments, baked goods, soups, candies, bologna, frankfurters, sausages, pet foods, oriental dishes, Cajun recipes, and more. As an object of controversy, chile has been claimed by its boosters as a possible cure for cancer and studied by its detractors as a possible cause of the disease. Capsaicin, the compound which gives chile its bite, has earned the damnation of the American Civil Liberties Union for its use in mace sprays. At its heart, though, chile is much more than an ingredient in sauces, salsas and sprays.

Utilized with beans, tortillas, and its close relatives the tomato and potato, chile has transformed the culinary temperament and character of the North American diet. Burritos and tacos, spiced with chile, are gaining a foothold alongside hamburgers and hot dogs. Jalapeño-topped nachos are a popular treat in stadiums, restaurants, and bars. In the supermarket, nacho cheese chips and tortilla strips accompanied by salsa lure shoppers. Chile has ended forever the dominance of the ketchup-laden hamburger and the onion-dipped plain chip.

Behind this shift are a number of sweeping economic and sociological changes. The surge in immigration to the United States from Third World nations produced a multitude of ethnic eateries in cities where *salsa mexicana*, Indian curry powder, and Thai peppers are all standard fare. As people from chile-using cultures settle in the various regions of the United States, their food, if not always their presence, becomes increasingly accepted.

From virtually the very beginning the chile pepper had an international character and flavor. Scientists think the fiery food originated in the hill country of Bolivia or Brazil and then was spread by seed-carrying birds to Mexico and other regions of the Americas where it became a staple of the Aztecs and other peoples. Centuries later chile was a prize of European expansionists, bagged with the gold Columbus and succeeding colonialists carried back with them to their sponsoring kings. In a short time, chile seeds appeared in Asia and Africa.

Prized for its versatile properties, chile has been a symbol of empire building and empire dismantling. The Aztecs demanded chile from subject tribes as tribute and utilized the scorching smoke of the pepper as a means of political control and torture. Much later, Chinese Communist revolutionaries, led by the notorious pepper-lover Mao Ze Dong, sang a tune composed in honor of a rebel chile fed up with the oppression of the vegetable kingdom. On their marches to overthrow warlords, Kuomingtang bureaucrats, and Japanese invaders, the guerrillas composed their own song to the imaginary Red chile that organized other members of the vegetable family in collective revolution. Ironically, the ardor of the nationalistic Chinese Communists for the chile was the result

of an embryonic imperialism that uprooted the world. After the European conquest of the Americas, seeds hopscotched the globe and were cross-pollinated in a circular breeding pattern that connected Mexican chile to Peruvian chile to Hungarian chile to New Mexican chile to California chile and so on.

One of the major chile-growing centers emerged in New Mexico, where a debate raged on the origin of the treasure of the Land of Enchantment. Was chile a result of the Pueblo Indians' trade with the indigenous nations of the Mexican interior? Or was its presence a consequence of the Spanish-Mexican colonization of New Mexico at the end of the sixteenth century, brought with the *conquistadores* from the Mexican heartland? Whatever the truth, the chile pepper became an essential part of the New Mexican culture, celebrated in paintings and artwork, praised in poems and songs, and eaten with abandon at virtually every meal.

From the late sixteenth century, chile was a source of food and communal strength for the Native American and Spanish-speaking New Mexican farmers. Every year they pitched in to work the acequia ditches that nourished the fickle chile plants, creating a rhythmic harvest cycle from the season of hand-planting seeds to the stringing of chile *ristras* and the stewing of red chile at Christmas time. Chile picking and the making of *ristras* were family affairs, bringing together relatives and *vecinos* in a shared cultural activity.

Even the gringo conquerors were charmed. Peppers were purchased by U.S. soldiers and, in 1847, an officer ordered seed to be planted for the troops at an army outpost. A territorial New Mexican newspaper later applauded the U.S. Congress in 1863 for approving road-building, an activity which in part would enable "the transportation of chile colorado." Not everyone was as thrilled. In an 1871 report to the Secretary of the Interior, Professor Cyrus Thomas noted the northern New Mexican chile crop. "I beg to be excused," pleaded Thomas, "unless I can have my throat lined with something less sensitive than nature's coating."

Subsequently, fewer farmers grew chile in the northern villages Thomas observed, but the crop expanded in the southern section of the state. Curiously, European immigrants from France, England, and Austria (countries not known for their spicy cuisine), aided by New Mexico State University (NMSU) researchers and plant breeders of Mexican and Japanese descent, were leaders in blazing the path of the commercial chile industry. Over time, New Mexico-grown chiles were tailored to fit the market. Now, long greens are for chile rellenos, enchilada sauce, and stew. Cayennes are for powder and Louisiana hot sauce, jalapeños are for nachos and salsa, and the mild varieties are used in paprika.

In New Mexico, where in 1965 the chile was proclaimed the state vegetable, and where stinging, walloping names like Barker's Extra Hot flourish alongside sweet ones like the R-Naky, the pepper blossom is topped off by the dollar sign. Between $230 million and $300 million of them stacked up annually in the early 1990s in the thick of the Great Chile Boom. Thousands of people earned their livelihoods by planting, picking, processing, and peddling the pepper pod. At one point, more New Mexicans depended on chile for their paychecks than on the California electronics plants relocating to the Albuquerque area.

The pepper occupied farmers, who mulled over the sprouting seeds, strained the backs of pickers who rode for hours in rickety buses to reach the fields, tickled the noses of cannery workers who counted chiles like sheep, and weighed down the cargoes of truck drivers who

even honked at the cellblocks of the Albuquerque jail. It brought tips to the pockets of waitresses who repeated the query "Red or green?" like a broken record and, of course, filled the stomachs not only of New Mexicans but of a growing flock of culinary enthusiasts worldwide who just could not get enough of the stuff. Thousands of New Mexicans and visitors from places as far-flung as Brooklyn and Hawaii flocked to yearly chile-honoring extravaganzas. These included the Hatch Chile Festival, the Santa Fe Wine and Chile Festival, the Texas-New Mexico Chile War cook-offs, and Las Cruces's own Whole Enchilada Festival, where a processing company donated hundreds of pounds of peppers to make giant, eight-foot-long enchiladas.

If outsiders could not visit New Mexico to sample its chile, the pepper was taken to the outsiders. State promoters, anxious to sell the Land of Enchantment to visitors and investors, delegated an ambassadorial role to the New Mexico chile. In a modern rerun of the old Santa Fe railroad trans-country produce trips, Albuquerque tourism boosters with chiles packed in their hip-pockets boarded an Amtrak train and headed to Kansas City where the pods were used in sales pitches to clients. In 1991, when New Mexico got its chance to exhibit a giant Christmas tree outside the White House, lights shaped in the form of red chile peppers dangled from the spruce's branches. NMSU Dean John Owens called chile the "magic" plant and New Mexico the "magic kingdom."

Nurtured by university researchers, farmers, and state boosters, New Mexico chile found its niche in international agribusiness. The pepper became a centerpiece of the New Mexico Economic Development Division's strategic plan during the most recent administration of Governor Bruce King. "Adobes, Green Chile and High Tech" was the slogan coined in the state capital of Santa Fe. As any self-respecting chilehead knows, New Mexico is the center of the U.S. chile universe. But this status was not always the case. It was a timely convergence of twentieth-century agricultural innovations, international economic trends, and the realities of an underdeveloped Mexico on New Mexico's doorstep that put the land of the red and the green on the pepper throne.

Prior to the advent of the NMSU program, it was in the swampy lowlands of Louisiana where the mass U.S. commercial industry actually got off its feet—most likely as plunder from the 1846-48 Mexican War when historians think returning U.S. soldiers came home with seeds of the Tabasco chile. The war booty spawned a Louisiana hot sauce business that made its mark in the 1850s before being interrupted by the Civil War.

After that conflict, a Louisiana banker by the name of Edmund McIlhenny encountered little left on his Avery Island plantation save for a few sturdy Tabasco chile plants. The resourceful businessman went on a mashing spree, blending the red peppers into a hot sauce and, in 1868, launched his world-famous Tabasco sauce. Soon one-dollar bottles of the flaming stuff went to customers in New York and Europe. The McIlhenny Company was among the first to chart the path of the U.S. chile business. Like the Tabasco kingpins, the others were also distantly situated from the garden-like plantings that prevailed in a chile-loving New Mexico whose time was yet to come.

At the turn of the twentieth century, chile was nationally valued not only as an ingredient in hot sauce but also as a zesty additive to ginger ale and as paprika. In 1905 the U.S. Department of Agriculture (USDA) attempted to launch a paprika industry to compete with Spain and Hungary by sponsoring an association of growers in Florence County, South Carolina. The USDA supplied the farmers with seed and directions to cultivate the mild paprika.

Around this time, a pimiento pepper industry emerged in Georgia and California. Still another major pepper-producing region was New Jersey, which in 1926 led the nation in production with 7,500 acres. The state was mainly known for its sweet bell peppers, but it also produced a "mild hot variety" pepper aimed at the New York City area. The Gulf Coast of Louisiana hosted a vibrant pepper-growing industry, growing 2,850 acres in 1926 for delicacies that included Tabasco-laced oyster sauce. Today McIlhenny's few dozen or so acres of Avery Island Tabasco chiles are among the surviving stands in the state.

Next to Louisiana, California was the second major staging ground of the U.S. commercial chile industry, supplying two-thirds of domestic dried chile by the 1930s and maintaining a lead over New Mexico until the mid 1970s. Actually, much of California commercial chile had a New Mexican origin from seeds taken to the Golden State by Emilio Ortega at the dawn of the century and reborn as the Anaheim chile created by H. L. Musser in 1903. In 1906, Ortega opened a processing plant near Los Angeles to can the Anaheim, now one of the most profitable items of Nestle. Ortega subsequently expanded to the lucrative salsa market, spreading the message through Hollywood actor Jack Palance's commercial "Mex to the Max." California's valleys produced other jewels. Walker Foods, founded in 1914, specializes in the cascabella or yellow hot variety. "(We're) the largest processor of yellows in the world. God's the one that grows them," touted General

Manager Mitchell DeWitt. And Cal-Compack, the so-called "Cadillac of the red chile industry," made its debut in the 1940s.

Yet time was running out for both California and Louisiana. In the 1960s the McIlhenny Co. went south to grow peppers because of plant diseases ruining the Louisiana crop and the availability of inexpensive labor. In the Dominican Republic, Colombia, Venezuela, Guatemala, Honduras, and Mexico the hot sauce heroes found "a bunch of nimble fingers ready and willing" to pick the hand-harvested Tabasco, according to Paul McIlhenny. In the search for new fertile plots, the distinctive red McIlhenny Tabasco chile was even cultivated briefly in New Mexico's Mesilla Valley.

Meanwhile, California's chile plantations fluctuated between four and seven thousand acres, affected by insects, disease, and virus outbreaks in older growing areas; urbanization in places such as Orange and Santa Clara counties; and drought, international competition, and the perceived threat of farmworker unionization. This led California and Louisiana processors to search for new sources of chile, whether in New Mexico, Baja California, or Delicias, Mexico. Southern New Mexico benefited from the "burn-out" of the older mass market producing areas in Louisiana and California.

The evolution of the Louisiana and California industries is important in understanding the rise of the New Mexico chile empire because it characterized an industry-wide pattern of periodic scrambles for disease-free soil and cheap, compliant labor. New Mexico also gained from the decline in paprika production in politically turbulent parts of Europe, the Mideast, and Africa, as well as from the U.S. Food and Drug Administration's phase-out of synthetic FD&C Red No. 2 dye in the mid-1970s. This opened a new opportunity for producers of the mild red paprika used as coloring.

In the late 1960s and early 1970s, conditions were ideal for the crowning of the New Mexico chile king. A sandy loam soil nourished a fertile ground in which a chile culture had taken root. The mid-range elevations of four to five thousand feet, freshened by summer rains, welcomed a generally friendly sun, usually neither too cold nor too hot for the sensitive skin of the chile. The Elephant Butte Irrigation District, a massive government-built project, channeled a reliable water source from the Rio Grande, offering cheaper water rates compared to California's. NMSU's pepper labs, then under the direction of Dr. Roy Nakayama, gave a dynamic boost to research and development. Across the state line in Texas, Mexican foods manufacturers provided an easy, proximate mass market. And last but far from least, the closeness to Mexico guaranteed a never-ending stream of low-cost labor.

Still, the vitality of New Mexico's chile industry as it approached the twenty-first century was questionable, influenced by economic forces far beyond the famed sunsets. What began as a business initially regionalized by a few wheeling and dealing traders ended up being shaped by the largest giants of international agribusiness. The farmers' fate rested in the hands of these companies, many of which also bought chile not only from New Mexico but also from California, Arizona, Texas, China, India, Mexico, Colombia, and Zimbabwe. The New Mexico chile-growing industry had ceased being an essentially local business as more farmers lined up to sign contracts with the packers and the processors. It was a fundamental change in the nature of the business, from the roadside stands and direct sales of yesteryear to the sorting lines of big corporations. It signified the changing identity of the chile farmer, who was less likely to be a planter utilizing hand-me-down skills and seeds passed on by his father and more likely to be a grower aware of world financial and commodities markets, hybrid seeds and chemical inputs, and technological advances. In southern New Mexico, chile played a huge role in carving out the modern face of agribusiness. Simultaneously, it helped change the demographic and social makeup of the southern counties, drawing in a new wave of Mexican immigrants who founded unincorporated communities called *colonias*.

The worker *colonias*, brimming with a youthful population, helped keep a vibrant Spanish language alive in New Mexico and renewed the historic economic-cultural link with old Mexico. Filling mesquite-scaped lots on the desert's edge, the *colonias* became the scene of struggles over what many people in the United States took for granted: decent housing, sewage, water hookups, and paved roads.

At the same time, the chile industry created the conditions for what was one of the most militant labor movements in the state since the "Salt of the Earth" strikes in the Silver City mines in the 1950s. The chile picker protests were perhaps the inevitable culmination of an industry that grew from its modest, cottagelike beginnings to a complex farm-factory system. Similar in some respects to the great cotton era that preceded it in the southern counties, New Mexico chile underwent a boom only to face a shaky future at the pinnacle of its fame.

Follow the history of chile and one can trace important contours in the history of New Mexico. The journey of the New Mexican chile mirrored the history of the state and milestones in its development. Accordingly, the social and economic function of chile continued to

change. The pepper went from a regionally consumed crop in the Rio Grande Valley, north and south, to a commodity bought and sold in the farthest corners of the globe. From a defining cultural item of the New Mexican homeland it became an icon and mass marketing tool, plastered on the ads of the large corporations that appropriated more and more of the harvest. From an emblem of a fairly egalitarian rural New Mexico, chile was transformed into a crop that signified a growing division between commercially successful farmers and less successful ones and called attention to class divisions in the countryside.

There exists a myth of New Mexico chile as a cute, picturesque memento grown in patches here and there by a weathered, quaint people. While on the surface chile symbolized the Chicano, Mexicano, and Native American core of New Mexico, it also exemplified an economically poor New Mexico whose destiny was in the hands of large, out-of-state-based institutions, government or private.

In the final analysis, chile became one more New Mexican resource like cattle, copper, and uranium, to be bought and sold by the new caretakers of the colony. The final years of the twentieth century were another crossroads in New Mexico's chile country, a time when the North American Free Trade Agreement, uncertain new technologies, threatening plant infestations, and overproduction jolted the confidence of chile's overseers, leaving farmers and farmworkers wondering what lay in store for them. This book is a chronicle of their struggles and triumphs and their successes and failures in a business that began as a New Mexican staple and was then ushered out of the Rio Grande Valley to stamp its bite on all corners of the shrinking planet.

The Blossoming of the Chile Culture

2

It was in the name of the King of Spain that the staff of the chile empire was first firmly planted in the red earth of New Mexico. Late in 1598, an exhausted caravan, weary from months of travel in ox-carts, halted at the Indian Pueblo of El Yunque on the Chama and Rio Grande rivers. The 400 Spanish and Mexican sojourners rested after an arduous trip begun in Santa Barbara, Mexico. They then braved the wasteland of the Chihuahuan desert, waded the ford at El Paso del Norte, and followed the meandering Rio Grande past the thick stands of woodland, or bosque, then alive with jumping fish, turtles, bear, and beaver. Others had arrived before them, also as representatives of the King, but the men and women under the leadership of Don Juan de Oñate had a different mission: to establish a permanent settlement for New Spain on the isolated northern frontier of the New World empire. In their necessary provisions were chile pepper seeds from the heartland of colonial Mexico.

Nearly 400 years later, on a tiny patch of land below the snow-capped peaks of the Sangre de Cristo mountain range and not far from the spot where Oñate's settlers erected the first Spanish capital of New Mexico, 102-year-old Don Esquipula Vigil contemplated another season of chile planting. In his rituals of planting, irrigating and hoeing, Don Esquipula was practicing skills which had been handed down to him and thousands of other New Mexicans ever since Oñate's caravan initiated a full-blown chile culture in El Valle de Chama. The old farmer used seed he religiously saved after each harvest.

Born in 1892, Don Esquipula had worked many jobs—as a migrant worker, sawmill hand, carpenter, farmer, and rancher. But when asked what crop he continued to grow in his garden, even at his advanced age, he unhesitatingly replied, "chile." Chile had become a staple of Don Esquipula and his *paisanos* up and down the Rio Grande, Chama, and Upper Pecos valleys. Springtime marked the start of the annual chile season, ushered in by the planting of wetted seed, which frequently had been soaked in manure, a quarter-inch deep in the soil. The summer months, cooled by the afternoon deluges from rain-bloated clouds bursting over the chile fields, were a period of back-bending labor spent thinning and weeding the fragile plants.

In August or September, chile was picked green and consumed fresh, or roasted, peeled, and hung out to dry. In the weeks ahead, the remaining pods, now a matured red, were hand-picked and left out in the sun to dry. There they graced the landscape with a beautiful crimson shadow as seasonal as the changing colors of the aspens on the high mountains, where the winter snowpack held the spring water for the streams and rivers that supplied a system of irrigation canals, or *acequias*, that sustained the chile, corn, bean, squash and fruit crops.

Culturally, the crop was of major importance to the lives of the Native American and Spanish-speaking New Mexicans. Cooperation was key for sharing the acequia's waters and family participation paramount in the tedious tasks of picking, drying, and stringing. Such events were occasions for community get-togethers, celebrations, and parties. The pepper was perhaps as important to the New Mexicans as the potato was to the Irish and perhaps surpassed its cousin of the *solanaceae* plant family in value.

In this harsh land with its alternately hot and cool climate, chile, whether powdered, dried, or fresh, spiced up stews and sauces and flavored beef, goat, deer, and sheep meat. Specialized dishes such as the stuffed *chiles rellenos* or red-chile soaked *carne adobada* became New Mexican specialties. People developed an indestructible pride in their chile. Each village claimed to grow the best, each home to prepare the finest. Places like Chimayo, San Juan, Velarde, and Puerto de

Luna became synonymous with the fall chile harvest. Eventually, there developed such a personal attitude toward chile that many scoffed at the claims of gourmet restaurants or sophisticated food processors to deliver the greatest. Insiders knew the best was in home recipes and that life without chile was practically unthinkable.

Growing chile, however ubiquitous an occupation in New Mexico, was nevertheless a tricky proposition even under the best of circumstances. The pepper was a fragile plant which could be terminated prematurely by field rodents, blown to the four winds, snapped up by a late or an early frost, or mowed over by a hailstorm. A deep pride was felt at the conclusion of a fruitful growing season.

The inseparability of the New Mexicans from their chile was something outsiders, especially Washington bureaucrats, had difficulty grasping. When federal relief aid flowed into New Mexico during the depths of the Great Depression, food packages lacked beans and chile. Reports of colds and health ailments increased, and observers claimed school children's health fared better once chile was restored to its rightful spot on the table. Hispanos and Native Americans alike valued their chile as an item of consumption, barter, and sale. Tied together in a long string of dried red pods called *ristras*, chile commanded a handsome exchange rate, bringing a supply of meat, potatoes, wheat, blankets, jewelry, and even eagle feathers in return. Chile was a reason for the Navajos and Apaches to visit the Rio Grande Pueblos and trade.

Chile's appeal transcended the different cultures in New Mexico and did not escape the notice of certain newcomers setting foot in the territory and state, both the early tourists whisked to the Pueblos and Hispano villages and the artists who eyed the intriguing land. Almost immediately, the founders of what would later be a billion-dollar tourist industry capitalized on the curious sights and smells of the chile pod.

"There are no more picturesque scenes in the entire state of New Mexico than the gray adobe houses, adorned with long strings of red chiles suspended from the roofs to dry in the warm sunshine, late in the fall," claimed the authors of one tourist brochure from the early twentieth century. "It is a picture familiar to every resident of this state,

A New Mexican Icon: Chile *ristras* at the Santa Fe Farmer's Market.

and one that many celebrated artists have painted. Their canvasses have sold for large sums in eastern galleries, but no artist can picture the savory taste of the succulent chile, which grows to such rare perfection in the fertile soil of this productive state."

For good measure, the brochure's writers added instructions on the preparation of New Mexican chile, especially cautioning novice cooks on the pitfalls of chile con carne (actually a Texas creation) and practically begging them to take delicate care in making sure the chile was correctly prepared in order to avoid the consequences of slackers who, unwilling to put in the labor needed to make a good chile pulp, stirred up a "sloppy concoction unfit for the human stomach." After Spanish-speaking northern New Mexicans colonized southern Colorado in the mid-1800s, a vibrant trade developed. Naturally cherished was the New Mexico-grown chile, packaged in five-foot-long *ristras de chile*. From Cundiyo,

Chimayo, and other towns, "fruit wagons," or *carretas*, loaded with chile and other produce headed north to the cool country of Colorado, where the temperatures and elevation were not kind to capsicum. Shipments of chile were sold or exchanged for wheat and potatoes, crops the southern Coloradans specialized in raising. Yet the trade did more than just keep the people happy through the winter; it solidified the independent-minded *manito* culture of northern New Mexico and southern Colorado.

At the turn of the century, Don Esquipula joined the wagons and knocked on the doors of villagers in Trinidad and Trinchera, where good luck could fetch a hefty $1.50 a string. One year he remembered earning the enormous, rewarding sum of $70 for his trouble.

For the young Vigil, who immensely enjoyed the mountain vistas and roadside horses he glimpsed, the weeks-long trips were both a rite of manhood and an economic imperative.

He was part of a generation of New Mexicans for whom the perennial treks northward spelled adventure and survival. "We just used [chile] for ourselves," remembered Vigil. "But after a little while, we left to sell chile in Mora [New Mexico], in Colorado, selling *ristras*."

In a society that was changing from a traditional subsistence economy to a modern capitalist one, chile was destined to become a cash crop—and an important one to boot. But not any old *ristra* would do. A quality *ristra* had to be the right size, the right color, and the right wrap. "A string, to bring top price, must be at least five feet in length, must be closely strung, and have very few moldy peppers in it," observed New Mexico agricultural economist P. W. Cockerill in 1944. A *ristra* not tied and prepared correctly was the catalyst of much haggling and argument.

Nevertheless, chile was only a supplemental—if significant—source of cash. Possessing small plots of a few acres or so, northern and middle Rio Grande Valley farmers could not support a growing population solely from their chile and other harvests. So, commencing in the late 1800s, an epic, annual migration overtook the Rio Grande Valley as young boys and men left their homes to seek seasonal employment as shepherds, potato pickers, beet harvesters, and miners in the states of Colorado, Utah, Wyoming, and Montana.

A modern train, the Denver, Rio Grande and Western Railroad, servicing Colorado and northern New Mexico, hastened the yearly outflow, transporting people and peppers to points north. The train earned a nickname, "the Chili Line," the origin of which, according to various accounts of the time, had to do with either the hot cargo on board destined for Colorado or the conductor's habit of announcing "chile stop" for lunch break. Passenger Forest Crosen added

another explanation when on one of the train's last runs he was struck by the trackside adobe houses "all flaming red with drying chile, exclaiming at the sheer beauty of it, realizing why some wit long ago had called the railroad 'the Chili Line.'"

Don Esquipula and his friends hopped aboard the train and connecting railroads with the stern motivation of finding work up north, frequently stowing away and hiding from the clubs of the railway bull inspectors. Once, on one of the "tramping" excursions, he lost a friend to the merciless grind of the locomotive wheels.

The northern New Mexicans greeted the departures and arrivals of the "Chili Line" with great fanfare. Susie Martínez of Chimayo, New Mexico, recounted how her father's trips to the sheep camps were eagerly anticipated.

"When the 'Chili Line' arrived in Española the people all gathered there, and it was a big thing," said Martínez. "It would blow its horn and the people would gather there because they were coming back home with a little money and that meant a lot to them."

While the men were laboring in the north, the remaining family members, usually women and children, were left behind to nurture the chile plants until the men came home.

The founding and flourishing of the "Chili Line" was another milestone in the economic transformation that had descended on northern New Mexico and southern Colorado by the dawn of the twentieth century. With the U.S. conquest and the opening of the railroads, big capital put its stamp on the daily lives of the villagers. Investments in ranching, farming, mining, and timber were made throughout the region. Merchants appeared on the scene acting as middlemen who traded and sold imported commodities of all kinds and accepted, often on credit, the products of the land. Charles Ilfeld, the Las Vegas, New Mexico wholesaler, epitomized the new class of outside commercial intermediaries. A German immigrant, Ilfeld became the largest wholesale trader in New Mexico. Thousands of New Mexicans exchanged their goods and ran up their credit with the one-time ox-cart-driving trader.

As an Ilfeld company executive observed in the 1920s, the enterprise, in imitation of the New Mexico state motto, "shall grow as the time goes on." And indeed it prospered, buoyed by the new mines, the new lumber mills, and the large-scale irrigated farms. The new fortunes were made possible by an indigenous labor force and customer base. Thousands of New Mexicans spread across the workplaces of the region to power the wheels of industry and purchase the products of commerce. And as they migrated, they brought their acquired tastes with them. So it was that a new demand and bigger distribution of chile was realized.

But in a cash-strapped society dependent on cyclic migrancy, it wasn't always possible for the farmers to sell directly to the consumer and get the optimum price for their beloved pods. Several mercantile outlets run by non-Hispanic merchants opened shop in Española and northern New Mexico and bought *ristras* from the small farmers to resell them to other sellers in the Southwest. In an arrangement akin to the company store, they paid the growers between 35¢ and $1.50 per string, depending on the market situation. *Ristras* were exchanged for flour or other "stuff that you didn't raise," according to Paul Romero of Velarde, whose father unloaded carloads of *ristras* at one popular mercantile shop. The merchants, of course, traded their goods for chile at a slightly higher price than would have been charged had cash exchanged hands.

One big middleman was the Bond and Nohl Company, based in the heart of the Española Valley and owned partly by the family of big-time sheep rancher Frank Bond. As wholesalers, the Española merchants turned the red chile over to other brokers and retailers. Bond and Nohl also handled green chile and powder ground up at its Española mill. The company's business benefited from a stream of Colorado mail orders sent in from Telluride, Erie, Walsenburg, Trinidad, Durango, Denver, etc. Interest was keen, with one outfit eagerly writing to Española to "get some real chili business for you this season." At times people could hardly wait for their chile. "Please send good, large strings as the people seem to want especially large ones," wrote Carpio Lucero of Denver's Spanish-American Investment Company in 1922. "Please rush . . . I want it here Saturday." Bond and Nohl northern chile, trumpeted by the company as having "the reputation of being the best grown in New Mexico," was also shipped to places such as Winslow, Arizona. And to dispel any doubts, the Rio Grande red was touted by the company as superior to California's, which "cannot compare with New Mexico chile either in quality or strength." Chile fortunes rested with the mining economy, since a good portion of the pods went to miners in the coal districts of southern Colorado, Gallup, and Magdalena, where Spanish-speaking New Mexicans and immigrants like the Iraqis (who called themselves Assyrians) were a sure-sell clientele. When strikes hit Colorado mines in 1922, Bond and Nohl wrote to a distributor in the Rocky Mountain state explaining the stoppages would affect the chile prices.

The early 1920s were a tough market and Bond and Nohl floated prices according to production, consumer demand, and competition.

Among the rivals were the "fruit wagons" hauling green chile and door-to-door peddlers, who, in 1922, "hurt the sale of chile" for a company middleman. In this climate, Bond and Nohl wheeled and dealt, wholesaling at different prices for different quantities at different times for different people. The northern merchants were not above cutting a few corners or bad-mouthing a competitor. In November 1922, Bond and Nohl offered Las Vegas, New Mexico businessman Obaido Maloof *ristras* at 70¢ per string, a price Bond and Nohl suggested would give Maloof a "good profit . . . as they are strings that are slightly smaller in length than the others or have the same length but are more loosely packed and do not contain the same number of chile pods." The same year, a Colorado customer wrote to Española mentioning another seller who was offering *ristras* for 10¢ less a string. Bond and Nohl replied that a reliable source had told them the man was mixing up old strings with new ones and that some people had rejected the *ristras* "on account of being rotten and packed very loosely." A mid-1930s USDA study concluded that Bond and Nohl, along with two other companies, Reuth and Kramer and the Murhage Brothers, had "monopoly control" over the chile market through their combined purchase of 38,000 *ristras* out of 60,000 produced annually in the Pojoaque, Santa Cruz, and lower Chama valleys. The *ristra* merchants were the temporary kings of the New Mexico chile trade, dominating the commercial sale of at least 700 to 900 acres of chile produced annually in the Upper Rio Grande Valley between the early 1930s and early 1940s, the period of time that could be described as the beginning of the end of the north's Classic Chile Era.

"Chile Land" was one nickname ascribed to northern New Mexico, and the region's reputation for its legendary crop outlived its dominance of the New Mexico pepper industry, remaining etched in the memories of locals. When New Mexico Democratic Senator Dennis Chávez faced a tight 1960 election race, someone was heard to say in the midst of the nervous murmurs during the vote-counting, "Wait till the Chili Line comes in." The ballots from the northern villages arrived and Chávez won his seat.

In the interim, amid the boom years and bust years, a near-disaster struck the chile fields, raising the possibility of the unthinkable. A fearsome disease descended on the rows, forcing many New Mexican farmers to face the seemingly uncontrollable wrath of Mother Nature. Few at the time knew that their future was in friendly hands, those of a once-poor Mexican orphan, hard at work on a scientific experiment, hundreds of miles to the south in the sleepy town of Las Cruces, New Mexico.

Notes

1. "El Camino Real," radio series produced by Común, Inc., Albuquerque, NM, 1986.

2. Jocelyn Lieu, "New Mexico Chiles," *New Mexico Resources* (College of Agriculture and Home Economics, New Mexico State University), Autumn 1989, 16.

3. Arthur L. Campa, "Chile in New Mexico," *New Mexico Business Review*, April 1934, 61.

4. Esquipula Vigil and Longhino Vigil, interviews by author, Cundiyo, NM, February 1994.

5. José Ramos Oyengue, San Juan Pueblo elder, interview by author, San Juan, NM, March 1994.

6. Joe M. Clark, "Chile for Health," *New Mexico Magazine*, September 1941, 46-47.

7. State Land Office and New Mexico State Tourist Bureau, *New Mexico Cookery*, 1916 and 1939, 1, 21.

8. Jean Andrews, *The Peppers* (Austin: University of Texas Press, 1984), 70.

9. P. W. Cockerill, *Economics of the Production and Marketing of Chile*, Bulletin No. 314, Agricultural Experiment Station, New Mexico College of Agriculture and Mechanic Arts, 1944.

10. John A. Gjerve, *Chili Line: The Narrow Rail Trail to Santa Fe* (Española, NM: Rio Grande Sun Press, 1969).

11. Roscoe Fleming, "The Chili Line," *New Mexico Magazine*, November 1941, 24, 40.

12. William S. Greever, "Railway Development in the Southwest," *New Mexico Historical Review*, April 1957, 151-203.

13. Susie Martínez, interview by author, Santa Fe, NM, October 1993.

14. William Ilfeld Papers, New Mexico State Records Center and Archives, Santa Fe (hereafter cited as NMSRCA).

15. Paul Romero, interview by author, Santa Fe, NM, September 1993.

16. Frank Bond Papers, Center for Southwest Research, University of New Mexico, Albuquerque.

17. U.S. Department of Agriculture, *Handling of a Cash Crop (Chili)*, Regional Bulletin No. 46, 1937, cited in Marta Weigle, *Hispanic Villages of Northern New Mexico* (Santa Fe, NM: Lightning Tree, 1975), 229.

18. *Santa Fe New Mexican*, 5 May 1974.

Saint Chile

FABIÁN GARCÍA AND MODERN CHILE

García's Garden ▪ Number 9 Rules ▪ The Dreaded Chile Wilt Disease ▪ A World-Famous Chile Breeding Program

There was a time when the prospects of a young Mexican child, Fabián García, must have seemed pretty bleak. Orphaned as a toddler by the deaths of his humble Chihuahuan parents, Ricardo García and Refugio Ribera, he was born into the pre-Revolutionary Mexico of 1871, at the dawn of the dictatorship of Porfirio Díaz, when landowners and business lords in cahoots with North American and European corporations held sway over a great mass of dispossessed workers who toiled relentlessly in the fields, mines, and railroads. García, who was destined to become a true giant of New Mexico agriculture and is known as "The Father of Chile" (or more correctly now, "The Great-Granddaddy") was fortunate to have a caring grandmother, Doña Jacoba, who like millions after her peeked across the Rio Grande for a better life. In 1873 the houseworker bundled up Fabián and headed to the hilly Apache country of south-central New Mexico, a rugged terrain still beset by hostilities between the settlers and Native Americans.

One of the boy's earliest memories was the day he and his buddy Juan were hunting quail in the boondocks outside the town of Mimbres. It was late in the day and they were happy to have bagged three birds. Suddenly Juan's lips started trembling, and Fabián looked up to see a party of Apaches passing near them. "I felt my hair stand up straight," García later wrote. "Without saying a word to each other we started on a run as fast as we could toward town."

In Fabián's tenth year, his grandmother landed employment in the Mesilla Valley home of Thomas Casad. This move to the southeast changed her grandson's life. A great landowner and fruit grower, Casad once owned 21,000 acres of the old Brazito land grant in the Mesilla Valley and was a well-endowed citizen of a developing Doña Ana County. His fortunes crested prior to the furious land sales and great migrations from the south and the east that temporarily divided the valley into a patchwork of generally small farms years before family member Darwin Casad

> *"Fields were plowed with walking plows and cultivated by mule power . . . Chile, beans, and onions were not the first-class, improved products of today."*

—FABIÁN GARCÍA, THE "FATHER OF CHILE"

threw a portion of the local populace into an uproar when he shot and killed a Mexican share-cropper over an alfalfa harvest dispute. Casad's wife took Fabián under her wing and sent him to Las Cruces College, the forerunner of the New Mexico College of Agriculture and Mechanic Arts (later NMSU). Dr. García regarded her as responsible for his success.

Luis Álvarez's father knew García, and Álvarez himself met the man once or twice. As the story is told in Álvarez's words, García was asked what he wanted to do with his life. "Education, I want to go to school," was the young Fabián's reply. Graduating as one of five members of New Mexico A&M's first class of 1894, García attended graduate school at Cornell University before returning to Las Cruces for employment as a professor of horticulture and as head of the Agricultural Experiment Station, a post he held from 1913 to 1945. For a while, he had the distinction of being the only Mexican faculty member at a university constructed in the middle of a Mexican population. He is credited for developing new strains of onions, pecans, and a hybrid chile—the famous Number 9—that was the commercial favorite in New Mexico between the early 1920s and 1950s. From the beginning, New Mexico A&M leaders vested great confidence in García, with one finding him "an invaluable administrative official" in a young institution beset by disorganization. "He did a lot for New Mexico, no question about it," said Hatch farmer and acquaintance Ben Archer.

The motivating factor behind the birth of No. 9 was the need for a commercially cannable variety. The local chile, learned Dr. García, wasn't suited for the Mesilla Valley Canning Company, in which the assembly line was hampered by irregular chiles that didn't fit into the can exactly right. What was needed was a pod that could be roasted easily, hand-peeled, and canned. A milder chile amenable to gringos' tender taste buds wouldn't hurt, either.

In 1907 the budding "father" of the chile business initiated the years-long research and cross-breeding that resulted in the release of the new improved No. 9 chile. He obtained seed from *chile colorado* first brought to the valley from California in 1902 by Theodore Rouault, the operator of the Mesilla Valley Canning Company, and *chile negro* brought from Mexico in 1903 by Francisco Rivera of San Miguel, New Mexico. A third type, Chihuahua *pasilla*, was added to the experiments. From then on, García played with the pollen.

Even at this formative stage in his career, it was apparent that Dr. García was on to big conquests, and he gradually became a player in the business and professional circles of late territorial New Mexico. The professor caught the eye of a young Las Cruces high-society woman, Julieta Amador, the daughter of the well-connected merchant Martín Amador, who sold goods up and down the old Camino Real between Chihuahua and Santa Fe, and a romance was kindled between the child of poverty and the child of wealth.

Julieta, a prolific postcard writer before and after their marriage, sent her scholarly beau love-filled cards from her many trips to El Paso and Mexico—all written in Spanish—with such disparate subjects as pre-Columbian ruins, portraits of wavy-haired females, and, naturally, an early automobile winding its way along the "splendid country roads near El Paso, Texas, through alfalfa fields irrigated from the Rio Grande." In 1907, the same year his historic chile experiments began, Fabián and Julieta were married in Las Cruces, beginning a 13-year union that ended tragically before the bride was able to witness the best-known accomplishment of her husband's landmark career.

In the ensuing years, Dr. García's hopes for a new, widely accepted chile were delayed by disease-inflicted setbacks and errors. Finally, in 1921, after two decades of grinding effort, he officially announced the chile hybrid No. 9. "Our idea at that time in improving the chile was to produce a pod that would be as smooth as possible, straight in shape, shoulderless at the stem, and as fleshy as possible," he wrote.

Coincidentally, No. 9 stood up against the chile wilt fungus, or the blight as it was called then, better than the native strains. No. 9 set the framework for the NMSU chile breeding program, and succeeding horticulturists tailored chiles to fit in cans, to repulse wilt, and to satisfy the dietary sensibilities of non-New Mexicans.

Ever since the halcyon days of No. 9, "the tin can (has) commanded the chile industry," later summed up former NMSU chile breeder, Dr. Jaime Iglesias. No. 9 elicited widespread positive response from New Mexico farmers. Dr. García's Agricultural Experiment Station supplied eager growers with new seed, but it was the New Mexico A&M Cooperative Extension Service, started in 1914, that made sure it flowered. Although No. 9 was developed with the interests of the canners at the Mesilla Valley Canning Company in mind, it was hundreds of miles to the north, in the Middle and Upper Rio Grande valleys and the Upper Pecos Valley, where the new chile first made its real mark. In those years that was where the bulk of New Mexican chile was harvested, not always an easy task. Farmers hand planted seed, hand cultivated young plants, and hand picked pods, which were smaller than today and yielded less produce.

In the 1920s Extension agents in four north-central New Mexico counties advised farmers on the latest chile-farming techniques and brought them seed and thousands of transplants. These multiplied the small farmers' fortunes. In order to avoid any possible confusion, Dr. García furnished growing instructions written in Spanish.

Other growers were assisted by farmers like Mr. Griego of Sena, who saved 75 pounds of No. 9 seed and dutifully handed it out to his neighbors. A product of science, No. 9 had the air of yet another modern gizmo meant to benefit mankind in an age of progress. Accordingly, the Extension organized youth "garden clubs" in such places as San Felipe Pueblo and in Bernalillo, Valencia, and Taos counties. No. 9 was the draw, and a new generation of chile farmers was taught how to raise the crop successfully. But kids will be kids, and sometimes it was the parents who had more fun. A 1923

Extension report noted that the youth club in Taos County had faltered, as the children herded goats instead of tending chile. Nevertheless, the old folks took up the slack and the program was deemed "a great success."

García's No. 9, paradoxically better suited for the longer growing season of the south, was crossed with the native and Anaheim varieties and it contributed to the heyday of the chile economy in the Middle and Upper Rio Grande valleys. A 1924 report submitted by García to the Extension director noted that chile production, fostered by No. 9, had recently increased 300 percent, and crop yields in Santa Fe County had doubled to the point where it was easily the "main cash crop for truck gardeners."

No. 9's results were "remarkable," according to a 1933 Extension report to New Mexico governor Hockenhull. Pods doubled in size and acquired a uniformity permitting growers to receive "better prices than they used to get before the chile crop was improved." García's chile improvement program "has done much to save and improve the state chile crop," concluded the Extension in 1933. Enthusiastic farmers gathered in villages such as Puerto de Luna to talk chile and mull over the future as suggested by No. 9.

But growers confronted a serious challenge—the first of many fungal diseases that fell under the rubric of "chile wilt." First noticed in 1908, the wilt captured widespread public attention three years later when plants turned sickly, withered, and lost their foliage. The horror was particularly acute for those growers waiting to pick the chile red, in its final mature stage. One newspaper account noted the wilt was wreaking havoc in the Alameda and Los Griegos areas of then semi-rural Albuquerque, where chile was a significant money-maker: "One day the crop looks all right and the next morning many of the

plants will be wilted on the ground." Frank Durand, a Pajarito grower, wrote to New Mexico A&M, "I am obligated to pick my chile while green in order to save any at all."

Nobody knew what had struck the chile fields. On the Pecos River, farmers thought chemicals from the American Metals Co. might be responsible. Insects were suspected. Lime was sprayed on chile to no avail. The horticulturists and biologists at A&M began tests that identified the wilt and led to resistance breeding. Yet the pathogens spread, gaining notorious nicknames like chile wilt, blackleg, and the blight. Observers noted the tendency of wilt outbreaks to be worse in wet years when poorly drained fields proliferated. In bad years, such as 1930, an estimated 50 percent of the statewide chile crop was destroyed by the wilt. Assisted by his colleagues at the college, García turned his attention to combating the menace and devised alternating irrigation and new methods of thinning and land leveling combining the native and level-ridge cultivation methods that seemed to stave off the worst plagues.

In the Upper Pecos Valley, farmers heeded his recommendations and in 1932 picked the best chile crop in a decade. Others weren't always as ready to abandon tried-and-true methods passed down from one generation to the next, but Dr. García and Extension personnel persisted in propagating their up-to-date farming techniques. "During all these years my neighbors who would not follow the instructions of the Agricultural College have had a total loss of their chile," wrote Ramón Madrid of Villanueva, New Mexico. "From one acre this year I harvested 6,000 pounds of green chile and about 1,500 pounds of ripe (red) pods."

Not content to remain behind a desk, Dr. García was employed as a part-time horticulturist by the Extension Service because of his "point of contact with the Spanish-American people." He broadcast the hot word on the Extension program on the original KOB radio, and he toured widely, sharing his chile skills and university-grown chile plants with farmers in places such as Socorro, Valencia, Mora, Rio Arriba, and Santa Fe counties. In 1930 he was a passenger on the historic agricultural train, "The New Mexico Farm and Home Special," sponsored by New Mexico A&M and the Santa Fe Railway. This famous train was a rerun of similar specials launched in 1912, when 33,000 people crowded 66 towns to view the miracles of modern farming. But New Mexico's rural landscape had changed in the intervening years, populated by an influx of settlers and faced with the unknowns of the Great Depression.

A&M president H. L. Kent, Dr. García, and a cast of other characters logged 52 stops on a feverish two-week trip that originated in the Mesilla Valley and snaked across the track up to Capulin and back. This route one day took them only a few hours to the north of a Santa Fe train and bus wreck near Isleta Pueblo. Nineteen people were killed in the wreck.

The 1930 Special was the trip of a lifetime. For men like García, it was the culmination of a long career spent ensuring the greening of an arid New Mexico. For others, like the later famous Extension specialist and New Mexico cookery expert Fabiola C. De Baca, it was the initiation of a life's work in the diverse reaches of a tough but rewarding countryside. Chugging through sunlight and snow clouds and over terrain that ranged from the high mesa of Santa Fe to the burning plains of Portales, New Mexico A&M professors and Extension staff delivered the latest in farm science to intrigued spectators. Navajo livestock raisers, Spanish-speaking farm-

ers, and Anglo ranchers all turned out in the thousands to marvel at the eight-car "traveling county fair" that exhibited wonders such as "pure" university-invented seed, a 2,100-pound bull, and a modern farm home kitchen designed to ease the drudgery of rural life. From his pulpit, Dr. García conveyed the bilingual gospel in English and Spanish on matters like "Crop Improvement with Special Reference to Chili and Wheat."

The Santa Fe newspaper responded to the excitement by inserting a complimentary editorial on the Las Cruces professor of chile fame and his cohorts, stating that it is "a little hard to estimate the value of these men and their associates to the people of New Mexico for a generation past. Undoubtedly, they will get a substantial reward in heaven." In Dr. García's life, one detects that blend of populism and conservatism that was a hallmark of the so-called Progressive Era of the early twentieth century.

Doña Ana farmer Carl Nakayama, one of the thinning ranks of an older generation of rural New Mexicans, recalled García as a "compassionate man" who always had time for the common folk. As a youngster, Nakayama accompanied his father on visits to Dr. García's office at the College for advice on raising fruits and vegetables. "You know there's lots of so-called experts in their fields that don't realize that questions that seem simple to them are a concern to us," said Nakayama. "And (Dr. García) would really patiently explain and answer our questions."

Perhaps more than anything, Dr. García had an unbridled faith in education and in a world where, as he once wrote, "investigation, agitation, and discussion are the characteristics of this age and an indication of progress." In order to best understand the impact and context of Dr. García's work, it is essential to understand his

Saint Chile at the Helm of Power: Fabián García (second from right) with unidentified officials in Mexico City, circa 1920s.

place in the economic and social milieu of the times. The first decades of the twentieth century were bellwether years for his home base of southern New Mexico, the epoch when farming grew from small to large production as new railroads and highways eased the delivery of produce. Just to the north of the Mesilla Valley, the huge Elephant Butte Dam was under construction by the U.S. Bureau of Reclamation, and it promised a controllable source of irrigation. On the farms, tractors began replacing mules and manpower. And in the corridors and classrooms of New Mexico A&M, new revelations flowed from the deductions of bright, energetic scholars. For Dr. García, the flip side of scientific discovery was business development, and he was quick to put his money into enterprises supported by research that the college

conducted. In a 1930 notebook he scribbled "agriculture is the foundation of human life and the inexhaustible source of all true income." Dr. García invested in oil, real estate, the farmer-financing Bowman's Bank ("Santa Claus has a bank account" was one company slogan), the First National Bank of Doña Ana, a ranch owned jointly with in-laws Clotilde and Antonio Terrazas (scions of the Chihuahua landlord family), the Mesilla Valley Fruit Association, and, unsurprisingly, the Mesilla Valley Canning Company, one of two green chile canning companies in the United States at the time.

Luis Álvarez remembered García as a frugal, "funny man" who was always saving something. One year Álvarez was cultivating a tomato patch for the college when the second-in-command walked up to check.

"What are you doing, Luis?" asked the supervisor.

"Why, isn't that the patch you wanted me to cultivate?"

"Yeah, yeah, but look at the horse."

"What's the matter with the horse?"

"It's sweating."

"Yeah, it's working."

"If Mr. Fabián sees you he'll can you, he'll run you away."

According to Álvarez, García "didn't want the horse to get hot." Another quirk, remembered Álvarez, was the professor's habit of having his car's gasoline tank half-filled so in case of a fire the whole thing wouldn't "burn up."

While García and his researchers perfected onions, chile, cotton, and other crops for local farmers, First National and other financial institutions provided the wherewithal for the farmers to succeed and earned profits from the myriad of modernized agricultural enterprises blossoming in the valley. Realizing the gold mine at their doorstep, A. Love of the Las Cruces Chamber of Commerce began collecting donations for García's Agricultural Experiment Station. A power triad consisting of farm, finance, and fellowship evolved in Las Cruces and the college. It encompassed individuals who were simultaneously involved in the construction of the Elephant Butte Dam, the founding of NMSU, the opening of banks, and the establishment of large-scale commercial agriculture. These movers and shakers, guided by an overlapping class of financiers, large ranchers and farmers, and high-ranking university officials, consummated a revolving set of business relationships. Bankers forked out the dough, growers planted the seed, and New Mexico A&M staff assisted with the technical aspects.

A system that has survived to this very day began with men like Quaker Hiram Hadley, the first president of New Mexico A&M and head of the Las Cruces Chamber of Commerce. Hadley was emulated by others like farmer Oscar "Alfalfa King" Snow, a classmate of García's and 1894 graduate who ran a 1,000-acre farm and served as the first director of the First National Bank of Las Cruces, the lending institution whose "main source of income was land, land owned by farmers and ranchers." Others followed his lead. They included H. L. Kent, NMSU president and First National Bank stockholder; Frank Papen, First National Bank president, NMSU Foundation, and state representative; and Kenneth Black, dairyman, regent, and banker. Black had a Scottish grandfather who was so enamored of the red chile *ristras* he saw hanging from Las Cruces adobe homes that he decided to stay in the United States.

New Mexico A&M's academic, experimental, and extension divisions spouted a hundred fountains of knowledge. College personnel plunged into the controversial work of constructing a new drainage system in the seepage-prone Mesilla Valley, gave technical advice to canners, founded the New Mexico Crop Improvement Association to distribute high-quality seed, uplifted the dairy industry, formed vegetable growers' associations, pushed cotton as the number one cash crop, and supervised the placement of Mexican contract farm laborers called braceros in the 1940s. Central to this project were the agents of the New Mexico A&M Extension Service, which brought Dr. García and agricultural science to the field.

The Extension and New Mexico commercial agriculture grew up together, enduring both good times and bad times. Agents like J. W. Knorr, praised as a "hustler" who netted "splendid results," organized the New Mexico Farm and Livestock Bureau to efficiently channel the latest research. "The county agent as the Farm Bureau manager is the captain of America's organized soldiers of the soil," stated a University publication. A private growers' organization, the Farm Bureau rose to become the preeminent political voice of agriculture. A song written to the tune of "Last Night on the Back Porch" by a Mrs. Yoast, the Extension secretary, perhaps expressed the sentiments of both parties at a 1925 Farm Bureau banquet:

> When the fields are dry
> And the stock all die
> And the farmer sure feels blue
> Then the cow and the hen
> And the pig in the pen
> Are the ones that help things thru;
> But when the crops are full
> And the fruit trees all
> With blossoms are aglow
> Then you work and smile
> And feel life worth while
> In sunny New Mexico. . . .

The Extension directed the sunlight's rays on farmers. For example, when Sandoval County chile farmers in the 1950s wondered how in the world to sell their chiles to the legions of gringos swooping in on the Land of Enchantment, they turned to the Extension for help. It was more than happy to oblige. An Extension circular, "Chile," was published, full of anecdotes, histories, and recipes. Sales and production increased.

Back in the laboratory world of Las Cruces, García and staff dabbled in the exotic. As the world plunged head-long toward war in the late 1930s, paprika varieties were obtained from France and Hungary. Thanks to the USDA, 18

strains were introduced to New Mexico A&M from Europe and Asia.

The new chile types carried such un-New Mexican names as White Casaba, Jubilee of Honor, Louisiana, Hungarian, Brown's Spanish, and Brown's Hungarian. Subsequent test plantings produced good outcomes, presaging the day when New Mexico-grown paprika was destined for the international spice trade. What might have been judged as the esoteric doings of scientists wrapped up in their own experiments actually had a commercial impulse. Large chile processors wanted a mild chile and New Mexico sorely needed one in order to compete on the market. Meanwhile, tests were underway to improve No. 9 to meet those specifications and outwit the recurrent wilt. Success was partially achieved in 1950 when García's successor, Dr. Roy Harper, announced the No. 6 variety, which had about half the pungency of No. 9 along with a better shape and smoothness to "permit a high proportion of it to be used in canning fresh chile." Strangely, the reign and demise of No. 9 dovetailed the peak and end of García's career. Only a few short years after Grandpa Chile left this world, so did the No. 9. In its place came other types, including Harper's processor-favored Rio Grande and the 6-4, which was snatched up by a cannery. All of this was owed to Dr. García, whose work in establishing a chile breeding program at NMSU established this Las Cruces institution as the leader of chile research in the United States and, indeed, the world.

Prior to his death, García was widely acclaimed in the United States and abroad. In the mid-1920s, he turned down an offer from the Peruvian government to establish and head an agricultural school there. In addition to being listed in *Who's Who in America*, García belonged to several academic fraternities, joined the Farm Bureau, and was a director of the Doña Ana county fair. His name was on the membership rolls of the Knights of Columbus and the Alianza Hispano-Americana. As an advocate of Mexican-American education at a time when the academy was of a whiter hue, the one-time poor orphan quietly supported the college careers of an undetermined number of young Spanish-speaking students at New Mexico A&M by providing them with money from his own pocket in their times of need.

Though the learned García circulated comfortably within the professional elite of his time, he remained a Mexican in an Anglo-dominated establishment and he encountered cultural stereotyping. While ailing in an El Paso hospital in 1944, García received a letter from A. B. Youngblood, the administrator of the U.S. Department of Agriculture Experiment Station in Washington, D.C. Youngblood, who knew the New Mexico A&M official, asked for biographical information that could be used by USDA public relations writers to spin stories for Central and South American publications. Playing on the *indigenismo* movement of the day, Youngblood said, "I recall that you are part Yaqui and part Spanish, all of which seem to have made a most excellent Spanish-American out of you. We are proud of you." Youngblood urged García to emphasize his Indian heritage so his biography would be "as pungent as your chili con carne (a Texas creation) and hot tamales, or your peppers themselves." The USDA administrator also requested a photo like "the one you had made when you were running around with women folks down there." García's friend A. S. Curry wrote back that the professor was unable to reply at the time.

As he neared the end of his life, García reflected on the changes that had overcome his Mesilla Valley, many of which were attributable to the work of the Chihuahua-born horticulturist and his colleagues. "Fields were plowed with walking plows and cultivated by mule power," García remarked to writer Margaret Page Hood. "Cotton was an unthought of crop. Chile, beans, and onions were not the first class, improved products of today."

As his health deteriorated, the years finally took their toll on the old stalwart. But García was not one to quit easily. "The old gentleman became older and older as I knew him and finally he got to where he couldn't get around, but he still wanted to work," recalled John Augustine, a former Doña Ana County Extension agent. "He would show up at the office and keep pushing people to get things done. He was a doer, that old man."

García's recurrent personal tragedies contrasted starkly with his professional achievements. His only child, a son, died in infancy. His wife, Julieta, passed away in 1920 at age 38. In 1945 misfortune struck again. The aging chile breeder was admitted to McBride's Hospital in Las Cruces with Parkinson's Disease. The college regents were forced to retire him, but García's portrait was hung deferentially in the Extension office building.

Yet even from his hospital bed, García kept up his unwavering interest in agriculture, writing letters to farmers in which he asked about their harvests and conferring with New Mexico A&M officials about Experiment Station business. Friends found him in surprisingly good spirits, willing to joke and tell stories of early Las Cruces and its prominent families such as the Amadors. Martha Montes Skaggs, a friend and visitor to his room, remembered García reflecting humorously on his marriage into the wealthy Amador family. "They were a little aristocratic and he made fun of himself for marrying into that family, because I don't think he considered himself an aristocrat to begin with," said Skaggs.

On August 6, 1948, the third anniversary of the Hiroshima bombing and almost 41 years to the day he married Julieta Amador, the old professor died. On the very same evening the summer commencement was held at New Mexico A&M and news of García's death "cast a gloom" over the celebration. The bells tolled at his beloved college in the shadow of the Organ Mountains, characterized by graduates Mary Alice Will and Lise Courtney as "a vivid spot of green under the blue New Mexican sky with Tortugas [mountain] grey and earthly in the background."

A generous García donated the bulk of his personal wealth, estimated at a minimum of $100,000, to NMSU, directing that most of it go toward student housing for "poor boys." He implored university officials to "not forget poor students with Spanish names." In his will García urged the school to "not charge a high rent for the rooms. Help the poor students. I was a poor boy and I know what hardships are."

In death, the work of García loomed over the chile industry larger-than-life. In 1974, he was declared the Patron Saint of the International Connoisseurs of Green and Red Chile. This Las Cruces-based group celebrates his birthday as an official holiday.

Notes

1. Fabián García Papers, Manuscript 71, Boxes 1-12, Rio Grande Historical Collections, New Mexico State University (hereafter cited as RGHC).

2. Mrs. Humboldt Casad, "Old Timers Stories," interview by Marie Carter, 1937, Works Progress Administration (WPA) File #197, NMSRCA.

3. Bertha Mandell Chandler, interview by Marie Carter, 27 June 1937, WPA File #197, NMSRCA.

4. *El Paso Times*, 26 May 1916; *Rio Grande Republican*, 2 June 1916.

5. Luis Álvarez, interview by author, Mesilla, NM, August 1993.

6. *Report of Dr. G. E. Ladd to Honorable Board of Regents, New Mexico College of Agriculture and Mechanic Arts*, 4; *Report of the Work of the New Mexico College of Agriculture and Mechanic Arts January 1, 1909-February 1, 1912*, 18-23, Gov. William C. McDonald Papers, Expandable 1, NMRSCA.

7. Ben Archer, telephone conversation with author, October 1993.

8. Marriage Records on Doña Ana County, New Mexico Book A (April 1905-December 1908), Doña Ana Chapter DAR, 1971-72.

9. Fabián García, "Improved Variety No. 9 of Native Chile," Bulletin No. 124, Agricultural Experiment Station, State College, NM, February 1921.

10. Dr. Jaime Iglesias, interview by author, Las Cruces, NM, August 1993.

11. Early issues of *Extension Service News and New Mexico Extension News*, the publication of the New Mexico A&M Cooperative Extension Service, State College, NM, carried reports of the success of Number 9 chile in the field. See: April 1922, 4; May 1922, 4; September 1922, 4; October 1922, 4; June 1923, 4; October 1923, 4; July 1928, 7; October 1932, 3; October 1933, 3.

12. *9th Annual Report of the Cooperative Extension Work in Agriculture and Home Economics, For the Year Ending June 30, 1923*, C. F. Monroe, Extension Director, Gov. James F. Hinkle Papers, NMSRCA, 72.

13. *11th Annual Report of the Cooperative Extension Work in Agriculture and Home Economics, State of New Mexico, For the Year Ending June 30, 1925*, C. F. Monroe, Extension Director, Governor Arthur T. Hannett Papers, NMSRCA, 89-90.

14. *19th Annual Report of the Cooperative Extension Work in Agriculture and Home Economics, For the Year Ending June 30, 1933, Extension Project No. 8, Horticulture*, W. L. Elser, Director of Extension, Governor Hockenhull Papers, NMSRCA.

15. "Minutes of a Program Planning Meeting at Puerto de Luna, December 6, 1939," *County Land Use and Agricultural Planning Report for New Mexico 1940*, New Mexico A&M Agricultural Extension Service.

16. John William Knorr, "The Disease of Chili" (bachelor's thesis, New Mexico College of Agriculture and Mechanic Arts, May 1913), RGHC.

17. R. F. Crawford, "The Etiology and Control of Chile Wilt, Produced by Fusarium Annum," *New Mexico College of Agriculture and Mechanic Arts and Agricultural Experiment Station Bulletin #223, June 1934*, Introduction.

18. *18th Annual Report of the Cooperative Extension Work in Agriculture and Home Economics, June 30, 1932*, Vol. 1, Gov. Seligman Papers, NMSRCA, 503.

19. Fabián García, "Reduction of Chile Wilt by Cultural Methods," *New Mexico Agricultural Experiment Station Bulletin 216*, December 1933, Introduction, 14-20.

20. *New Mexico Extension Service, Annual Report 1933 Extension Project No. 8, Horticulture*, H. C. Stewart, Extension Horticulturist, Governor Hockenhull Papers, NMSRCA.

21. *15th Annual Report of the Cooperative Extension Work in Agriculture, For the Year Ending June 30, 1929, No. 8*, 56, Governor Hockenhull Papers, Reports to the Governor, 1927-29, NMSRCA.

22. "New Mexico College of Agriculture and Mechanic Arts June 30, 1912 Report," *Report of the Work of the New Mexico College of Agriculture and Mechanic Arts*, 2, Governor William C. McDonald Papers, Exp. 1, NMRSCA.

23. A few newspaper accounts of the 1930 agricultural train: *Albuquerque Journal*, 3 April 1930; *Socorro Chieftain*, 5 April 1930; *Gallup Independent*, 4 April 1930; *Santa Fe New Mexican*, 9 and 11 April 1930.

24. Carl Nakayama, interview by author, Doña Ana County, NM, November 1993.

25. Charles F. Coan, *History of New Mexico*, Vol. 3 (Chicago and New York: American Historical Society, 1925), 41-42.

26. George B. Anderson, *History of New Mexico: Its Resources and People*, Vol. 2 (Los Angeles: Pacific States Publishing, 1907).

27. Leon C. Metz, *Southern New Mexico Empire* (El Paso, TX: Mangan Books, 1991), 8, 23, 62, 81, 158.

28. Tom Barry and Jim Frazin, "New Mexico Agriculture and Ranching: Its Present and Future," *Who Runs New Mexico?: NMPE Power Structure Report* (Albuquerque: New Mexico People and Energy, 1980).

29. *New Mexico Farm and Ranch*, June 1970, 4.

30. *New Mexico Farm Courier*, October 1918, 10.

31. *New Mexico Cooperative Extension News*, January 1962, 7.

32. *51st Annual Report of the Agricultural Experiment Station of New Mexico, College of Agriculture and Mechanic Arts 1938-39* (State College, NM), 64; *53rd Annual Report of the Agricultural Experiment Station of New Mexico, College of Agriculture and Mechanic Arts 1941-42*, 65.

33. R. E. Harper, "An Improved Variety of Chile for New Mexico," New Mexico A&M Agricultural Experiment Station Press Bulletin 1041, April 1950.

34. *66th Annual Report of the Agricultural Experiment Station of New Mexico 1954-55; 69th Annual Report of the Agricultural Experiment Station of New Mexico 1957-58*.

35. Lelia Collins, interview by author, Las Cruces, NM, March 1994. Mrs. Collins's father, G. R. Quesenberry, was an extension director in the late 1930s. Earlier he was recommended by Dr. García for the Peruvian position, but he also declined the job.

36. Margaret Favrot, interview by author, Las Cruces, NM, April 1994. Ms. Favrot's uncle ran McBride Hospital, where she visited the sick Dr. García as a personal friend. She was also a very close friend of Dr. García's secretary, who knew of the professor's personal financial help given to students.

37. George Edmonds to Governor John E. Miles, 30 December 1938, Governor John E. Miles Papers, Correspondence, NM State College A&M 1939-42, NMSRCA.

38. Margaret Page Hood, "Trial and Error Farmers," *New Mexico Magazine*, May 1944, 10-11.

39. John Augustine, interview by author, Las Cruces, NM, February 1994. Augustine was the Doña Ana County extension agent circa 1940 and as such knew Dr. García.

40. Martha Montes Skaggs, interview by author, Las Cruces, NM, February 1994. Mrs. Skaggs was another personal friend of García's who visited McBride Hospital.

41. Mary Alice Will and Lise Courtney, "A History of the New Mexico College of Agriculture and Mechanic Arts" (bachelor's thesis, New Mexico A&M, 1929), RGHC.

42. Frances French Papers, Ms. 6, Box 1, Folders 3 and 11, RGHC.

43. Constitution of the International Connoisseurs of Green and Red Chile, Chamber of Commerce, Las Cruces, NM, n.d.

College Chile

NEW MEXICO STATE UNIVERSITY AND THE RISE OF THE CHILE EMPIRE

A Japanese-New Mexican Chile Inventor ▪ Bob Hope and Ronald Reagan Become Chile Lovers ▪ The Globetrotting Aggies Promote Chile

A legend in his own time, Fabián García was a hard act to follow. Nevertheless, his successors proved more than capable of building on his legacy and of creating one of their own. Next to Roy Harper, Dr. Roy Nakayama is most renowned in chile country; this is for releasing the 6-4 variety popular among processors; the R-Naky, named after his wife; and, of course, the Big Jim. Every modern industry honors its birthplace and its founding fathers, and chile is no exception. Steel has Pittsburgh and Andrew Carnegie, the auto has Detroit and Henry Ford, and chile has Las Cruces and its horticulturists.

Still another figure in the ongoing ritual of chile creation was a gregarious, blue-eyed chile plant breeder and California transplant named Dr. Paul Bosland. The capsicum expert par excellence, who possessed the moniker "Chileman,"

Dr. Bosland was the fourth in a prominent line of principal chile breeders at NMSU who were charged with the task of crossing pollen to create stronger, bigger, brighter, and disease-resistant varieties of chile.

Dr. Bosland's war room in his spicy scientific mission is the greenhouse at the University's Fabián García Science Center, where three to four thousand chile specimens flower in a veritable jungle. These include not only the standard chiles familiar to New Mexicans, but also a visually enticing array of hot and cold capsicums that includes yellow leaf mutants, spinach leaf mutants, and plants with leaves growing upside down, all members of a mutagenesis line created to map chromosomes for plant breeding.

In the early morning hours, Dr. Bosland's staff steals into the water-dripping, hollow buzz of their lab to emasculate the "best of the best" chile plants chosen for improvement, snipping the anthers away from the flowers and gently touching the stigma with male pollen. Each one is tagged and given a number that is kept in a pedigree book "just like horse breeders" do. Six to eight months later, seed is produced and surveyed for 25 different traits. Color, size, shape, and strength are noted. A food industry association, the American Spice Trade Association, assigns numbers to each color grade. Bosland and company are like a picky panel of beauty contestant judges: if any one of their 25 criteria isn't up to par, the hapless plant is rejected for further trials. If, on the other hand, the chile shows the desired qualities, it is a candidate for more experimentation.

If good fortune prevails, a new plant variety might even make it into someone's lipstick or onto someone's chile cheese fries. Out of 40,000 plants involved, calculates Bosland, only one makes it to the prestigious slot of new variety of the year. "My job is to ask, 'Five to seven years from today what is the industry going to need? What kinds of plants?'" he explains. Like García before him, "Chileman" even proposed a green chile ideotype for processing. The fruit is 11.4 centimeters in length and 2.5 to 3.8 centimeters in width, with uniform pungency and wall thickness. Bosland and his colleagues in the public and private chile worlds, men such as Dr. Ben Villalón of the Texas Agricultural Experiment Station and Phil Villa of California's Ortega Co., spent decades in their laboratories and experimental plots shaping and following pepper trends to suit the tastes of the industry and their booming legions of customers. Perhaps their greatest challenge was overcoming the *phytophthora* root rot fungus, a job Villalón assessed as "a Herculean task that may never be achieved."

So, with the chile world's eyes upon him, Bosland combed the world beyond for a wilt-resistant pepper he could cross with a New Mexican one in order to outwit the root rot. "Chileman" even teamed up with Max González, an NMSU Guatemalan graduate student, and ventured to remote regions of Guatemala, retracing the adventurer Paul Stanley's tracks in search of the key to the super chile.

The NMSU chile breeder remembered a cool reception on the part of the peasants; one could only surmise that the *campesinos*, residing in a country where 100,000 had died in a long-running civil war, probably scorned the pair as but the latest in a line of anthropologists, missionaries, or CIA operatives. González's Spanish succeeded in easing the *campesinos*' fears, recalled Bosland, but the NMSU chile breeders fell short of their expected goal, possibly because of rain-forest cutting and the subsequent elimination of the mysterious chile they sought. By a stroke of luck, much of Bosland's research was spared the smoke of a December 1992 fire that broke out in NMSU offices, which was caused by a spilled flammable. Nevertheless, by 1993, Bosland reported that a wilt-resistant red chile, or at least an 80 percent resistant one, was just around the corner. Seed for this type of chile was brought to NMSU in 1984 from Morelos, Mexico, by Dr. Jaime Iglesias, a collaborator of Bosland's. The insistence of processors that chiles be not only wilt-resistant but that they contain a certain heat level as well complicated the effort of the Never-Ending Search for the Almost Perfect Chile.

An inherent tension in Bosland's or any plant breeder's job was the contradiction between the demands of industry and the peculiarities of nature. The land is measured by its need for biodiversity, while the market is conditioned by its short-term desires to make a buck. Monoculture, the growing of one crop in one area, is frowned upon by knowledgeable farmers, agronomists and scientists. Well-known difficulties result from pest infestations, which are typically handled by chemical spraying, an act that kills other beneficial species and introduces a whole new set of problems into the ecosystem. Moreover, the expansion of capitalist agriculture over a large area ushers in collective headaches not easily alleviated in an increasingly individualistic farm culture. Weeds become everyone's downfall but remain the responsibility of an individual owner. Harvesting crates and dirty tractors that contain insects and fungi contaminate entire production regions but are in the ultimate control of a sole farmer or corporation.

Over the years savvy agriculturalists have developed sowing patterns and irrigation methods that curb pestilence and disease. Once, speaking before growers, Bosland cautioned them to take care of their cultivating and irrigating practices, in order not to encourage the wilt. "Resistant varieties aren't the silver bullet. We'll get you a resistant variety, but you have to be a good farmer. . . . we'll never have the perfect chile, it's an impossible dream. What we'll do is give you something to work with." But in the real marketplace, where, for instance, the cost of installing efficient drip irrigation systems ran at about $1,000 per acre, growers might hesitate in a situation of stagnating chile prices.

For Bosland, the fundamental problem he and the chile industry confronted in the horticultural realm could be defined by what was termed the "Red Queen Hypothesis," drawn from the Alice in Wonderland fairy tale in which the protagonist "runs very fast to stay in the same place." Remarked Bosland, "We're running like crazy to keep up in terms of breeding

new chiles for tolerance." Inventing the latest chile is an ongoing, life-long task. Diseases change and strike even the resilient varieties. "We always have to be in a constant struggle to increase resistance to the adverse conditions of spreading chile wilt," said Dr. Iglesias, echoing Bosland's statement about the importance of growing practices to beat the wilt. And wilt is just one of a host of maladies afflicting chile across the globe.

As the research and development arm of the chile industry, NMSU researchers and scientists were employed to solve the whole range of pepper-related problems. Craig Liddell, NMSU plant pathologist, arrived in 1989 to find the tomato spotted wilt virus the rage of the year. Then, three years later, in 1992, it was the pepper mottle virus. According to Liddell, the disease was accidentally discovered when a processor tried to roast a batch of chile and was instead greeted with a batch of exploding pods. For two weeks successive roasting attempts ended in similar messes before NMSU was finally called in to investigate. A few short years later, in 1995, it was the curly-top virus, spread by a vector, that frustrated growers. In a short period, Liddell witnessed chile wilt shriveling plants, bugs hopscotching diseases across fields, and pepper weevils eating up profits. "It's like the plague in medieval Europe," concluded Liddell. "I can guarantee you that in three years there will be [another] one of these things that pop up."

Far from being the quaint headquarters of what otherwise might be viewed as a Southwestern oddity, Dr. Bosland's NMSU, the state's land grant agricultural college, is actually a nerve center of a burgeoning international industry. His main task is to keep New Mexico, the land of the chile, on the throne of the pepper industry, a business that has helped to move the United States's formerly lackluster cuisine into conformance with the ethnic diversity of both the 50 states and the larger world in which chiles are a first-class passenger on land, on sea, and in the air. In 1992, statistics compiled by the U.S. Department of Agriculture reported that $60.4 million worth of peppers were imported into the United States, a 41.7 percent monetary leap over the previous year. U.S. exports, on the other hand, were $8.9 million for 1992, but growing.

A smorgasbord of chiles was served up on the North American plate from Mexico, India, Pakistan, Costa Rica, China, Chile, Colombia, the Dominican Republic, Hong Kong, Spain, Morocco, and Israel. Moreover, the chile caravans journeyed both ways: New Mexican and Southwestern peppers were sold in Canada, Australia, Europe, and Mexico, among other places.

"We look at [NMSU] as an international center for chile research here, not just as a New Mexico provincial point of view [on the industry]," comments Dr. Bosland. "Our first goal of course is to keep New Mexico farmers competitive in this international market. . . ." Outside the NMSU lab is a chile garden that engages visitors and that features Thai, Japanese, and Chinese peppers which, Bosland is quick to note, are all of Western Hemispheric origin, carried to their new lands by free traders of the mercantile and imperial eras. In today's world of tariff-free markets and NAFTA and the WTO, chile is among products enjoying an old, boundaryless history. Inside, germ plasm from nations such as Colombia and Ecuador is a vital part of NMSU's collection, preserving the chile species for the future.

Bosland clearly has his work cut out for him. He is entrusted with the strategic position of keeping a New Mexico chile industry viable at a time when world economic forces could help make or break the kingpin role in the United States of the Land of Enchantment's pride and joy. He was a driving force in the effort to found an international center for chile research and propagation, which it was hoped would be supported financially by corporate and private donors whose contributions would earn them a plaque in a "chile hall of fame." All eyes were on Bosland, not the least reason being because of the record compiled by his predecessor, "Mr. Chile" himself, the late Dr. Roy Nakayama. Similar in some characteristics to the founder of the NMSU chile breeding program, Nakayama, too, hailed originally from modest circumstances and later achieved fame for his agricultural accomplishments. And like Dr. García, he pursued his career with zeal. Described by former colleagues as "quiet and unassuming," "brilliant," and "excellent," he is considered the creator of the majority of commercial chiles grown and sold in New Mexico after the 1950s and up until the 1990s.

Writing in a 1977 issue of *Horticulture*, author John Neary likened the three-and-one-half-acre plot where Big Jim chile was developed to the Trinity Site atomic bomb testing ground for physicists. Nicknamed "Mr. Chile," Nakayama was the son of a Japanese farmer who settled in the Mesilla Valley in 1918. His immigrant father came to New Mexico from Nebraska where he grew to detest the harsh winters after 10 frigid seasons.

When John Nakayama was approached by a partner and asked to share in a land deal in the developing Rio Grande Valley of south Texas, he headed south with his pregnant wife and first son, Carl. The trip was delayed in El Paso by his wife's health problems. The elder Nakayama,

A Red Chile Queen in southern New Mexico.

looking for a way to earn money, heard about available land in the Mesilla Valley just to the north. He also learned there were about 20 Japanese and 30 Chinese families residing in Las Cruces at the time. "So he took the train and came to Cruces and leased a plot of land and we stayed here ever since," said his oldest son, Carl. Almost by a fluke, the best-known chile creator of modern times was a New Mexican instead of a Texan.

Born in 1924, Roy was first exposed to chile by his father, a man who developed a reputation as one of the best fruit and vegetable farmers anywhere. Nakayama senior depended on Roy and his siblings to pick chile, carry boxed cantaloupes to the wagons, and execute other farm tasks. While working, he taught them to respect the land.

Generally well-received members of the Mesilla Valley community, the Nakayamas were nevertheless scorned by some neighbors in an outburst of World War II anti-Japanese racism. But others backed them as friends and citizens. The young Roy dashed off to join the U.S. military and was captured in the 1944 Battle of the Bulge. Ironically, while the future benefactor of the Hatch Valley chile industry was languishing in a German prisoner-of-war camp, Italian and German POWs were laboring on Hatch area farms. Returning home, Nakayama earned his bachelor's degree at NMSU in 1948 and his graduate degrees at Iowa State University.

Except for a two-year stint at the California Department of Agriculture, he worked as chief chile breeder at NMSU from 1950 until his retirement in 1984.

In the beginning, however, pecans were Nakayama's passion, a vocation that sent him to Mexico to advise farmers there on raising a respectable bag of nuts. This infatuation lasted until "he realized he had to spend full time on chile because there was too much work to do," according to brother Carl.

Dr. Nakayama arrived on the scene at a time when wide-scale cross-fertilization of varieties like García's No. 9 was disturbing its size, shape, and pungency. Heat was hard to gauge and pod size unpredictable. An ugly chile mess sat on the table. To clean it up, Dr. Nakayama pulled in seeds from South America, Europe, and any other suitable place he could find and crossed them with New Mexican chiles, commenting that "a new gene pool can do wonders for new flavor and qualities."

Devoted to his chile research, Nakayama meticulously tended up to 1,500 experimental plots. He completed an enormous amount of study and cluttered his office with piles of paper. Keen to grower and processor needs, he labored to develop chiles with uniform sizes, higher yields, and machine-harvestable characteristics, a goal he would have to leave for others. "Their suggestions were included in the breeding program," he said of the commercial influence in shaping NMSU's research. "We paid attention not only to the people who eat chile, but also to the growers and processors . . . if they couldn't grow it economically, if they couldn't process it economically, the price would go up."

Nakayama claimed that he never gained personal profit from his chile creations, though his upbringing on his father's farm in the opening years of Mesilla Valley agribusiness clearly led him to recognize the value of NMSU to the farming community. "If people back then had access to the information they have now, my father wouldn't have been as poor as he was," Nakayama told writer Neary. "He didn't have a nickel. The farmer could have been so much better off."

Dr. Nakayama's releases indeed made some better off, and the chile industry cherished his work at the University for benefiting members in and outside of New Mexico. In 1983 the California Pepper Improvement Foundation bestowed a certificate of appreciation on Nakayama for his contributions. The horticulture professor's passing in 1988 was a somber moment in the chile belt. "He'd really have to be called the father of the chile industry as we know it today . . . he provided a real service that is impossible to measure in dollars and cents and was a fine person," said Farm Bureau Vice-President Bob Porter.

Before his death, Nakayama was an active member of an NMSU-based organization that popularized chile, the International Connoisseurs of Green and Red Chile. The idea for a chile-promoting club was hatched by former NMSU President Gerald Thomas and University public relations man Dave Rodwell. Dr. Thomas arrived in Las Cruces in 1970 from Texas, where the Terlingua chile cook-off was the type of high-profile event he wished to see in New Mexico. Surveying the chile scene, he thought "there wasn't enough visibility" to the growing chile industry. The new NMSU CEO set out to change that.

One day in early 1973 Thomas invited 25 people to the historic La Posta restaurant in the Mesilla Valley, where in the back room the

"International Connoisseurs was born," according to first member and ex-Executive Director Jeanne Croft. Among the early members were processor Louis Biad, farmer Ray Enríquez, and Marian Black of the dairy and banking family. Croft considered Thomas an "astute" organizer for reaching out to the various sectors of the agricultural industry and drawing in "all the key people together to start the organization." NMSU and the processing industry provided financial support for a jumbled bag of activities and antics that sent Connoisseurs traipsing all over the world, in Croft's words, "to educate the uninformed of the world to the joys and mystique of the chile culture."

On a diplomatic mission, the Connoisseurs were joined by the Hatch Chile Festival Queen on their state visits. In five years, the group grew from 25 members to hundreds in the Las Cruces area alone and formed chapters, or pods, throughout the United States. The NMSU head honcho himself created the Prairie Pods in South Dakota, the Palouse Pods in Iowa, and assisted with the Bureau of Pods in Washington, D.C. Connoisseurs were soon found in all 50 states and in 17 foreign nations. As chile missionaries, they recruited new members who received a regular, recipe-laced newsletter, sold thousands of cookbooks, conducted gourmet cooking classes, held chile eating contests, sent chile "care" packages to members of the military, competed in tortilla tosses, and were among the first to popularize wet T-shirt contests.

Celebrities were drawn in to the rave. Lawrence Welk, Vikki Carr, José Feliciano, Bob Hope, and the musical group Alabama were among the initiated. Touching ground in California, the ambassadorial Amigos group of New Mexico businessmen inducted Governor

Ronald Reagan. On one occasion in the 1970s, Thomas and company flew "I don't know how many pounds of chile" into Washington, D.C. for a bash featuring the likes of Senator Pete Domenici, Senator Joseph Montoya, former Vice President Hubert Humphrey, and, according to Thomas, a tipsy Speaker of the House, Carl Albert.

Jeanne Croft, also a New Mexico Department of Agriculture marketing specialist, defined the once 3,000-strong Connoisseurs as a "tongue-in-cheek" organization, but it nevertheless functioned to get the word out about New Mexico's sizzling pride and joy. Once, Croft got a telephone call from a distraught producer for Armed Forces Radio Network in Europe who asked her to recite the Connoisseurs' Pledge of Allegiance to Chile over the air. She did, and it made the soldiers smile.

The scientific side of the chile-breeding program was reemphasized during Thomas's presidency. The private sector's input was enhanced and food processing firms donated money. Grants from companies such as Old El Paso Foods complemented state and private tax dollars obtained for the program by influential friends like New Mexico Republican Senator Pete Domenici. Appearing on the scene in 1987, Dr. Paul Bosland filled the shoes of Dr. Roy Nakayama. In a relatively short time, Dr. Bosland's staff claimed noteworthy accomplishments. In 1991 they released the new, high-yielding Nu Mex Joe E. Parker, Nu Mex Sweet, and Nu Mex Bailey Piquín varieties. The machine-harvestable, hot piquín chile was selling for almost $10 per pound in supermarkets and could yield super profits of up to $10,000 per acre. By producing more chile on the same amount of land, these cultivars give growers more bang for their buck. The Las Cruces chile designers also did their part for the New Mexico tourist industry by releasing ornamental chiles such as Nu Mex Sunglo and Nu Mex Sunflare for the *"mini-ristras"* visitors to the Land of Enchantment stow away in their suitcases. While NMSU's chile breeders released the latest peppers for a voracious industry, Croft and other New Mexico Department of Agriculture (NMDA) employees embarked on a globe-trotting sales blitz. In-house demonstrations of chile products were done in stores and restaurants. In the beginning people in places like Boston were cool. "'Yuck, we've tasted Texas chili,'" Croft recalled people in the Pilgrim beachhead saying. "We thought we were in a foreign country, but in a few months people were buying it."

In a short time, NMDA marketers were in genuine foreign republics, selling at shows and restaurants in Paris, London, Hong Kong, Singapore, and Malaysia. By 1991 the pitches netted an estimated $10 million in exports. And to head off any befuddlement about what to do with the chile, videos instructing the preparation of Southwestern dishes were produced in 12 languages.

Spearheading the capsicum conquest, NMSU and the NMDA enlisted a range of talents and departments. Nowadays, the Extension continues giving farmers advice on crops and planning, the Plant Genetic Engineering Laboratory transfers genes for the high-tech chiles of tomorrow, professors travel to China for chile discussions with government big-wigs, and the NMDA peddles products at trade shows and a New Mexico "Country Store." Nationally, the NMSU chile breeding program is reinforced by other public and private concerns, most notably the Texas A&M program where Dr. Ben Villalón changed the chile industry with his creation of a mild jalapeño back in the early 1980s. Private companies with significant seed development capabilities include Cal-Compack, Ferry-Morse Seed Company, and Petoseed Company. Transnational and local companies including Dow Chemical, American Cynamid, and DuPont, as well as the area's Farmer's Market and Supply, donated the chemicals and seed. But clearly it is at that small plot in the Mesilla Valley named after Fabián García where much of the cutting-edge research and development of chile is in progress. Glancing back, it would be impossible to imagine the contemporary New Mexico chile industry without the scientific and business skills of NMSU. While the horticulturists concentrated on crowning superior cultivars, the Extension Service helped farmers "test-tube" fertilizer and chemical pesticide experiments.

Raised on the premise of the Green Revolution, a new generation of farmers, processors, and agricultural college personnel had their day after the Second World War. The work was of immense importance in increasing the yield of green chile from one good acre from about five tons in Dr. García's times to six to twelve tons toward the end of the century. The publicly supported college was the modernizer of a much-lauded chile industry that captured the fancy of many inside and outside the Land of Enchantment. And perhaps nowhere in New Mexico was the chile fervor and the brouhaha more splashy than in the Hatch Valley, the cradle of New Mexico's Great Chile Boom.

Chile Cultivars Developed at NMSU 1921-91

BREEDER	YEAR	CHILE	USES
Fabián García	1921	Number 9	Green, sun-dried red. Crossed with native chile in the north. Medium hot.
Roy Harper	1950	Number 6	Mild canned green, red
Roy Harper	1950s	Rio Grande	Canned green
Roy Harper	1956	Sandía	Hot green, popular in open market stands
Roy Nakayama	1950s	6-4	Standard, mild canned and frozen variety
Roy Nakayama	1975	Big Jim	Standard chile rellenos
Roy Nakayama	1982	R-Naky	Mild, paprika
Roy Nakayama	1960s 1984	Española Improved Española Improved	Suited for northern New Mexico
Paul Bosland, Jaime Iglesias, S. D. Tanksley	1988	NuMex Sunrise NuMex Sunset NuMex Eclipse	Ornamental chiles
Paul Bosland	1991	NuMex Joe E. Parker	Mild green and red
Paul Bosland	1991	NuMex Sweet	Mild, paprika
Paul Bosland	1991	NuMex Bailey Piquín	Crushed pepper
Paul Bosland	1991	NuMex Sunburst NuMex Sunflare NuMex Sunglo	Chile mini-ristras and wreaths
Paul Bosland	1991	NuMex Twilight	Ornamental pot plants and gardens

Note: Other varieties not specifically developed by NMSU are grown in New Mexico, although many have been crossed with the college seed at one time or another. These include Cuarteles, Chimayo, El Guique, and Velarde, all native cultivars in the north; Barker's Extra Hot; the mild Sonora; and the numbered cultivars designed for color shade developed by private companies such as Cal-Compack.

Principal Sources: New Mexico Cooperative Extension, New Mexico State University, New Mexico Farm and Livestock Bureau.

Notes

1. "Chile heroes," *New Mexico Resources* (NMSU), Autumn 1989, 23.

2. Fabián García, "Chile Culture," New Mexico College of Agriculture and Mechanic Arts Press Bulletin #405, 14 January 1922.

3. John Neary, "The Big Chile," *Horticulture*, March 1977, 69-73.

4. Carl Nakayama, interview by author, Doña Ana County, NM, November 1993.

5. Linda Harris, interview by author, Las Cruces, NM, November 1993. Ms. Harris is a former NMSU employee and acquaintance of Roy Nakayama.

6. "Breeder Recognized for Developing Tasty, Mild Chili," *New Mexico Farm and Ranch*, March 1983, 20, 31.

7. "Mr. Chile Peppers Market with Improved Plants," Associated Press wire story, *Albuquerque Journal*, 22 March 1987.

8. "Chile Pioneer Roy Nakayama Dies," *Albuquerque Journal*, 13 July 1988.

9. Dr. Gerald Thomas, telephone conversation with author, August 1993.

10. Jeanne Croft, telephone conversation and interview with author, Albuquerque, NM, August-September 1993.

11. Ricardo Rael, Domenici staff person, telephone conversation with author, September 1991.

12. Dr. John Owen, untitled presentation, New Mexico Chile Conference, Las Cruces, NM, February 1993.

13. Dr. Greg Phillips, NMSU, telephone conversation with author, July 1993.

14. Dr. Robert Lansford, NMSU, telephone conversation with author, August 1991.

15. Craig L. Mapel, "The New Mexico Chile Industry 1991-92," New Mexico Department of Agriculture report, 1993, 2.

16. Petoseed Company, Southwest/Mexico Technical Bulletin, n.d.

17. *The Packer*, 10 October 1992.

18. *29th Annual Report, NMSU Cooperative Extension Service*, n.d., 45, 48.

19. *NMSU On-Farm and On-Ranch Demonstrations, Reports 1-10 1954-63, Fifth Annual Report 1958*, Cooperative Extension Service and Department of Agricultural Sciences, NMSU, 8.

20. Paul W. Bosland and Max González, *Chile Pepper Breeding Program, New Mexico State University 1991 Report*, NMSU, 21.

The Hatch Valley

CHILE CAPITAL OF THE WORLD

Royal Ostriches and Chile ▪ Galas and Gripes ▪ Franzoy's Fascination ▪ Festival Friends

Hatch, New Mexico, is the unlikely center of an empire. The tiny agricultural community, with an official population of 1,084, is tucked snugly away in southern New Mexico's Rio Grande Valley. "Hatch is not noted as the movie capital of the world," once commented local politician and farmer William Porter. Summer, though, is a lively season, a time when residents don their Sunday best and mingle outside the battery of churches. Roadrunners dash across the two-lane highway dotted with onion skins from Boston-bound bulbs. And travelers taking the shortcut to Tucson or Los Angeles crowd the counter at the Franklin Avenue Dairy Queen, served by young Mexican helpers flipping burgers and stirring shakes to the pace of Spanish and country and western radio hits.

Normally, Hatch's residents quietly go about their principal business of producing vegetables, fruits, and especially chile peppers for the world's tables. For decades Hatch chile was a Southwestern secret.

Word of the pepper's power slowly sizzled and filtered outside the Land of Enchantment's borders, until it was celebrated in the *New York Times*, photographically honored for future generations in *Smithsonian*, and publicized to millions the world over in *Reader's Digest* and *Sunset* magazine.

Hatch is the old warhorse of the New Mexico chile industry, which is the country's largest. Expanding from a once-local cottage industry, Hatch chile has been sold on the shelves of upscale Harrod's in London, displayed in Tokyo trade fairs, and cherished in the sands of Saudi Arabia during the Gulf War. "(Hatch) chile is the best chile in the country," boasts one matronly resident. "It has a different flavor."

Hatch's long-standing claim to fame is apparent every Labor Day weekend when thousands flock from as far away as New York and California with one treat in mind—the annual Hatch Chile Festival and its bounty of sizzling green and red peppers, which have put Hatch on

"California chile kinda' tasted like grass . . . it don't have no flavor."

—JUNE RUTHERFORD, DAUGHTER OF COMMERCIAL HATCH CHILE PIONEER JOSEPH FRANZOI

the food connoisseur's map as the self-proclaimed "Chile Capital of the World." Sponsored by companies like Coca-Cola, the chile festival kicks off with a parade down one of the village's two main thoroughfares. Under the heading of themes like "How Chile Won the West," an honor guard consisting of war veterans leads the way, trailed by contingents from the 4-H Club, the Future Farmers of America, the Doña Ana County Sheriff's Posse, and many other organizations. Colorful and creative, the entrants are proud witness to the days and weeks villagers take to prepare for the festival.

One First National Bank of Doña Ana County float had chile peppers—instead of money—growing on "trees." As the parade winds through town, whipping up a carnival-like mood, children snatch up candies thrown on the blistering, late summer pavement. Batman and Cat Woman cruise past on a motorbike, followed by saber-holding and musket-toting cavalry and infantrymen from the nineteenth century. Clowns on a "Jesus Loves You" float roll by, blessing the crowd. A low-rider brakes his red Mazda truck, jacking the vehicle up and down in the middle of the road with a hydraulic lift. The Hatch Chile Princess for the year extends regal waves from atop a classic Mustang car. Two Ronald McDonalds run up and down the street, giving out souvenir pens inscribed with the simple message of "Chile: Gotta Have It."

Not far from the parade hoopla, but distant enough from wandering tourists' eyes, is another side of Hatch. Flanked by an old silvery cotton gin and overgrown railroad tracks are two cement barracks where seasonal farmworkers in town for the onion and chile harvests pay $2.50 per night to rest their heads on old, dirty mattresses. Plywood walls fashion crude rooms, and the absence of air conditioning inside one windowless building renders the midday swelter outside a welcome relief. Buzzing flies add to the constant din of running showers, chatter, and Spanish-language radio. Away from the commotion, 32-year-old Hugo Ramírez of Chihuahua City, Mexico, was laid up in a bunk with a cut foot he suffered after emerging from a swim in the Rio Grande River. The injured worker admitted he hadn't visited a doctor because he didn't know where to find one. The wound, added Ramírez, had further delayed his goal of sending money home to his parents, a problem compounded by unpredictable mail delivery, low wages and high expenses. "In Mexico, you're in your house and all, you don't have to pay rent. Here you have to pay for everything."

Outside, the parade rolls on. Once it ends, the throngs hop into their vehicles and jam the road to the old Hatch airstrip where the festivities continue. Western fiddlers and Mexican dancers entertain the hungry crowds, shoppers sample chile products, and viewers admire the chile-themed crafts, landscapes, and wildlife art sketched and painted by Valley artists. While some find diversion in pitching horseshoes or inspecting the shiny chrome at the car show, others line up on a hill to fire away at clay targets. With rifles popping in the background, a tall, bearded man, decked out in the outlaw black of Western desperadoes, invites passerby to purchase his books about Old West criminals. "Before chile, there were outlaws," he yells.

Inside the covered pavilion that provides relief from the scorching sun, the seats fill up in anticipation of the grand event of the season. Signaled by the appearance of a Veterans of Foreign Wars color guard and the rising of the crowd to sing the "Star Spangled Banner," two of the Valley's nubile young women take the stage to be crowned the year's Red Chile Queen and Green Chile Queen, respectively. Visibly honored by the coronations, they read statements praising the vital role chile plays in the economy of the Hatch Valley. The Red Chile Queen even admits to having one addiction—to chile. "It's that powerful," she adds.

Back in the barracks, the chile pickers wash off after a hard day's work. A fortyish Mary Kittredge, wearing a fading checkered shirt and work pants, relaxes at a wooden table after a hard day of harvesting jalapeño chiles. A Durango, Mexico, native, Kittredge worked at a Colorado meat-cutting plant for $7.10 per hour before being laid off and arriving in Hatch during the summer of 1991. The mother of three children, including a son in the army at Ft. Ord, California, Kittredge likes picking chile but wishes the harvesters were paid more money than the minimum wage of $4.25 per hour. Some of her roommates, scrubbing the dirt off of their bodies after a day in the fields, readily agree. They complain that piece rates for each bucket

of picked jalapeños dropped from $1.30 in 1990 to 85¢ in 1991. "Let's say the work isn't easy, because you work hard enough and they pay very little," chimes in Pablo Ramírez, a resident of Juárez, Mexico, who's been traveling to Hatch for three years. Another man, hurriedly stuffing a suitcase, loudly bursts out that he's had enough of the low pay and is bound for California in a bus to find work in construction.

For barracks workers like Kittredge and Ramírez, a typical day of back-bending labor in the chile fields begins around six a.m. and lasts anywhere from four to ten hours—weekends often included—depending on the size and condition of the field to be picked and the wait for the distribution of the daily payroll. For many, an early day commences at the Hatch Pic Quik store for a wakeup shot of morning coffee. Joined by other workers bussed in for the day by El Paso-based farm labor contractors—the middlemen between the chile picker and the chile grower—they're forced to wait in line to purchase coffee. "In the morning, you have to go fast to get coffee," said an irked Kittredge. "You go inside and they tell you, 'You get out, there're five people in here. No more. You have to wait outside.'" When clearly more than five people were inside the store on the day of the chile festival—in violation of a sign displayed on the front that prohibits more than five customers inside at a time—a counter clerk was asked what the warning meant. "Oh, that's the farmworkers," he nonchalantly replied. "They come here in the morning. We can't fit them all in."

Whether the employee knew it or not, he was only verbalizing the ambivalent attitude of some longtime Hatch Valley residents toward the thousands of field hands and their family members drawn to the region because of an unprecedented boom in chile and other labor-demanding crops.

The largely Mexican field workers were in fact but the latest wave of immigrants to transform this remote section of southern New Mexico into one of the most fertile and profitable agricultural regions anywhere. A vintage small town, Hatch is actually the commercial hub of the Rio Grande and Las Uvas valleys of northern Doña Ana and southern Sierra counties. Known commonly as the Hatch Valley, the area is home to several thousand people who populate the farms, small houses, apartment complexes, and *colonias* of Hatch, Rincon, Placitas, Rodey, Milagro, Salem, Las Uvas, Garfield, Derry, and Arrey. For the sightseer it is a pleasant country excursion along the old highway that slices the valley in two, delineating a long strip of desert oasis past miles of dairies, chile processing plants, cabbage and onion patches, pecan groves, cotton gins, and the ubiquitous chile fields, whose red fruits emblazon the autumn landscape. At times alfalfa scent is in the air, hovering over the remaining stands of cottonwood trees.

Every now and then, the visitor is treated to an unexpected sight. Drivers near Rincon were startled to see ostriches strutting their feathery stuff on the roadside. Ever keen to diversification, local farmers delved into the exotic, importing young chicks hatched from African eggs; the birds' eggs, meat, and feathers brought high prices in specialty markets. It was only a matter of time before green chile ostrich burger or stew became the next rave. The long-necked, pecking birds became a part of the landscape, just like chile, and attracted nearly as much curiosity. Military aircraft buzzed the Royal Birds farm, scaring the gregarious creatures. Enraged ostrich ranchers on the ground cursed and shook their fists at the rude fly-boys.

Permanent settlement of the Hatch Valley dates back to the last century. Long used by the Mimbres Apaches, valley lands were claimed by Hispanos from northern and central New Mexico in the early to mid 1800s. González, Trujillo, and Apodaca were among the first names to make their mark on this marshy section of the Rio Grande. In order to survive on their small farms, the settlers worked cooperatively to build community irrigation ditches, or acequias.

The coming of the railroad in the last quarter of the nineteenth century helped spur growth in the region, and by 1882 the town of Rincon, now a sleepy shell of its former self, boasted a reputation as that "wicked town" where gambling, whoring, gunfighting, and thieving attracted a seedy element. In those days, cattle were the commodity of choice and rustling the preferred occupation of more than a few. The formative years of the Hatch Valley, however, were not all scenes of smoke and sin. Life acquired a mundane character as settlers went to work, attended church, or organized social functions with their neighbors.

"Most people were like those you see in a *Little House on the Prairie* type thing," writer and historian Bob L'Agoe is quick to add. A few miles from Rincon, the village of Hatch (named after a U.S. Army general) was originally founded in 1880 as a flag station on the Santa Fe Railroad. Its fertile lands, coupled with the demise of the railroad, eventually allowed Hatch to overtake Rincon in terms of importance. The valley's cultivators, however, had one sticky problem to contend with—the Rio Grande. In springtime, the river ran wild with run-off, frequently overshooting its banks in a natural occurrence beneficial to soil and vegetation but disastrous to human agriculture.

Even today, water continues to wreak havoc for farmers and residents. In summer, instantaneous thunderstorms appear from nowhere and pound the streets and fields with buckets of rain, sending farmworkers scrambling for shelter and growers to the altar praying that the downpour doesn't damage their fragile, ripening chile plants. At the junction of Interstate 25 and the Hatch turn-off, where an arroyo slopes into the Rio Grande, a surging stream of run-off crashes into the river and produces a surrealistic swirl of turquoise and crimson that flows furiously south toward the Mesilla Valley, the notorious "red water" feared by chile planters.

Yet the worst threats posed by nature's angry outbursts were mitigated in the early part of the century with the christening of the Elephant Butte Irrigation District and the construction of the Elephant Butte, Caballo, and Percha dams. The federally backed irrigation and flood control project permitted the take-off of commercial agriculture in the Hatch Valley and southern New Mexico. Soon, word got out, in the words of one Valley chronicler, of "fertile land for the taking." It was in the years between 1917 and 1947 that the bedrock of the Hatch Valley's agricultural and chile industries was laid. Cotton became the favored crop, and between the end of World War II and the early 1960s this fluffy plant was picked mostly by Mexican contract workers known as braceros. From the rural districts of northern Mexico, thousands of field hands were shipped north from the Ft. Bliss or the Rio Vista reception centers in El Paso and housed on individual farms in Hatch and across southern New Mexico and in old POW camps in Las Cruces and Artesia.

Alongside the braceros were the illegals who crossed the Rio Grande in substantial numbers. Their importance was underscored in 1947 when the Farm Bureau contracted to have illegals legalized as braceros. The braceros built up the cotton industry by weeding, hoeing, and picking

the plant. From the late 1940s to 1964, they earned 30¢ and then 60¢ an hour for their work and $2.25 per 100 pounds of cotton picked, though the premium Pima brand brought up to $3.50 for every 100 pounds. Eventually machines and the Farm Bureau program's cancellation made their presence in the Hatch Valley temporarily unnecessary.

At cotton's peak in the early 1950s, 24,000 Mexican braceros were officially reported as working in New Mexico. They not only worked cotton, but harvested apples in the Mimbres Valley, tomatoes around Deming, and other vegetable crops statewide. The Mexican farm hands were quartered in small adobe houses provided by growers, most of which are now gone, and provided with beds, blankets, pots, pans, and medical insurance.

Raúl Delgado was laboring as a bracero in Donna, Texas, in the early 1960s when a letter from Doña Ana County arrived that announced a search for cotton workers. Like others, this Chihuahua migrant worked the farms during the day and socialized with compatriots in the off-hours. Delgado found a more lively Hatch Valley then, a place where the working men on weekends could enjoy diversion at one of a half dozen cantinas, at the billiard hall, or at the two movie houses, where the Spanish-language films of Cantinflas, Raúl De Anda, Luis Aguilar, and Pedro Infante played.

Another bracero who arrived years before said the farmworkers' money went a lot farther in those days. "You could buy two shirts with one dollar," he remembered. "Food didn't go up," added Delgado, who calculated that $6 purchased food for an entire week.

Delgado continued in Hatch after the bracero program and became one of the few ex-contract workers anywhere to purchase a small farm and settle in the community. His life is more sedate in some ways now, more harried in others. Video rental outlets have replaced the theaters, cutting out a common meeting ground but reaffirming the centrality of home and family. And Delgado is kept occupied searching wherever he can for buyers of what is now his chile crop.

The end of the bracero era coincided with the decline of the Hatch cotton kingdom as international economic competition, falling prices, and the pest-borne effects of monoculture all made the crop less profitable. But chile was waiting in the wings. Although Spanish-speaking New Mexicans began growing chile after settling the upper Hatch Valley in the 1800s, it wasn't until the present century that the crop became important enough to enshrine the Hatch name in the chile hall of fame.

An early trailblazer, and indeed the man whom many cite as the father of the commercial Hatch chile industry, was an Austrian immigrant of Italian background named Joseph Franzoi. According to June Rutherford, Franzoi's 69-year-old daughter, her father relocated to this country in the early 1900s to escape the military draft in empire-mad Europe. Securing work first as a miner in Michigan, the young Franzoy (as he later spelled his name) and his family headed for the silver and copper ore mines of the mineral-rich Southwest. There, amid the nervousness of his wife Celestina, Franzoy labored under conditions in which there were "too many accidents, too many people getting killed." With visions of farming and experience growing grapes and silkworms in Europe, Franzoy bought land in the New Englander-settled town of Salem just north of Hatch, cleared the marshy *bosque*, and learned from his neighbors in 1918 how to farm the arid real estate.

Franzoy possessed other skills as a photographer and a language enthusiast, and he soon added Spanish to his Italian, German, and English skills. He was one of the first immigrants to join a community of native-born Hispanic farmers eking out a living on the land. "Everybody was poor, nobody had nothing," was the way Rutherford described her family's first years in the Valley. When the Franzoys took root in the Hatch Valley, there were a few chile patches "here and there," said Rutherford. A traditional method of preparation and consumption, *chile pasado*, involved the roasting of green chile which was then peeled and hung out to dry.

"The first time [Papa Franzoy] ate chile, he thought they poisoned him," chuckled Rutherford. But the adventurous Austrian was enthusiastic and began attending dinners that featured a New Mexico A&M Extension agent who gave presentations on chile growing. Franzoy was one of the first farmers to obtain a power tractor and in 1924 took the bold step of seeding 10 acres of chile, a large amount for the time. In those days, chile was sun-dried on roofs, hillsides, and irrigation embankments, a practice largely abandoned in the south now, though a careful gazer can still spot random heaps of chile sunning on a roof.

Still a novice, Franzoy was coached in chile growing by Doña Ana County Extension Agent Stockdale. Notified of the goings on in the Hatch Valley, Dr. Fabián García popped in to inspect Franzoy's chile. After finding he could raise a crop, Franzoy returned to the mining districts of Silver City, Bayard, and Santa Rita. But instead of donning the miner's cap for the pits, he wore the produce seller's hat, peddling his chile and vegetables to hungry workingmen in his former haunts. When not shipping by train, Franzoy loaded up his green stuff aboard Model

T trucks and endured day-long excursions over dirt and gravel to reach the miners' camps in the mountains. His oldest son, Alex, tagged along and remembered times when trips lasted two or three days, especially when the rains washed in and changed their schedule. "Roads was pretty rugged, mostly cow trails then. We used to have a time in the [wet] season," he said.

The elder Franzoy was pivotal as an early New Mexico connection to California chile distributors and he racked up dealings with a company called Chile Products. By the 1930s, the young June was helping her father sack chiles bound for Los Angeles. Slowly, Hatch chile and the Franzoy family were making their mark on the national scene. Locally, Joseph Franzoy and his descendents influenced the course of Hatch history through their participation in the Farm Bureau, Elephant Butte Irrigation District, Soil Conservation Service, and the Garfield cotton gin cooperative.

A large clan, the Franzoys intermarried extensively with other top Valley chile farmers, including members of the Riggs, Lytle, Carson, Biad, Berridge, Lack, Benvie, and Gillis families. Today they are the dominant farm families in the Hatch Valley and control much of New Mexico chile growing.

In the early days, chile harvesting and preparation for shipment was a long, drawn-out process, often taking weeks before the pod was ready for the sack. June and the other Franzoys carpeted the hillsides with drying red chile, creating an annual repainting of the New Mexican countryside. But there was always the prospect of rain ruining the canvas. "Hell, it was pretty but you had to work like everything. You had to do it, you know, early in the fall, because of the weather," she explained. "It was not as clean as it is now because you know how it was then, but

people weren't as conscious. There wasn't the Food and Drug on your neck all the time like it is now. People knew how to wash things before they ate it." Sun-dried chile hosted rodents, birds, and spiders on the piles. Rains created molds. As one 1949 New Mexico A&M report noted, "officials of the Food and Drug Administration (FDA) have warned growers that the mold content must be reduced or eliminated if the crop is to be sold on the open market." Restrictions on sun-dried New Mexico chile were such that processors in adjacent El Paso were compelled to purchase dried chile hundreds of miles away in California. The solution to this dilemma lay with the artificial dryer once tried in El Paso County and then in vogue in California. The artificial dehydrator, a tunnel-like machine using gas or butane-powered blowers to slowly dry a ton of chile in a 24-hour period, made its appearance in the Hatch Valley of the late 1950s and early 1960s, when the late Fred Riggs Sr., the late James Lytle Sr., and the Biad family cranked up machines.

While the machines put an end to the splashy, red landscapes of days of yore, they complied with FDA regulations designed to ensure insect and bird-dropping-free products in the supermarket. "It gave New Mexico a chance to compete with California," remarked Ernest Riggs, the son of Fred Riggs Sr. and the manager of Cal-Compack in Las Cruces. At last, the animal problem was solved at drying time but remained an issue at the growing stage. "Some of our fields we have so many deer in, we can't even harvest the fields," said Ernest Riggs's sister Mary Gillis, who wed Dencil Gillis and operated the dehydrator-run Mesilla Valley Chili Company. "We also have coyotes that eat the chile. They'll just take it and they bite tips off and eat it."

The dehydrators brought new business and enthroned families like the Riggses and Gillises as industry leaders. Gillis's Arrey plant acquired the Barker Extra Hot seed variety from a famous Las Cruces farmer of the same name and sealed its red fire in plastic bags. The Mesilla Valley Chili Company claimed trademark rights on the blistering chile, but many others sold it under the Barker Extra Hot name anyway. Eventually New Mexico chile growers set up more than two-dozen dehydrating units, choosing names like Kit Carson Chile Products (Nick Carson), Tres Hermanos (Franzoys), and Sun Products (J. W. Donaldson). Victor and Louis Biad, belonging to another Austrian immigrant family, had three plants in the Mesilla and Hatch valleys; they employed more than 100 people. The dehydrating technology even attracted an unlikely, self-proclaimed helper of the small chile farmer in 1992: Canadian tobacco dryer magnate Gabe DeCloet. The urbane DeCloet was contacted by a New Mexican interested in DeCloet's dryers (7,000 sold worldwide) for the chile industry. Intrigued, DeCloet, with the advice of Dr. Jaime Iglesias, modified the dryers slightly and placed four south of Deming.

While Hatch growers pioneered the shift toward artificial drying, they also worked to innovate at the fresh end of the chile trade. The future June Rutherford married a man in 1942 who would also have a memorable impact on the New Mexico chile industry: her first husband, James Lytle, Sr. Learning the tricks of chile growing from June's dad, Lytle was soon hooked on the pepper trade. In the 1950s he began working with NMSU's legendary chile breeder Roy Nakayama to develop a bigger green chile pod amenable to the labor-saving machinery of an area cannery. Lytle, Sr. passed away in 1970 before witnessing the fruit of his experiments,

but June kept the torch burning. Four years later, Nakayama released the Big Jim variety, which as any chile aficionado knows is the preferred pepper for the New Mexican *chile relleno*. The final years of the Big Jim experiment coincided with the downturn in Hatch cotton production and the increase in commercial chile cultivation, geared for the changing tastes of a culturally and ethnically changing nation.

Local businessmen seized the time to launch a promotion. One of the key figures was the late Clayborn Wayne, a former New Mexico A&M agronomist, ex-secretary of the New Mexico Crop Improvement Association, decorated World War Two veteran, and pesticide-fertilizer salesman. Wayne was a respected member of the Hatch community, having opened the Farmer's Market and Supply store in 1947. He couldn't have picked a better time and a better place. Optimism was sweeping the agricultural world, driven in large degree by the boom in chemical pesticides derived from war-related research. Wayne's one-stop private business offered the farmer seed and livestock feed, fertilizers, pesticides, and even a crop-dusting service to put the bug-killing chemicals to use. An astute observer of market trends, Wayne got involved in helping farmers move away from the cotton economy to a more diverse market. "He wanted people to learn that there was more than one type of chile," said his widow Alice. "He spent a lot of time promoting it." Hatch patriarch Ben Archer, an 86-year-old pecan rancher who has the local clinic named after him, similarly credits Wayne for advancing the fortunes of Hatch chile. "(Wayne) has done more for that angle than just about anyone else," remarked Archer. "We started growing chile, quite a bit at the time. Several of us thought we should do something to help the farmers."

In 1971 Wayne and Archer were members of the first Hatch Chile Festival committee, a group backed by the local Chamber of Commerce to get the word out about Hatch chile. The first festival was wildly successful, recalled Archer, and drew several thousand more people than expected. Wayne then went on to become a founder of the International Connoisseurs of Green and Red Chile, serving dutifully as a dedicated member who never "missed a meeting," according to one-time Executive Director Jeanne Croft.

But in order for the Hatch chile boom to flourish, bigger outside markets were needed. This requirement was met in the 1970s by California, Texas, and Arizona-based food processors including Cal-Compack, Universal Foods, Fiesta Canning Company, La Victoria, and the Santa Cruz Chile and Spice Company, firms that ensured the growth of the Hatch industry through their purchase of the fiery product.

"California chile kinda' tasted like grass, it don't have no flavor," commented Rutherford on the shift in the business from the Pacific state to the Rio Grande Valley of Hatch. "Chile has gone so far ahead, you look back and you can hardly believe it. They even buy chile from New York." Once the table-top fare of Hispanic growers and later their immigrant neighbors, Hatch chile became a commodity in "hot" demand: it not only put the valley on the map of international cuisine, but it transformed the social and economic relationships of the population as well. And, like any big business that descends on small, rural communities, chile gradually changed the nature of daily life in the Hatch Valley by attracting new settlers whose interests sometimes clashed with those of previously settled people. Hatch would never be the same.

Notes

1. William Porter, testimony to U.S. Commission on Agricultural Workers, Las Cruces, NM, 23 October 1991, *Hearings and Workshops before the Commission on Agricultural Workers 1989-1993 to Accompany the Report of the Commission*, Appendix 2, 783.

2. *Albuquerque Journal*, 12 December 1989.

3. *The Courier* (Hatch, NM), 29 July 1993.

4. *The Courier*, 3 September 1992.

5. Author's observations of the Hatch Chile Festival, 1990-93.

6. Hugo Ramírez, interview by author, Hatch, NM, August 1991.

7. Mary Kittredge, interviews by author, Hatch, NM, July and August 1991.

8. Pablo Ramírez, interview by author, Hatch, NM, August 1991.

9. Hatch Valley Friends of the Library, *History of the Hatch Valley* (Hatch, NM: n.p., 1989).

10. Bob L'Agoe, interview by author, Hatch, NM, September 1992.

11. *New Mexico Farm and Ranch*, May 1971.

12. June Rutherford, telephone conversations and interviews with author, Hatch, NM, August 1992 and September 1993.

13. Alex Franzoy, telephone conversation with author, January 1994.

14. *New Mexico Farm and Ranch*, March 1960, 27.

15. Ernest Riggs, interview with author, Las Cruces, NM, August 1993.

16. Mary Gillis, interview with author, Arrey, NM, October 1993.

17. *Research for New Mexico Agriculture: 60th Annual Report of the Agricultural Experiment Station, College of Agriculture and Mechanic Arts*, State College, NM, 31 December 1949, 29.

18. Joel A. Diemer, Buddy Stewart, and Rosanna C. Álvarez, "Food Processing in New Mexico," NMSU Agricultural Experiment Station Report #653, February 1991.

19. Raúl Delgado and Faustino Ramos, interviews with author, Salem, NM, October 1993.

20. Gabe DeCloet, interview with author, Las Cruces, NM, February 1993.

21. Dr. Jaime Iglesias, interview with author, Las Cruces, NM, August 1993.

22. Amal Naj, *Peppers: A Story of Hot Pursuits* (New York: Alfred A. Knopf, 1992), 62-63.

23. Alice Wayne, telephone conversation with author, August 1992.

24. Ben Archer, telephone conversation with author, August 1992.

25. Jeanne Croft, interview with author, Albuquerque, NM, September 1993.

The Two Worlds of Hatch

CONFLICT AT EMPIRE'S CENTER

The 18-Wheeler Chile Express ▪ Settling Salem-by-the-Rio Grande ▪ The Great Chile Bridge Camp-Out ▪ Parade Protest

One man who can tell you just how far chile has come is Raúl Medina, a small farmer from Garfield. A quiet man whose voice is edged with baritone when he speaks, Medina is the proprietor of a roadside stand that sells vegetables and chile to the hungry traveler. In front of his rural home, friends from Acoma Pueblo sell handmade pottery.

Medina, who's grown chile for more than 40 years, has watched the transformation of the valley chile industry from the days of horse-drawn plows to the power tractor. "I've driven many a team of horses," he laughs. In his time, Medina has felt the weather get "hotter," competed with more growers, and observed chile "double or triple" popularity from the days when it was "mostly the Mexican people who were going for it, because it was so spicy and everything." Surrounded by strings of chile *ristras* he calls *pico de pájaro*, or "bird's beak," Medina pauses to help a customer find a sack of Big Jim. Then the chile elder resumes his recollections of the old days:

"It was really very small pods, and then somebody came up with the Big Jim variety, which is a very thick, beautiful pod, and somebody else started coming up with some of the other varieties . . . yet making it worthwhile so you could have a nice pod that wouldn't be so hard for somebody to pick. For the farmer, he would have a large return, in other words, on his crop."

During the months of August and October, between the last thundery outbursts of the rainy season and the bodings of autumn, visitors drive to the Hatch Valley to stop at outlets like Medina's. They pick out a decorative *ristra*, sample a burning jalapeño, or buy a big, bulging sack of green chile and have it roasted for the long months of winter when only the freezer contains the memories of the fall's harvest.

In many important respects, the Hatch Valley was simply unprepared for the Great Chile Boom of the 1980s and 1990s. A labor intensive crop, chile demands lots of sweat and blood all the way from thinning, weeding, and

> *"Everyone who used to work here knew each other, and now they're people from California . . . there're cars here with Miami license plates."*
>
> —HATCH CHILE PICKER

irrigating the crop to the final harvesting, which itself could involve multiple pickings from the first ripe green peppers of the season to the last stand of red in the frosty days of winter after the pod had changed colors. At the same time chile spiraled in production, other labor-intensive vegetables such as onions, lettuce, and cabbage became favorites of valley farmers.

Consequently, greater numbers of Mexican agricultural workers, responding to the clarion call of the Hatch chile empire, flocked to the region, only to encounter a crisis in affordable housing. Like other rural towns in the 1980s, Hatch did not have enough housing, schools, health care, or recreational facilities. Many chile pickers continued to endure the arduous daily bus ride back and forth from the labor recruitment site in El Paso, but others naturally chose to settle with their families in close proximity to work.

The Valley's population mushroomed in the wake of the 1986 immigration reform that legalized formerly undocumented workers. Seizing on a clear-cut opportunity, in the Hatch Valley salesmen subdivided lands into smaller plots and sold them off in pyramid schemes in which one subdivision ended up as a collection of tiny properties. The lots sold for up to $17,000 each, payable in monthly installments that many of the low-income agricultural workers could afford. Unfortunately, the properties did not have utilities.

By 1992, an estimated 10 to 20,000 people lived in the unplanned Doña Ana *colonias* that stretched from Arrey in the north to Chaparral in the south. Near Hatch, the Salem *colonia* was born, home to between 600 and 800 people. In the windy weeks of spring, dust storms kicked up along the dirt roads; in the wet weeks of summer, flash floods created a muddy mess. Through it all, the Salem residents rose to bend in the fields, sack onions in burlap bags, or stand for hours in the chile dehydrators, sorting the good pods from the bad ones. They packed their kids off to school, saved money to send home to Mexico when possible, and prepared for the winter lull in the agricultural work cycles, when food stamps or government donations sustained them. They dreamed of finding full-time work with a farmer, perhaps laying irrigation pipes or operating machinery.

Still unincorporated, Salem is a jumble of small homes and trailers set up in clusters along winding, dirt roads. Children play on street corners and a video rental outlet services the entertainment needs of residents. On certain Saturday nights, in vivid contrast to the quiet slumber of nearby Hatch, Salem comes alive with the sounds of popular Mexican *banda* music and partying. Young men and women, outfitted in the best dresses and cowboy hats and boots they can afford, strut in style, just as they would if they were back in a Chihuahua town.

Together, immigrants sought a burst of joy in the depths of Trailerville, a new, low-cost community model slapped onto the sands of a growing New Mexico where accessible housing was still a storybook tale for many. The trailers varied in size, shape, and condition, featuring everything from comfortable quarters to vermin-infested dregs. At one spacious trailer, a group of men from Zacatecas, Mexico, shared the rental for $20 each per week. Nonetheless, they had no electrical outlet and were forced to run an extension cord to an adjacent structure.

Initially neglected, the Salem *colonia* drew the attention of politicians, planners, health experts, and code enforcers, especially after President Bush's 1991 proposal for a free trade agreement with Mexico directed attention to the border. Some, like Greg White, a Doña Ana County planner, worried about fecal contamination of groundwater supplies from leaking septic tanks, a pollution problem cropping up throughout the state of New Mexico.

The County of Doña Ana filed and then settled suits in 1994 against *colonia* developers, hoping to force the desert-lot real estate salesmen, including former U.S. Attorney Bill Lutz, into building roads and basic infrastructure at their own expense rather than the taxpayers'. The settlements provoked an outcry from New Mexico state legislators, who worried about future state financial support in the absence of concomitant private sector outlays.

But while officials argued about where to stop the buck, *colonia* dwellers articulated a voice for their own interests. Some Salem residents turned to the activist arm of the Roman Catholic Church and to organizer Antonio Luján for help. In 1989, they founded the Farmworker Project, a church-funded, grassroots group dedicated to community health awareness, voter registration, and political empowerment. The group's young head was Rubén Núñez, a 30-year-old native of Juárez, Mexico, and a onetime farmworker himself.

Sitting in a back room of the project's office in a frame house off a Hatch side street, Núñez recalled coming to Hatch 10 years earlier to escape the stress of urban life. Remembering his first thoughts of Hatch as "pretty," Núñez added that much of the excitement occurred when the teenage sons of a prominent farm family blocked off the main drag downtown and held impromptu drag car races.

Now, Núñez had put aside the field hoe for the organizer's pen and was at work forming health and youth committees, holding events to bring together Valley newcomers and old-timers, advocating for sewage and water systems and parks, and urging newly legal *colonos* to apply for citizenship so they could vote and influence the affairs of their community. "We don't deny there are problems of alcoholism or that kids are beginning to drop out of school," remarked Núñez, "but I see a community that's trying to leave these problems behind, and many people participate in the projects we've had here."

As the seasonal and migrant farmworkers streamed into the Valley, tensions developed over jobs, schools, and housing. The barracks and local motel were packed to the brim, scores of farmworkers—including entire families—sought shelter under bridges over the Rio Grande, and busloads of exhausted workers were ferried to and from El Paso on a daily basis. Early conflict surfaced in 1988 when citizen complaints of single, male farmworkers supposedly boozing it up and urinating on the street while whistling at women reportedly led to the ouster of the police chief for alleged negligence in carrying out his job.

Friction spilled over into the public schools. Decades earlier Hatch was known as having the most unused, available classroom space in the region, with about 1,000 students in the Valley school district and ample room for 300 more young minds. In 1991, State Representative William Porter testified to a federal commission meeting in Las Cruces that the school system was having difficulty absorbing new students, remarking that 150 new students meant a crisis for a small rural system. One school calendar year later, Hatch Schools Superintendent Cecil Davis declared, "We're worried because we don't have any more rooms . . . [The students] are coming from families that work in the fields." In the first enrollment release of the 1994-95 school year, authorities reported 1,373 pupils and were still counting.

Dependent on one another for their livelihoods, newcomers and old-timers co-existed at the workplace but usually socialized separately. Teresa Ramos, a health educator, former school board candidate, mother of two, and daughter of a Hatch cotton picker from the 1950s, spent time discussing the issue with teachers in the Hatch schools: "From what they [teachers] see, and from what I've been able to see myself, people tend to stay in their little groups. You especially see this in the kids who are entering the school system. If you're new and have been here for two or three years, even the Mexican American who has been here, or is a first-generation Mexican American, it's a totally different society to them. They don't seem to interact as well. If you even compare the farmers with the Mexican Americans who've been here for years, 20 to 30 years, there's not much mingling in that either."

Other controversies raged: locals disagreed about whether to declare Hatch itself a *colonia* eligible for federal assistance, mulled the wisdom of a private prison near the town, and debated the migrant educational program, an issue that drew a bevy of sharp-tongued legislators.

Already involved with the farmworker community, the Roman Catholic Church sponsored a 1991 Las Cruces hearing in a bid to find joint solutions for the burning issues of housing and wages. From that hearing, a loosely organized group emerged to tackle the housing crisis. Its members included Bishop Ramírez of Las Cruces, State Senator Mary Jane García of Doña Ana County, Rose García of the non-profit Tierra del Sol, Inc., housing development corporation, and social service providers. An immediate goal was to establish, with state support, an emergency encampment for 250 farmworkers. Initially, the group claimed to have the support of New Mexico Governor Bruce King and the state National Guard, which could provide tents, water, and electricity.

Governor King's spokesman, John McKean, voiced qualified support for the project, emphasizing that the Governor's stamp of approval was contingent upon tent city organizers obtaining permission from the appropriate state, federal, and local authorities. "It's a tough situation we need to work on and clear up," King told a Santa Fe reporter. "My heart goes out to them (the farmworkers), but it's too much to ask the taxpayers of New Mexico to take care of them. It's a big problem for everybody." King was later voted out of office, and homeless farmworkers remained a fact at the end of his term. The tent city idea foundered after two Hatch farmers rejected a proposed site as being too close to their land and the U.S. Department of Labor decided it would not meet housing standards. An alternative site owned by the Bureau of Land Management (BLM) near Rincon was likewise turned down because the federal agency was concerned about creating another *colonia*, and it was too close to an old landfill with hazardous methane gas.

The Mexican government entered the fray and formally requested the tent city in a letter to then U.S. Secretary of the Interior Manuel Luján, the overseer of the BLM. Luján's department replied through a lower-level official and repeated its opposition to the Rincon site,

though one BLM spokesman pledged his office's cooperation in finding federal land for a permanent housing project.

In the middle of the tent city deadlock, Núñez and the Farmworker Project protested when a representative from the Doña Ana County Building Inspector's office drove up to Salem in June 1992 and red-tagged 20 small trailers, giving the 60 to 75 occupants 90 days to pack up and move out. According to Inspector Tommy García, the trailers were not legal dwellings under housing codes, were potential health hazards because of overcrowding, and were fire dangers because of extension cords running in all directions from the campers. Salem *colonos* viewed it differently: They con-

Breakfast in the Barracks: Farmworker housing in Hatch, New Mexico, early 1990s.

Below the Bridge: Farmworkers in Hatch, New Mexico, early 1990s.

tended they had nowhere else to live and would be forced to join the ranks of homeless farmworkers. "They're going to put us in a place where there's no water, no place to cook; they're going to put us along the river or under a bridge. Then there will be health problems," predicted Núñez.

García relented and let the deadline pass without fanfare, leaving the Salem trailer dwellers unmolested. His logic concurred with Núñez's: "More or less it'll evict them and leave them without anywhere else to stay. We decided to back off because there's no place to go."

Actually, there were a few places to go, all of them on the cold ground. Hidden from the traffic on Interstate 25 just a stone's throw away,

the bridge over the Rio Grande offered a refuge for upwards of 60 farmworkers who called it home. There, gang and braggart graffiti covered the bridge's concrete columns, open beer and food cans littered the ground, and black patches were burned into the ground where workers had prepared themselves a meal. Creeping gently by, the Rio Grande teased the willows on the banks where men and women peered into the river before jumping in for a bath or a swim.

In addition to the regular "tenants," off-duty workers like Sharon stopped by to crack a brew or shoot the bull with friends. A husky, loud blonde from Chicago, Sharon seemed out of place amid the Chihuahuahense accents chorusing around her. But as her story unfolded it soon became clear that she had been initiated into the lifestyle of the agricultural worker. The big woman had left the Windy City for Mexico in the spring of 1992 and become stranded in Hatch when her car broke down. Thinking that she would earn a few bucks and be on her merry way, Sharon landed a job at a Las Uvas Valley onion packing shed as a quality control inspector. There, she put in double shifts, with a two-hour daily break, and she developed a pair of swollen feet. Today, however, she was taking a break and sipping beers with friends. "I go home and go to bed. I ain't got no time for boyfriends. There ain't time for nothing, nothing."

In spite of her endless days, Sharon managed to make friends, and she discovered that she did not have to go to Mexico at all: Mexico had come to her. She was especially touched by Juana Bujanda, a woman whose three-year-old granddaughter was killed that year by a car while standing near an onion field. After two and one half months, Sharon was ready to go home. "All I want to do is go to Chicago, because this isn't it."

But for others at the bridge, there were no such feelings. For them, it was nothing less than a second home. Early one summer evening, three veteran chile pickers sat talking on the tailgate of one man's truck, chatting and watching the sunset, a pastime which was only upstaged by a young man popping in a cassette tape and singing along, remembering that girl back home. The elder of the trio got up and started picking trash off the ground, piled it into a van, and then drove off. His friend, a talkative man attired in old work clothes and sporting a full, slightly graying beard, was apologetic: the local dump had been closed to them and garbage was accumulating underneath the bridge.

Originally from Ciudad Juárez, they said they had been coming to Hatch since 1978 or 79 as one stop in an annual cycle of onion and chile plantings, cleanings, and harvestings, beginning in February in the southern Mesilla Valley and culminating in the fall at Deming and Lordsburg to the west. As in previous years, they were living in the back of a pickup and returning home on weekends for family visits. Still, they counted themselves lucky to have at least a semblance of a roof over their heads, mentioning that they were fortunate to have a vehicle to sleep in and not be compelled to sleep on the ground as others were.

In town, the accommodations in the barracks or in the hotel were too crowded for the men. "They can't move," said the bearded man. "Thanks to God, we've got our furnishings and in this we live, we sleep and we got room." But in their view, something was different this year and a strange scent of change was looming over town. Work was scarce, and on some days the men could only find part-time harvesting jobs which netted them 10 or 15 dollars. "Now there are many strange people one's never seen. There's more tension in town," asserted the bearded man. Perking up, his buddy quipped that he couldn't believe the places people were coming from to work the chile harvest, lured by false stories of high wages to be made in the harvest. "Everyone who used to work here knew each other, and now they're people from California, other places. Some people have come from Texas and even from Miami. There're cars here with Miami license plates." Worse yet, added the bearded man, many would-be chile pickers were arriving at a time when decades of plantings were taxing the soil and making the pickings less bountiful than before, thus complicating an already competitive labor market. "You know the land gets tired over time always planting the same seed, the same seed," he mused. "It's necessary to vary the seed."

The conversation then turned to the nitty gritty of agricultural economics, with the bearded individual adding that in 13 or 14 years he'd only seen piece rates for each bucket of picked green chiles go from 45¢ to 60¢—though chile sales had skyrocketed during the same time. He stated that the labor contractors were getting the extra money the workers should have been earning. "It's better to work directly with the farmer, because the money the contractor earns should go to us." Suddenly, the mood got lighter as other men pulled up. A shaggy little dog, appearing lost, wandered down the dirt escarpment leading to the highway. One man leaped out of his car, grabbed a piece of a branch that resembled a cigar, and tried to stick it into the bearded man's mouth. "Fidel Castro," he announced to a round of laughs.

Talk then turned to possibly leaving Hatch for the green chile harvests in full swing near Deming and Lordsburg to the west. The men debated, weighing the advantages and disadvantages of waiting two weeks in Hatch for the start of the red chile picking compared with striking out and heading for Luna County. One consideration, noted the bearded man, was the easy access the Rio Grande provided for baths right at their doorstep. "There's no river in Deming," he added.

On a daily basis, the dissatisfaction over wages expressed by the workers at the bridge existed as an undercurrent of resentment. But sometimes long-standing grievances broke out into the open. This happened at the 1990 Hatch Chile Festival. That was the year the El Paso-based Border Agricultural Workers Union rolled

into town. A feisty, independent organization formed in 1984 by 100 workers from Mexico and the United States, the union staged the public protest as part of a regional strike action against labor contractors and growers in southern New Mexico and west Texas. Packing two old school buses with about 100 chile pickers, the union slipped into the official parade route, its members waving red union flags from the windows and passing out pamphlets to surprised onlookers. Displayed prominently from the buses' sides were enlarged copies of workers' pay receipts which showed earnings less than the federal minimum wage. The protestors distributed an open letter, which read in part:

HOW CAN THE CHILI GROWERS AND PROMOTERS OF THIS FESTIVAL CONTINUE TO BE PROUD OF THE CHILE CROP AND ITS FAME WHILE THOUSANDS OF FARMWORKERS AND THEIR FAMILIES CONTINUE TO ANGUISH DAILY BECAUSE OF THE MISERABLY LOW WAGES THEY RECEIVE?

In closing, the strikers' message asked the public to support the chile pickers, who were called "the real producers and the foundation of the New Mexico chile industry."

After the downtown crowds dispersed and headed for the sumptuous aromas blanketing the festival grounds, the protestors rolled up their flags and regrouped for a brief strategy session underneath the familiar Rio Grande bridge. There, they traded shouts of "*huelga, huelga*" (strike, strike) for bites of warm tortillas. Juárez picker Jesús Rodríguez was clear about why he was participating, despite a federally mandated increase in the minimum wage that spring. "We have expenses like the rent, the gas and all that. That's why we're supporting the strike, so they'll increase our wages to allow us to move forward with our families, to give us more support."

In addition to the strikers' principal demand of an immediate 25¢ to 50¢ hike for each bucket of picked chile (depending on the variety), the pickers demanded bathrooms and drinking water in all fields, enforcement of federal labor statutes applying to farm labor contractors, and an end to abuse of what they alleged was a mistreated workforce, which counted women and

Uninvited Guests: Protestors crash the 1990 Hatch Chile Festival.

children in its ranks. "Wages haven't changed in 10 to 12 years. At the same time the cost of living has risen," charged union coordinator Carlos Marentes. "So there's been a big deterioration in farmworkers' living conditions. Now you can find children less than 12 years of age working in the fields. They don't go to school because they have to contribute to the household income. There's a total indifference on the part of the chile industry, despite a rise each year in its profits. It's a multimillion dollar industry, but at the same time it's putting the farmworkers in a state of unbearable poverty."

Prominent chile growers were indignant. Don Hackey, the son of a Pecos, Texas, rancher who moved to the Hatch Valley in the 1940s, grew 400 acres of chile and had a hard time swallowing the tales of deprivation. As president of the farmer-organized New Mexico Chile Commission, the young Hackey was a spokesman for the state's pepper cultivators.

Noting that a USDA wage survey of several farms in 1990—including his own—claimed that the average worker made between $5.40 and $6.04 an hour, Hackey also questioned assertions of inhumane conditions prevailing in the fields. "They took isolated incidences or made up incidences. I don't know how many interviews I've given, but in fact if you're out there working in 100-degree heat with no water, would you go back the next day? Of course not, that's really stupid." As for wages, Hackey challenged the union's contention of windfall farmer profits, pointing out that most growers were locked into a set price for their product that was prenegotiated with the food processors who handled the final marketing and distribution of the chile or chile-containing products. The small raise growers received in 1990, he asserted, went to pay the harvesters their increase in the minimum wage. "Every single penny of it."

Also limiting farmers' income from chile, said Hackey, was the need to rotate chile with other crops every three to five years, making imperative a good profit from a year's harvest. But Hackey wished that growers, too, could get more money. "Honestly we need more . . . our inputs have gone up, you know, fuel and fertilizer and just man-hours. We don't get enough for our product. There's not much money to be made in the crop as in past years."

Hatch chile and onion grower Andy Núñez, a former director of international programs at NMSU, was even more strident in his disapproval of the strikers' demands and went so far as to vow to get out of the business altogether. The solution, he warned, lay with mechanical harvesters, which would eliminate field labor. "You never hardly see any hand labor in cotton anymore because it's machine picked. And these people are just going to price themselves out of a job, that's what it amounts to."

The 1990 chile protest gradually wound down with the harvest, but it left unresolved key issues that were to resurface two years later in a Mesilla Valley strike. In the interim, the Hatch Valley chile industry faced a number of other challenges that tested its claim to be "Chile Capital of the World." Hail and floods in 1991, monikered "Hurricane Salem," damaged some crops. The dreaded chile wilt disease affected other acreage, cutting into farmers' profits. Pepper weevils were in the neighborhood.

Farmworkers and farmers alike positioned themselves to get a chunk of an ever bigger but slippery chile pie. The New Mexico chile industry, once the domain of small farmers up and down the Rio Grande Valley, was international business. From the hybrids sprouted at NMSU there had evolved a complex web engulfing pickers, contractors, farmers, packers, primary and secondary processors, distributors, marketers, investors, lenders, and consumers. Each was a link in the chile chain. And each counted his pocket change in a jingle that began faint, grew audible, got louder, and climaxed in a noisy ring at the cash register.

Notes

1. Raúl Medina, interview by author, Garfield, NM, September 1992.

2. Jo Lytle, interview by author, Hatch, NM, September 1991.

3. Margaret Riggs, telephone conversation with author, October 1992.

4. Ken Smith, New Mexico Environment Department, telephone conversation with author, September 1992.

5. Greg White, Doña Ana County Planning Department, telephone conversations with author, July and August 1992.

6. Ramona Vallejos, South-Central Council of Governments, telephone conversation with author, August 1992.

7. Doug Durkin, Doña Ana County District Attorney, telephone conversation with author, July 1992.

8. Salem residents, interviews by author, September 1992.

9. Antonio Luján, Diocese of Las Cruces, telephone conversations with author, 1991-92.

10. Rubén Núñez, interviews by author, Hatch and Salem, NM, July and September 1992.

11. "Migrant Laborers Flood Hatch," *Albuquerque Journal*, 5 March 1989.

12. *Inside the Hatch Valley: A Study of a Rural New Mexico Community, Resident Instruction Series, No. 1, 1964*, NMSU College of Agriculture and Home Economics, Department of Agricultural and Extension Education, University Park, NM, 28.

13. William Porter, testimony to U.S. Commission on Agricultural Workers, Las Cruces, NM, October 1991, *Hearings and Workshops before the Commission on Agricultural Workers 1989-1993 to Accompany the Report of the Commission*, Appendix 2, 782.

14. "Migrant Workers' Children Boost Hatch Headcount 7%," *Las Cruces Sun-News*, 31 October 1992.

15. "Hatch School Population Still Growing," *The Courier* (Hatch, NM), 22 September 1994.

16. Teresa Ramos, interview by author, Salem, NM, September 1992.

17. "'No Colonias' Says Crowd at Village Meeting," *The Courier*, 18 March 1993.

18. "Doña Ana Board OKs Private Prison in Hatch," *Albuquerque Journal*, 10 June 1992.

19. "Spanish-Speaking Students Inundate Hatch, Parents Say," *Las Cruces Sun-News*, 16 June 1993.

20. *Albuquerque Journal*, 24 September 1994.

21. "Doña Ana Draws Fire on Colonias," *Albuquerque Journal*, 2 October 1994.

22. John McKean, telephone conversation with author, August 1992.

23. "Colonias: On the Edge of Forgotten," *Santa Fe Reporter*, 16-22 September 1992.

24. Rose García, telephone conversations with author, 1991-92, and interview with author, Anthony, NM, May 1992.

25. Daniel Talbot, U.S. Department of the Interior, letter to Honorable Roberto N. Gamboa, Consulado General de México, El Paso, TX, 16 October 1992.

26. Russell Lummus, Las Cruces Bureau of Land Management, telephone conversation with author, October 1992; "Minutes of the June 25, 1992 meeting of the West Texas-New Mexico Migrant Coordinating Sub-Committee, June 26, 1992," U.S. Department of Labor document released to author under Freedom of Information Act.

27. Tommy García, Doña Ana County housing inspector, telephone conversations with author, August and October 1992.

28. Sharon, interview by author, Hatch, NM bridge, July 1992.

29. Hatch chile pickers, interviews by author, Hatch, NM bridge, September 1992.

30. UTAF (Border Agricultural Workers Union) leaflet distributed at Hatch Chile Festival, September 1990.

31. Jesús Rodríguez, interview by author, Hatch, NM, September 1990.

32. Carlos Marentes, interview by author, Hatch, NM, September 1990.

33. Don Hackey, telephone conversation with author, October 1990.

34. Andy Núñez, telephone conversation with author, October 1990.

Pickin' the Red and the Green

THE WORLD OF THE CHILE PICKER

Gabriel's Hell ▪ The Bermuda Triangle ▪ New Wave Pickers ▪ Housing Fiascoes

The Organ Mountains cast a jagged stare at the neatly planted rows of chile in the Mesilla Valley south of Las Cruces, where about 100 men, women, and children are stooped over acres of ripe green peppers. As the morning sun breaks the gray mist, the workers slosh through mud to carry overflowing plastic buckets to waiting flatbeds where the containers' contents are dumped into wooden crates. On each of the tractor beds, a man hurriedly hands every picker a token, or *ficha* as it is known in field lingo, in exchange for his or her bucket. At day's end, the tokens are counted up to figure wages determined by a piece rate.

As the morning wears on, the pace of harvesting picks up. Field workers dash back and forth from the rows to the flatbeds, caking their bodies with mud. They are joined by soon-to-be disappointed latecomers hoping to find a vacant space to pick. Told there is no more work available today, the dejected job-seekers sit listlessly on a canal embankment and wait for someone to throw up his hands and call it quits. One wide-eyed 15-year-old, observing the scene with trepidation, promises to study hard at school so he won't have to pick chile for a living. An 18-year-old, Gabe Méndez, tall and well-built, surveys the field with a stern glare. The recent high school graduate once picked himself but chose to drive a tractor even though he makes about the same amount of money—the minimum wage. Thinking of the future, he isn't sure what he'll do with his life but considers a stint in the Marine Corps a good option for him.

One thing is certain, though—chile picking is not for him. "It's basically hell, that's what I call it, hell. All the mud, the water, the bugs, the insects, the humidity. It's all there." Yet for every Gabe Méndez, there are many others who say they enjoy picking chile and find it an honorable profession to work the land with their hands.

A green patch of Eden in the great Chihuahua desert zoned by a network of irrigation canals and pecan-shaded roads, the Mesilla

> *"We think those of us who work in the fields work harder than people who work in the factories. We're out of the house at five a.m. and out in the hot sun until four in the afternoon. Why do they pay us so little?"*

—NEW MEXICO CHILE PICKER, 1986

Valley is home to many of New Mexico's estimated 17,000 farmworkers. They inhabit the little towns of Sunland Park, Berino, Vado, Mesquite, Anthony, and San Miguel, places which, like the villages of the Hatch Valley to the north, underwent growth after the passage of the 1986 immigration law. Hundreds of other farmworkers arrive daily from El Paso, Texas, to the south, a 45-minute drive from the hub of the Valley at Las Cruces. Settled by Spanish *conquistadores*, El Paso today is at the bustling junction where the twin cities of El Paso and Ciudad Juárez, Mexico, collide in an uneasy marriage of the developing south with the developing north.

Set below a hill bearing the inscription "The Bible is the Truth," Ciudad Juárez is a booming center of the *maquiladora* industry. The *maquilas* are U.S. or foreign-owned plants erected on Mexican soil and enjoying the privilege of importing duty-free raw products for assembly in Juárez and eventual re-export out of the country to the United States and other markets. Called the "Paso del Norte" by economists, El Paso-Juárez is a hot, smoggy basin where hundreds of factories assemble clothing, electronic components, and auto parts and ship them to all corners of the shrinking planet. It's a metroplex that has served as a laboratory for the North American Free Trade Agreement (NAFTA) negotiated by the governments of Canada, Mexico, and the United States in 1990-92. The foundations for free trade trace some of their roots to the termination of the bracero program, the old Mexican agricultural guest worker system, in the mid-1960s. Concerned about the prospect of hundreds of thousands of citizens displaced from U.S. agriculture and having no equivalent means of support in the impoverished countryside at home, the Mexican government created the *maquiladoras*, in part, to absorb a potentially unruly labor surplus.

A quarter-century later, young women and men toil in 2,000 *maquiladoras* along the expanse of the U.S.-Mexico border, for weekly salaries that average between $24 and $40 (U.S. dollars). If anything, poverty has worsened in the Mexican *campo*, and agricultural workers show no signs of quitting their seasonal pilgrimages to the U.S. border. One of the busiest crossings for the *campesino* from the Mexican interior is at El Paso-Juárez. Passing into El Norte, many walk the short length of the Paso del Norte Bridge, or the Santa Fe Bridge as it is called by the locals, skirting the indigenous Mexican women hawking *chicle* or begging spare change, their babies in tow. For those without the legal papers, a makeshift ferry consisting of a small boat pulled across the knee-deep water of the Rio Grande by a lone entrepreneur awaits their business. As the crosser approaches the U.S. turnstiles with their notoriously fickle border inspectors, a large spray-painted message on a concrete river wall catches the eye. "For every Mexican treated badly in the U.S., we'll do the same to the gringo tourist," it warns. Once safely beyond the immigration agents and their drug-sniffing canines, the pedestrian enters the outskirts of the Segundo Barrio, a poor neighborhood in a poor city. Crowds flow back and forth in front of the cut-rate bus services that whisk passengers to Los Angeles, Albuquerque, and Denver, side-stepping the old freight yards while nearby Border Patrol agents nab an illegal and hustle her off in a ready jeep.

Inside the barrio, browsers meander through a two-block long, open-air flea market featuring used clothes, T-shirts, appliances, tools, and just plain junk, which vendors complain many people say they cannot afford. Taped music by Gloria Estefan and Los Tigres del Norte keeps the mood upbeat, though. On the surrounding streets, gang graffiti competes with the fading wall murals of the glorious Mexican past, the surviving and defiant testaments to the Chicano movement of the late 1960s and early 1970s that shook El Paso and the rest of the Southwest. The streets at the foot of the U.S. side of the Santa Fe Bridge hardly ever sleep, especially between the months of May and November when upwards of 800 seasonal field hands wait through the night to be recruited by labor contractors and hauled to the onion and chile fields of New Mexico.

Homeless farmworkers snooze on cardboard mats in front of peso-dollar money exchange houses and fill the "Bermuda Triangle," a concrete triangular median in the street. Now and then, off in the shadows, an amateur musical combo forms to play a *corrido* or two. Generally tranquil on most evenings, the bridge labor recruitment site assumes the air of a rowdy, red-light district on weekends when the party-goers return to El Paso from late-night Juárez nightspots. Speeding cars careen down the bridge in a screeching imitation of Bobby or Al Unser acting naughty, their occupants sometimes thoughtlessly jeering the chile pickers: "Hey, go get a job." Groups of youths trade insults and attempt to settle their differences with fisticuffs; they are only stopped by the scream of a police siren. Dog-bearing Border Patrol vehicles prowl by. But for the chile pickers peacefully gathered, it is just another long night in a long life of work. Some arrive at the bridge as early as 10 p.m., forced to come early from outlying Juárez *colonias* before the public transportation shuts down; others, hailing from outside the El Paso-Juárez area, sleep on the streets or in school buses and cars parked close by. At three a.m. the site is alive with clusters of farmworkers sipping coffee and chatting quietly. These provide protection from marauding gangs or muggers.

Then the shake-up begins as lines form in front of the old school buses owned by the contractors. Hoots and hollers roar out in the night at a straggling worker who chases a departing bus. The vehicle doesn't stop. At this point, the bosses decide who gets to climb the stairs and put in a day's worth of work—not unlike selecting a ripe chile pod for picking. The packed transports rev up their engines and pull away in a cloud of exhaust, sometimes commencing a six-hour daily roundtrip as far afield as Lordsburg or

Roswell in New Mexico. It is a routine even the greenest chile picker rapidly learns. First, a long wait at the bridge in the wee hours. On the bus at three or four a.m. for a ride to the field. In the field at sun-up. Hours of picking in the hot sun. A wait at the end of the day for the contractor to distribute the payroll. Deductions for rides to the field, burritos, cokes, and beers. Another ride back to El Paso. A couple of precious hours with loved ones. Then back again to the familiar bridge. Obviously, it's not a lifestyle conducive to family life.

"A lot of times Sunday rolls around and the kids don't even recognize us," one worker commented ruefully. "All week long. It's dark when we leave in the morning and it's still dark when we get home from work. . . . the kids say, 'Who is this man?'" Not surprisingly, the grueling routine takes its toll on the workers' minds and bodies, or as one young migrant in a sleeveless T-shirt put it, "if they don't eat well, sleep well, rest well, it's impossible."

Of course, few, if any, El Paso-Juárez chile pickers have medical insurance or a retirement plan. A few blocks from the bridge, Antonio Carrasco has studied what the cost of a chile picking career can entail. A special projects coordinator for the Centro de Salud Familiar de Fe, a low-income health clinic in El Paso, Carrasco sits in an office up the stairs from the crowded reception room and thumbs through a stack of statistics he compiled for a 1991 study of 400 west Texas and New Mexico agricultural laborers. The preliminary results revealed a grim state of affairs for a nation that prides itself on having the most advanced medical system in the world. Forty-two percent of these people test positive for tuberculosis, meaning they could later come down with active disease. Twenty-nine percent of the women were anemic, and some people showed abnormal cholesterol levels and possible liver problems. "Right here in El Paso the majority of farmworkers are malnourished," stated Carrasco glumly. "They're exposed to pathogenic diseases in the fields from hepatitis, from water, from overcrowded living conditions, and from having no food to eat in the fields while they are working. The state of health care here is one of the most deplorable that exists in the country right now."

Back at the bridge, most workers had more immediate concerns, such as putting food on the family table. Like their employer, the farmer, they are vulnerable to forces outside their control that determine their income—for example, the weather. The fierce summer rains often render a chile field a muddy pond impossible to pick, and floods and hailstorms can destroy weeks' worth of work forever. When the skies are clear in El Paso, they can be rainy in the New Mexico chile-growing belt, or vice versa, never permitting one to exactly know in what condition Mother Nature has left a planting.

Nevertheless, some contractors attempt to defy the rain gods and transport pickers to a mud-laden farm, only to be forced to return to the border with a busload of unhappy workers, who are compensated little or nothing for their long wait and fruitless trip. "There are parts that aren't rainy, that are good for working in," commented picker José Raygosa of El Paso, "but there are parts that are rainy. They bring people out there, but it's all soaked. We can't work like that." When workers waiting at the bridge are asked to tell about field work, they inevitably complain about pay. An examination of reported wages tells why. Surveys and estimates by three groups, the Border Agricultural Workers Union, Tierra Del Sol, Inc., and the Catholic Diocese of Las Cruces, reported that in the early

1990s the average annual income for a Texas-New Mexico chile picker was between $4,500 and $6,000.

Farmworker wages became a controversial issue in New Mexico, with NMSU releasing its own 1992 survey results which purported that workers in the chile harvest averaged between $5.30 and $8.30 per hour—well above the minimum and subminimum rates many workers and their advocates voiced grievance about. NMSU stood by its figures, defending them on the basis of interviews with 2,000 workers. But the Border Agricultural Workers, which itself claimed 3,000 members, retorted that none of its members had been contacted for the survey. Furthermore, added union leader Carlos Marentes, it was quite possible to earn high wages one day but drop

back easily to low wages the next when an unbountiful field was picked or the hours were short, thus making an accurate estimate only possible at the end of the season.

One longtime Hatch Valley picker scoffed at the notion of pickers raking in the bucks. "One can't say that I'm one of the best workers in the valley, but I'm not one of the worst, neither. When I make $30 or $40 these days, it's because other people made $10 or $12. But the way I do it is . . . I'm fast at the beginning, I work running, without any rest. Every moment we're working, without eating, without drinking." In a 1992 statement, the Catholic bishops of El Paso, Juárez, and Las Cruces pointed out that between 1981 and 1991 the cost of living rose 46.7 percent while the minimum wage increased only 27

Red Chile Picking 1970s Style.

Deautomated Red Chile Picking 1990s Style.
Note the absence of conveyor belts to ease the task.

wage, and the reality of receiving less than the minimum when paid '*por bote*' forces thousands of seasonal and migrant farm workers to live in dire poverty under inhumane conditions," contended the church leaders. Anthony farmworker Carlos Aguirre, for one, juggled costs to make ends meet for three daughters still in school. A heart condition prevented his wife from working; she had contributed previously to the family's income. "You have to make do with what you earn, no more," said Aguirre. "If you've bought milk, bath soap, then you don't buy meat, just beans and potatoes to eat."

Despite the obvious disadvantages of chile picking, more and more job-seekers arrived at the bridge and adjacent valleys in the 1980s and 1990s. There was Ramón Burrola, a jack-of-all-trades who put in a little farm work before journeying off to a Green Giant plant in Minnesota. There was 30-year-old Martín Valbuena, a former horse keeper anxious to speak in English, who turned to chile after his father was killed by a bucking bronco. There was Luz Corral and her teenage son and daughter, up from the apple country of Janos, Chihuahua, seated on the curb and waiting for their first season. The younger woman, her alluring eyes sparkling in the early morning blackness, had labored in a Juárez *maquiladora* for about $40 per week and now seized the chance

percent, and that hike occurred in one year, 1990, after a decade of no raises. For workers living in Mexico, this was a double whammy in escalating living costs, rocked by inflation in both the United States and in their home country, where prices spiraled skyward. "The disparities among the cost of living, minimum to make more money on the farms. Up in Hatch there was Jesús Solís, who wore a Los Angeles baseball cap and who stooped in the Hatch onion and chile fields with his family. A former truck driver who delivered the Mexican Embasa brand of chiles in the Los Angeles area before his employer went bankrupt, Solís fled the urban chaos of the California Southland for the deceptive tranquility of the Rio Grande harvests. Now instead of dropping off chiles picked by someone else, he harvested them for another person to deliver. And of course, there were the new, post-amnesty undocumenteds like the teenage mother who got in a week or two in the chile fields, bringing her five-year-old child to stay at her side and help out when possible.

Although the expanded onion and chile acreage in west Texas and southern New Mexico kept workers busy after the 1970s, there were gaps in the yearly work cycle of transplanting, thinning, weeding, and harvesting. The month of April, after onion planting but before chile weeding and thinning, is a rough time for many. "There's nothing, very little weeding in onions. We don't do anything," said farmworker Jesús Rodríguez. "Some look for work in construction, yard work, others in *maquilas* or in Juárez. Or (they) go to Nebraska, Kentucky, because there are people who send people to recruit here, and they go."

The work cycle picks up during the summer when field-cleaning chores require some labor. By summer's end, thousands are needed for harvest, a task which has not really changed since the beginning of the twentieth century when Dr. Fabián García noted that the job required some skill and stamina. The major difference is with work site mobility and product volume. The expansion of major growing areas outside the Rio Grande Valley proper, along with the corre-

sponding increase in acreage, demanded more workers who could move from field to field in the Texas-New Mexico "chile triangle." This area extended from El Paso County in the south, to Luna and Hidalgo counties to the west, to Doña Ana and Sierra counties to the north, and even over to Chaves and Eddy counties to the east.

Curiously, the job may have been easier for some pickers before the chile boom began reaching its apogee during the 1980s. Some farmers allowed pickers to load their buckets onto conveyor belts which shuttled the chile to the trailers, but the availability of cheap labor apparently discouraged that practice. At one time, not too long ago, fieldwork was supposed to be a spectacle consigned to a sad past as even sympathetic observers such as John Gregory Dunne, the author of a book on California's farmworker movement, predicted the demise of farm labor in favor of harvest machinery. Of course, their forecasts proved completely or partially accurate in crops like cotton and tomatoes, but as a 1991 Rand Corporation report underscored, greater numbers of field hands were flocking to America's fields to satisfy a consumer demand for cheap vegetables and fruits. It was under these circumstances that Mario Ortiz and George Sandoval competed for the same job on an El Paso street corner. Sporting an old cap over his graying hairline, Ortiz had been a bridge regular for 14 years, and a veteran of U.S. agriculture for even longer. Originally from Guanajuato, Mexico, the onetime undocumented worker first crossed into the United States in 1946 to follow the cotton (before he was replaced by a machine), tomato, grape, and now chile harvests, always one step ahead of the *migra*, or immigration department, before "fixing his papers" 16 years later.

It was September, the peak of the chile harvest, and Ortiz was picking the choicest fields around Deming and Hatch, trying to wrap up his stay before moving on to Michigan for the cherry and strawberry seasons. But much to his dismay, the year's earnings were disappointing. Large groups of people had entered the jalapeño harvest, he explained, and piece rates for each bucket had fallen to $1.25 or $1.30 from a high of $1.50 offered in previous years. "Now the salaries are lower than before. There's no work in the countryside here for many people."

Decades the junior of Ortiz, George Sandoval, too, waited patiently for the bus to the fields. A shy, young man in his 20s with sad, droopy eyes, Sandoval was a novice to the chile-picking profession, having only one month under his belt. Sandoval found himself at the bridge that summer after losing a job at a tire store in California. He located an apartment close to the bridge for his wife and baby daughter, but hampered by lack of experience, he discovered that his wages sometimes did not surpass the federal minimum. "And that's not right because you don't make enough money to support your family," griped Sandoval. Once aboard the bus, pickers like Ortiz and Sandoval settle in for a long ride. Initially, they pass the hillside neighborhoods of Ciudad Juárez that abut the muddy Rio Grande across from the old Asarco smelter in El Paso, a landmark industrial plant whose billowing emissions once earned the section of the city near the University of Texas campus the sooty nickname "Smelter Town." Minutes later they enter New Mexico, hugging the Mesilla Valley and its familiar dairies, truck stops, and the agricultural college at New Mexico State University, home of the "Aggies," a name emblazoned on Tortugas Mountain in white letters that twinkle in the struggling rays breaking through dark summer clouds pregnant

with rain. Traveling in the crisp hours of darkness, the farmworkers are largely invisible to the comparatively late-waking morning commuters who scurry to work on a diet of coffee and happy-talk radio.

Some buses then turn west on Interstate 10 toward the massive chile fields near Deming; others continue their journey north to the domains of the Hatch Valley, stopping at an immigration checkpoint so the border enforcers can check workers' papers. One of the closest stops is the fields near La Union on the Texas-New Mexico border. Down a country road stand two chile fields planted on either side of the pavement. One has been treated with herbicides and boasts weed-free rows of upright green capsicum; the other, overgrown with plant invaders, holds the remains of sun-baked, wilting jalapeños. In the middle of the weedy field, an older worker, his head shielded from the sun's rays by the trademark cap of the chile picker, is bent on his knees, examining each plant with careful scrutiny and picking only those red and green pods which have the squeeze of ripeness. He grabs a handful in a single stroke and tosses them in a plastic *bote*. But he shakes his head in frustration and apologetically explains that the farmer neglected this particular crop by not eliminating the weeds and ignoring consistent irrigation. Consequently, the pods are much smaller than normal. "It seems like we're picking nuts," he sighs.

A good amount of the chile in this region is delivered to the Mountain Pass cannery in Anthony, another New Mexico-Texas border town just up the road from La Union. Agriculture, whether on the assembly line or in the fields, is a prime employer in Anthony, a dusty town of 10,000 people, with about 6,000 people living on the New Mexico side and 4,000 in Texas. Anthony underwent a population boom in the 1980s as more agricultural laborers set down roots with their families. And the social conditions mirrored those of other border *colonias*: unpaved roads, homes without sewage hookups, overcrowded schools, and crime. An example of a fast-growing New Mexico of the 1990s, the growth of which was a constant, positive-sounding theme of economic growth boosters, Anthony had trouble finding enough employment for all its new residents. Enrollment in food stamp and welfare programs doubled in the early 1990s. For a while, many Anthony *colonos* were forced to live with the odors emanating from a neighboring dairy. In 1992, an activist group also initiated by the Las Cruces Catholic Diocese, the Citizens for the Improvement and Betterment of Anthony (CIBA), led a membership that included cannery and farm workers in a drive to empower the *colonos* through voter registration, funding for infrastructure upgrade, and the establishment of a youth recreation center.

One of the greatest needs for Anthony's residents was decent housing. Tierra Del Sol, a non-profit, Las Cruces-based corporation which builds housing for low-income agricultural workers, reported that in 1992 at least 300 families were on the agency's waiting list for housing in Anthony alone. Executive Director Rose García emphasized that the housing shortage in Anthony typified conditions throughout the chile-growing belt. "It's a real crisis in our communities in southern New Mexico, in the agricultural community. The sooner we begin to address it, the sooner the communities will begin to get benefit from it." Indeed, the housing shortage in southern New Mexico was only part of a worsening national problem. Well into the 1990s, farmworkers lived in caves near posh

Pebble Beach, California, golf courses, stayed in ravines below million-dollar homes in San Diego County, and slept at the doorsteps of money changers in El Paso.

Many obstacles were put in the path of advocates such as García. For instance, in 1990, García worked with the office of New Mexico Senator Jeff Binghaman and economic development and agricultural employer groups in the Pecos River Valley in an effort to find housing for pickers on the eastern edge of the chile belt. Two promising prospects were buildings owned by the Farmers Home Administration in Dexter and several hundred old dwellings at the Walker Air Force Base. The nascent campaign, however, stalled from almost the beginning when Tierra Del Sol realized it did not have the resources necessary to conduct comprehensive community development planning in the absence of significant outside support. By 1992 the federal government had auctioned off the former military homes to non-farmworker buyers, and the Farmers Home Administration (FmHA) declared its rules prohibited the leasing of federal property for temporary purposes. The Pecos River Valley failure foreshadowed the tent city fiasco in Hatch two years later. Bureaucratic agencies wrapped themselves in their own red tape, politicians moved on to other priorities, farmers claimed they could not afford to pay for expensive housing on their own, and local banks, many of which were profiting from the chile business through their loans to growers or processors, were reluctant to invest money in low-income farmworker housing.

Official recognition and ultimate neglect of farmworker problems was an old story in the Land of Enchantment. In the 1930s, the Works Progress Administration reported Dust Bowl refugees living in camps in both the Pecos and Rio Grande valleys. In 1953 a migrant issues meeting in Albuquerque debated housing and wages. Delegates at a 1977 farm labor housing conference in Lubbock, Texas, urged New Mexico to adopt a farmworker housing policy. In 1992 John García, Governor King's Chief of Staff, stated the governor's willingness to tackle head-on the southern New Mexico housing crisis. In 1993, more than a half-century after substantial numbers of field laborers entered New Mexico agriculture, thousands of workers remained homeless, curled up under river bridges or quartered in substandard dwellings. An exasperated Rose García later compared the sloth-like pace of housing development to the rapid response in sheltering the victims of catastrophes such as Hurricane Andrew in Florida. Apparently, government could mobilize quickly in natural disasters, but failed to get off the ground in the face of human ones.

Nonetheless, García plugged on in her bid to obtain "creative financing" from the USDA and other sources to open up low-income units whenever possible. In the spring of 1992, her group christened Tierra Encantada, "Enchanted Land," a 24-unit complex in Anthony specifically designed for farmworker families. The opening ceremony was a festive affair, replete with food, welcoming speeches, and a Spanish-language dance band. New tenant Leticia Hassel proudly led reporters on a tour of her family's modest, two-bedroom unit, showing off the spacious kitchen. Pride beamed from her rosy face as she pointed to a certificate one of her daughters received from elementary school for excelling in English as a second language. The 29-year-old woman remarked that the apartment was a major step up in the world for her and her husband, both of whom had picked crops. Her husband still labored in the fields, but the young mother now concentrated on homemaking and even dreamed of a time when they might own their own home.

Hassel was well drilled in the difficulties of raising a family while engaging in the physically exhausting demands of farm work. Although the majority of chile pickers are men, a substantial number, perhaps 30 percent, observers estimate, are women, and this includes many single mothers. The women workers had problems unique to their gender. Where to go to the bathroom in case of no portables? How to lift a heavy *bote*? What to do about the unwelcome advances of an employer or coworker? What to do with the kids on a workday? Yet, like the men beside them, more women farmworkers spoke out, becoming some of the strongest advocates for the chile pickers. As one woman in a La Union farm said, "We think those of us who work in the fields work harder than people who work in the factories. We're out of the house at five a.m. and out in the hot sun until four in the afternoon. Why do they pay us so little?"

Notes

1. Gabe Méndez, interview by author, Mesquite, NM, August 1991.

2. Peter Wiley and Robert Gottlieb, *Empires in the Sun: The Rise of the New American West* (Tucson: University of Arizona Press, 1982), 256-57.

3. Guadalupe Santiago, human rights researcher, interview by author, Ciudad Juárez, Mexico, July 1992.

4. El Paso street vendors, interviews by author, July 1992.

5. El Paso chile pickers, interviews by author, September 1986 and August 1991.

6. Antonio Carrasco, interview by author, El Paso, TX, August 1991.

7. José Raygosa, interview by author, El Paso, TX, August 1991.

8. Surveys of workers' wages by UTAF, Tierra del Sol, and Las Cruces Catholic diocese, 1990-91. UTAF was surprised when a 1991 study of chile pickers' earnings by University of Minnesota Professor Dennis Valdez showed an annual income even less than what the union had estimated.

9. Carlos Marentes, telephone conversation with author, August 1992.

10. *Albuquerque Journal*, 11 August 1992.

11. Hatch chile picker, interview by author, September 1992.

12. Recommendations of the Social Ministry, Catholic Diocese of Las Cruces, NM, 1992.

13. Carlos Aguirre, interview by author, Anthony, NM, July 1992.

14. El Paso workers, interviews by author, June 1993; Jesús Solís, interview by author, Salem, NM, June 1993.

15. Jesús Rodríguez, interview by author, El Paso, TX, March 1993.

16. Dino Cervantes, testimony to the U.S. Commission on Agricultural Workers, Las Cruces, NM, 23 October 1991, *Hearings and Workshops before the Commission on Agricultural Workers 1989-1993 to Accompany the Report of the Commission*, Appendix 2, 807, 810; *New Mexico 1970 Rural Manpower Service Report*, Employment Security Commission, New Mexico Employment Service, 20.

17. John Gregory Dunne, *Delano* (New York: Farrar, Straus and Giroux, 1967, 1971), 170, 196-97.

18. Associated Press wire story, 3 November 1991.

19. Mario Ortiz and George Sandoval, interviews by author, El Paso, TX, September 1992.

20. La Union chile picker, interview by author, September 1992.

21. Jay Caponigro and Citizens for the Improvement and Betterment of Anthony members, interviews by author, July 1992.

22. Rose García, telephone conversations with author, 1991-92, and interview by author, Anthony, NM, May 1992.

23. Associated Press wire story, September 1991.

24. Sigurd Johnson, "Migratory-Casual Workers in New Mexico," Press Bulletin 870, Department of Agricultural Economics, New Mexico Agricultural Experiment Station, State College, NM/Division of Social Research, Works Progress Administration, Washington, DC, 21 March 1939, 4-5; *New Mexico Farm and Ranch*, April 1953; Belaquín Gómez, ed., *Farmworker Housing Conference (1977) Proceedings*, NMSU Cooperative Extension, 1-2; John García, interview by author, Albuquerque, NM, March 1992.

25. Leticia Hassel, interview by author, Anthony, NM, May 1992.

Doña Lincha's World

THE LIFE OF THE WOMAN FARMWORKER

8

Single Moms in the Fields ▪ Chile Treks and Hideouts ▪ Involuntary Retirement of a Picker

Olga Sedano became a chile picker in 1980 or 1981, laboring alongside her brother and father. She mainly remembers it as hard work from which she earned as little as $13 per day. "I still didn't know how to work fast and the buckets were heavy and you got tired a lot. At times the trailers [flatbeds] were very far from where the people were at. There were bad parts in the fields where the chile was no good. They'd say, 'This chile's no good.'" One of the hardest tasks for women, in her mind, is hauling buckets across a field because "they're not as physically strong as men, but we have to keep doing it." She learned to put up with cold fingers from picking red chile in the cool season and burns from the fiery jalapeño and cayenne varieties, as well as the lack of drinking water for the workers in some fields, which forced many to drink from drains. Even when the workers managed to place ice over a bucket of water, the soothing refreshment often didn't last long because it melted easily in the hot sun and the

"towns are far away." Sedano says she was picking one day in the Hatch Valley when a fellow worker became dehydrated from the lack of cold water. "They didn't want to spend money on a bag of ice, and a man drank hot water and he began to feel very bad and entered a state of dehydration. If this man had been attended to right then, he would have recovered from dehydration. But no, he had to wait in the bus until everyone was paid and everyone got to [Hatch] to buy sodas . . . there was a hospital but it seemed they wouldn't treat him because he wasn't a resident. There was a woman that brought him to a hospital in Las Cruces, but he was in a state of advanced dehydration." Another time, Sedano watched a man turn sick and drop over in the field. A short time later he was dead.

Sedano's father died in 1987, leaving her the responsibility of taking care of her mother and supporting her own children on her meager wages. Though she shared the same frustrations over low pay and no sanitary or drinking facilities

> "*. . . I've never been bitten by a snake . . . they hide well in the onions, in chile. They're alive and hear and feel anyone who enters . . . they rattle and that's how we know they're there.*"

—LORENZA PRIMERO, VETERAN CHILE PICKER

as her male coworkers, as a young woman she faced a whole different set of problems. Often, there were no bathrooms where women could change their sanitary napkins during menstruation; many mothers had no money to pay for day care and were compelled to bring their children to the fields; and young, attractive pickers sometimes were the object of sexual pressure and harassment from labor contractors or others. "When a woman lives far away, like the women in Juárez, they have to arrive [at the Santa Fe Bridge] early, at midnight all alone, with the dangers there could be in the street . . . if they don't have a car, they have to get here in the morning and stay at the bridge, or stay with a friend [in El Paso] who lives near the buses."

During the winter and early spring, when the last dry red chiles have been shipped to market, Sedano and other single mothers are preoccupied with meeting their bills. "They are times that are very hard for us, because the rents are expensive here. Sometimes the landlords wait [for payment], other times they evict us from the house. At times we don't have electricity or water because we don't have anything to pay it with. We ask the government for help—food stamps

or whatever." After 11 years, Sedano is used to the rhythms of the chile harvest and has grown to like her work, laughing that she might even drive a tractor some day. "I'd like to work in the *campo* because my father taught me to love it. I like it a lot, a lot, this work. I would've liked to have other work, but I never had an opportunity to find good work because in the state of Texas there's lots of unemployment. I think I'm gonna continue in the fields."

One picker who has seen a little bit of it all is 53-year-old Lorenza Primero, called affectionately "Doña Lincha" by her friends. A tiny woman with a hint of mischief in her friendly eyes, Primero is part of the first generation of chile boom workers. Born and raised in Ciudad Juárez, she entered farm work in 1970 because the wages her husband earned at a Juárez furniture shop weren't adequate to support a growing family that reached 10 kids. A woman who has the weathered yet elegant skin of a long-time field hand, Doña Lincha has a reputation as one of the best pickers anywhere in chile country and has been known to tote 120 buckets a day. It is a record about which she is modest, and she scoffs at statements that she's perhaps the best around.

But she makes no bones about loving her work and likes picking all the different varieties of chile. "[Picking] isn't always good the first time, it could straighten out by the second time, depending on the water and the care the farmer gives the plant so the field is clean and weeds don't do damage to the plan." "I'm fearful of chile cayenne," she adds, "because it stings a lot and if it touches your clothes and your face, it's very hot."

Watching Doña Lincha pick is an exercise in coordinating eye with hand movements. Her tiny frame is practically hidden by the two-and-one-half to three-foot tall chile plants, but her trusty hands zap the ripe chiles off the plants and into the *bote* in almost the blink of an eye. A floppy hat shields her graying but thick hair from the omnipresent sun over the Florida and Hermanas mountains of Luna County, and Doña Lincha strips the plant with the stroke of a concert string virtuoso peaking solo. Then she moves on to the next plant. What rankles her is the demand some employers make for a *copete*, or chile crown, on top of the bucket. She calls the *copete* a "rip off for the worker" because the field hand is paid only by the bucket and doesn't get extra compensation for the extra pounds of chile topping. "If [the workers] don't put *copetes*, they [employers] say things or take away a token or don't give a token until the bucket is filled. Others don't do that and respect the rule of a *bote sin copete*."

On wet field days, Primero goes to work outfitted in special work pants to guard against the chilly rain droplets on the plants and the humid environment. "While entering [the field], you feel a little cold, but as you start to work fast, you don't feel the cold or the humidity." Of course, the sun usually has the workers sweating by mid-morning, but Primero is undaunted.

"We're already used to the sun, it doesn't bother us." The petite, engaging woman began her career as an illegal, a status she had for 16 years. She remembers a neighbor inviting her one day to pick onions in New Mexico. At first, she earned about $2.50 per day, "but for me it was a lot of money." One of her first bosses was the late contractor Jesús Manuel Ochoa, "may he rest in peace," who "taught me how to work, had patience with me, and later after many years fixed my papers." Another boss she recalls is Tony Portillo, who was run over by a trailer and killed. Before long, the budding chile picker was harvesting peppers for 25¢ a bucket, a piece rate that gradually increased to 35¢, then 40¢, then eventually the 50¢ or 60¢ paid by contractors today. Half her job as an undocumented worker, however, was to physically get to the fields.

She began crossing the Rio Grande to reach *el otro lado*, which would get icy in the fall months of the red chile harvest. "We were between 300 and 500 people. We had to take our clothes off and cross in groups, the men first, the women in the middle, our hands clutched together, because sometimes the water came up pretty high and we had to protect each other. After we crossed, the other men followed and we divided up into little groups so if the *migra* arrived they wouldn't grab everybody." On the other side, the workers rendezvoused with contractors' bus drivers who loaded them on board and delivered them to Mesilla Valley farms. "That's how we lived every day when we worked close to here, in La Union, Canutillo or Anthony, because we had no place to stay there."

Primero then got to know the farther outposts of the chile empire: Rincon, Hatch, Garfield, Deming. In Hatch, she gravitated toward the crowded barracks near the town's center; Deming was "more civilized," she said, remembering how she split the rent for a small trailer with four or five others and how they always had to keep an eye out for the vigilant *migra* (Border Patrol). But having a roof over her head, no matter how rudimentary, was a luxury in those secret days of chile picking. The *migra* was the workers' biggest problem, and its agents periodically scoured Hatch looking for unwitting illegals. Often, the bus drivers dropped the workers off at the edge of town to escape the Border Patrol's hawk eyes.

As a result, workers began camping out in the Sierra de las Uvas on the edge of Hatch, forming encampments which could total several hundred persons scattered about in small groups. It was a stay that frequently lasted for a few months for some. In the mountains, they cooked meals, rested together, and awoke to head back to the fields. Primero recalls sharing the ground with creatures that treated them as intruders, including a fair number of wildcats. "They growled at us a lot."

During this time, an underground railroad of sorts existed in Hatch to assist undocumenteds. "A lot of people helped us in Hatch, despite the fact that they were citizens or residents. They protected us and they advised us." One good-hearted woman for whom Primero developed a fondness went by the name of "Aurelia," who "always protected the illegal." The valley resident ran a boarding-house-like operation that acquired a name as a safe haven. "If you arrived and didn't have anything to eat, there was food at her place. Everyone ate, everyone slept and everyone rested." Aurelia financed her hostel by accepting $10 at the end of the week from workers and using the money to resupply the provisions for her new guests. This bed-and-breakfast-type service went on for many years

until Aurelia, not in very good health, was put in a Las Cruces hospital by her kids.

It was October 1985, red chile season, and it was not a good time for the ever-resourceful Doña Lincha and her friends. The *migra* was on a roll, catching illegals, deporting them, and then nabbing them again when they returned, often the very next day. Primero and two friends, Olivia and Gloria, decided to strike out on foot for Hatch from Juárez. They treaded the big mountain on the north side of the city where the Cristo Rey statue watches over the townspeople. Then they marched, "walking and walking" close to the Rio Grande until they reached Anthony—a good 12- to 15-mile hike. It was six or seven o'clock in the evening in Anthony and they stopped for awhile before resuming their march. A young man stopped his car. "'Where are you going?' 'We're going to Hatch,' Olivia replied. 'I'll give you a ride.'" But Olivia didn't feel well, continued Primero, and decided to go back, leaving Doña Lincha and her friend to get in the car with the stranger. Primero was in the back seat half-asleep and is fuzzy about a hassle that broke out between Gloria and the man. The stranger pushed Gloria into a cotton field, Primero rose to defend her, and the man got angry and left. The two women recovered and walked to Doña Ana seven miles north. At the village, they hitched a second ride, but only as far as Radium Springs a little way up the road. It was a moonless, pitch dark night, and the women "walked and walked" with only the faraway glow of the stars to guide them along on their journey to pick chile. The howls of coyotes were the only evidence of other life. Gloria wanted to rest but Primero said no, "the animals are going to get us." So they pushed forward, "walking and walking," and finally reached Rincon, about five miles south of

Hatch. By then, Gloria was crying; she didn't want to go any farther. A jeep passed but did not stop. Primero asked Gloria to use her loud voice to help flag down the next vehicle. To their luck, a car containing fellow workers cruised by and their *compañeros* recognized the two women's voices. The driver put the auto in reverse and gave them a ride to the house where they planned to stay. "Gloria was crying because we'd come from Juárez." It was early in the morning and the occupants were getting ready to go to work. Doña Lincha and her friend tried to rest, but they couldn't sleep because of the painful blisters on their feet. "We were thinking and talking about it and crying, because never before had we undergone such an experience of hard loneliness and danger on a dark road that was like an endless tunnel."

Doña Lincha and coworker on an El Paso contractor's bus.

Years later, Doña Lincha still travels the highways and dirt roads to the chile fields, but now with the confidence, gained by virtue of legalization from the 1986 amnesty program, of not being deported for trying to earn a buck. Most of her children have left home to start their own lives, leaving her a son, a daughter, and two young grandchildren to tend. When the onset of winter signals the emptying of the chile fields, Doña Lincha collects food stamps and cleans apartments in El Paso to help pay the bills. After

all these years, she is still poor, but she cannot envision a life outside agriculture since she is accustomed to waking early at three a.m. and being at the field as early as five a.m., a routine her body is accustomed to living. And she is adamant about the value of her work. "I like my work, and I've liked it ever since I started to be a *campesina*. Even today, I can't take a job outside the *campo*, I LIKE THE *CAMPO*." A sense of sadness grips her words as she adds that she is among the few of her generation who still frequent the bridge during the season. "We all knew each other, everyone, we were a group of 500 people. There were other groups [of workers], and when we began to get legalized too many other people came and we weren't able to earn a full salary. We made $15, $12, $18 at the most out of this salary, when we returned to bring our families. We didn't have enough money to legalize them, so we legalized ourselves with sacrifice, little by little, to the extent that the bosses lent us money to pay the [amnesty] fee. That's why I didn't legalize my kids, because it got difficult, there were too many workers and the work wasn't enough. The workers from 20 years ago are no longer around. The majority have moved away, others died . . . one died of cancer, others from hepatitis, others from tuberculosis. There are five or six of my old friends in Deming. They still work in the field. They are buying their lot and have bought used trailers They're Irene, Olivia, Pedro—three or four people have bought their trailers and brought themselves up. Because before we never thought they were going to do that."

The readily smiling Doña Lincha puts her life and those of her friends in perspective: "You know there's a lot of competition among the poor people in Juárez. As a mother of 10, I had to find work. If I worked six or seven months I could feed them all year. If I worked all year, great . . . but we never finished a whole year. That was the reason for crossing. We suffered . . . all of us who crossed had the goal of improving our lives." While the wages Doña Lincha is paid have remained flat for years now, she has witnessed other changes she says are beneficial to the workers. The Juárez-raised chile picker joined the Unión de Trabajadores Agrícolas Fronterizos (Border Agricultural Workers Union, usually referred to by its Spanish acronym, UTAF) in the 1980s and became a board member. Hardly any

UTAF activity, picket, or social service event was the same without the indefatigable Doña Lincha at the front. The union and legal services agencies, she said, are today an avenue for worker complaints where none previously existed. "Now with amnesty, you can contact Legal Aid, the union . . . the union helps us to know certain rules, helps us with letters, without self-interest," says Doña Lincha. More than anything else, Doña Lincha is a survivor, a fact she is careful to emphasize these days. "I don't have any problems with my health, although I've noticed that I don't have the same *rendimiento* I did when I was 30. The agility of my hands is slower where I feel a bit that I can't run with the buckets, so now I walk for fear of tripping, falling, hurting or hitting myself." "People who want to work more, to do more, run and want to do it fast, and that's when the accidents happen."

About the worst scrape Doña Lincha can remember was two years earlier in the Lordsburg area when mosquitoes bit a crew of workers weeding. Overall, picking was a risky occupation which involved possible heat stroke, dehydration, tractor injuries, insect and reptile bites, back and wrist disorders, urinary tract infections, hepatitis, tuberculosis, pesticide exposure, and anything else that could go awry under the sun. Then there were the instances when truly irregular, even freakish occurrences could put a chile picker out of the game. Take, for example, the story of Gloria Escovedo. Born to a *campesino* family in Durango, Mexico, in 1955, Escovedo moved to Ciudad Juárez with her family when she was just three years old. She attended school in the burgeoning border city while her father, a musician, put bread on the table by playing in different *conjuntos*, the familiar *norteño* bands that grace the border region with their distinctive guitar-accordion sound. In 1974, she crossed into the United States, introduced to agriculture as a chile and onion harvester in New Mexico and Colorado. It was a job she grew to love. "For me, farm work is a game. I like the countryside. I never got sick, and I like the people a lot. Many people didn't know how to work in the field and I helped them and showed them how to do it," she says.

At first Escovedo was surprised by the low pay, recalling how she first netted $7 a day, $14, $25, and then a little more after strikes organized by the Border Agricultural Workers Union. "I thought you could earn a lot more here than in Mexico," adds Escovedo, a big woman with a disarming smile.

Now field work is a memory of the past for the mother of five daughters, the result of being at the wrong place at the wrong time. Escovedo's forced retirement from chile picking happened in July of 1987 at the Placitas *colonia* near Hatch. The farmworker was driving back to the valley from Deming with friends in a van when the vehicle broke down outside of Hatch. The stranded motorists managed to get a ride to Placitas, where they got help to bring the van to town. It was late and the workers decided to spend the night in Placitas, a fateful decision for the young Escovedo. About 11 or 12 o'clock that night (Gloria doesn't remember the exact time), she heard gun shots. Rising to investigate, she peered out from the back door of the van where she had been asleep. Two bullets struck her, one in the left foot and the other in the stomach area. Bleeding profusely, the wounded Escovedo was rescued by an ambulance, which brought her to the hospital in Las Cruces. "They told my father I wasn't going to live, because they were going to cut off my foot, but they pumped enough blood back into me, I fought back, and they saved me." The doctors

placed plastic veins in Escovedo's injured leg and ordered convalescence in a wheelchair. She returned to Juárez and spent seven months partially recuperating at her father's home. But her recovery created new problems. When she was shot, Escovedo had just began the process of legalization under the amnesty program for undocumented workers. Since she was stuck in Juárez with no income, the recovering farmworker missed a chance to expedite her application, a costly endeavor requiring money and a presence Escovedo could not finagle.

Five long years passed since the wounding and Escovedo found herself in a worse situation. An artificial vein in her leg needed repair, but she had neither the money nor the status to undergo the necessary operation. One doctor told her she had a good chance of ending up in a wheelchair again. In the meantime, she suffered pain. "I walk for one or two blocks but at the third I can't because my foot hurts a lot." Earlier referred to a lawyer to get restitution, she once received small amounts of money from the attorney to pay doctors' office visits. The sympathetic lawyer left his job for parts unknown, however, and now Gloria only goes for medical attention "when I feel very bad." In between her bouts with physical discomfort, the former chile picker attempts to keep a family of five daughters intact. They range in age from nine to seventeen and all but one, who is a U.S. citizen and attends school in El Paso, reside with her father in Juárez. To survive, Escovedo relies on food stamps, a $62-per-month welfare check for her El Paso child, spare lodgings in friends' homes, and the generosity of some women farmworker *compañeras* who, like her, have very little.

A Las Cruces lawyer, Mario Esparza, filed a civil lawsuit against the individual who shot Escovedo, one Alex Martínez of Hatch. As it turned out, Martínez was firing away at other persons, whom he reportedly claimed had threatened him, when he accidentally hit Escovedo. Martínez served 18 months in prison for his crime. A local judge ordered Martínez to compensate Escovedo to the tune of $40,000 for her injuries, but the Hatch assailant was divorced by his wife, who received all his assets, according to Esparza. This put the latter in the proverbial position of trying to squeeze blood from a turnip. To her misfortune, explains Esparza, his client can't receive government victim's restitution funds or county indigent monies because she's not a U.S. resident, a status Escovedo missed obtaining due to her forced 1987 stay in Juárez. "It's one of the cases where she unfortunately fell through the cracks," Esparza sums up.

There is a tinge of bitterness in Escovedo's voice as she contemplates her odyssey from doctors to lawyers to consular officials to immigration authorities and social service counselors. "I have five daughters and I have nothing in the house. I've already sold everything I had that I bought when I was working. . . . I worked 13 years in the fields, and a lot of people never did and they got legalized. I didn't do it because I was in a wheelchair and I never had any money." More than anything, the disabled farmworker wants to have her health restored and get back to the beloved countryside. "Money doesn't interest me, it comes and it goes. What I want is medical attention and to be well."

For all her years of chile work, Escovedo had nothing to show. In her place came other chile pickers, drawn to a rapidly expanding chile industry in southern New Mexico, where increasingly large commercial farms predominated. The lure of the fields still beckons.

Notes

1. Olga Sedano, interview by author, El Paso, TX, April 1992.

2. Lorenza Primero, interviews by author, El Paso, TX, and Deming, NM, 1992-93.

3. Department of Labor, Occupational Safety and Health Administration (OSHA) Final Rule, 29 CFR Part 1928 Field Sanitation (Docket No. H-308) 52 FR 16050, 1 May 1987.

4. Gloria Escovedo, interviews by author, Las Cruces, NM, and El Paso, TX, February and April 1992.

5. Mario Esparza, telephone conversation with author, June 1992.

Growin' the Green and the Red

THE MAKING OF THE MODERN CHILE FARMER

Heatless Chile ▪ Wilt Attacks ▪ A River Tamed ▪ King Cotton to King Chile ▪
Chile Contracts and Contacts ▪ 91 Years with the Pepper

In many ways Robert Cosimati represents the past, present, and possible future of chile farming. Albuquerque born and bred, Cosimati relocated to Las Cruces in 1947 to assist his father in the liquor business. There he met his wife, Barbara Taylor, and her father, Anzlie Taylor, who introduced the young city slicker to the world of farming. As was typical in those years, Cosimati grew cotton and alfalfa. But when Cal-Compack, the Beatrice-owned California red chile processor, came knocking on New Mexico farmers' doors in the early 1970s, Cosimati switched gears and decided to enter the chile business. He quickly found out that growing chile necessitated a different type of farming than the one he had learned.

"It looks easy to plant the seed and grow the crop, but the average person doesn't realize what goes into it," remarks the Las Cruces farmer. Cosimati and his wife live in a gray brick house situated on a country lane encroached upon by an expanding, medium-sized city. A short, rough-hewn man with a gravelly voice, he expels bursts of slightly nervous energy in between puffs off his cigarettes.

Nominally independent, the New Mexico chile grower's fortunes are steered by corporations that define the amount and type of chile grown, review the crop with careful scrutiny, and set the price for the product. Close observers estimate that about 90 percent of the chile grown in southern New Mexico in the 1990s was contracted before planting. Typically, Cosimati devotes about 25 percent of his crop to green chile and the remainder to red. Since green chile pays more than red chile, green contracts are highly coveted and hard to come by, he notes. "Most of the plants we grow in this area have no heat. That's why some small growers will grow a four- or five-acre plot of real hot chile. Then this red chile that is hot will be mixed with the bulk of this chile that has no

> *"All farming is a gamble . . . and contrary to many beliefs, [that] if you plant a crop you make money. And that's not always the case."*
>
> —ALTON BAILEY, MESILLA VALLEY CHILE FARMER

heat, for processors or for consumers that want hot. It's a mixture."

The Mesilla Valley chile grower plants his seed in March and embarks on a nine-month season that becomes more complicated and stressful as the young chile plants mature and break the ground to greet the sun. The little chiles must be thinned by hand or machine, weeds eliminated, and irrigation done in just the right amounts and at just the right time. Summer, the rainy season, is when things get especially tricky. A nasty thunderstorm, for instance, often delivers muddy water down the Rio Grande and into the irrigation ditches used by Cosimati and other valley growers. Euphemistically termed "red water," the mud-laden river water seals the soil and doesn't percolate well into the ground.

"Ditch riders call and say, 'do you want to use it?' We'll say no, give it 24 to 48 hours," says Cosimati. If his chile survives the summer rains and hail, Cosimati begins harvesting the green around August 1, sometimes a little earlier and sometimes a little later, depending on the seasonal conditions. September spells the start of red chile picking, a phase which will last until the onset of Christmas. Before picking, the farmer inspects the crop to calculate the ratio of greens left to reds, and if 10 percent of the field is still green he will use a "man-made defoliant" that "kills the plant and forces the greens to go on ahead and go to red."

The biggest threat to Cosimati's crop is from a soil-borne fungus named phytophthora root rot—the notorious "chile wilt" that afflicts fields up and down the Rio Grande Valley. Outbreaks are worsened by poor rotation practices, bad water drainage, and rainy years. By the 1990s, a task force of growers warned the New Mexico legislature that, if not brought under control, chile wilt could single-handedly destroy the godsend of New Mexico agriculture.

In bad years, Cosimati might lose 20 percent or more of his crop to the wilt. "It hurts the pocketbook mainly, badly, because you're seeing so much of it over the Valley now that a lot of farmers are quitting chile due to that. They have no fields left that they can grow chile in due to the root rot and the wilt." The thought of losing a crop gives pause to the usually joking Cosimati: "It's depressing. I imagine it would be something like kinda' losing your wife." The wilt, however devastating, was but one difficulty routinely faced by Cosimati and his chile-raising neighbors. Water, the well of life in the thirsty Southwest, can also be the kiss of death for chile farmers. Crop insurance covered lost plants flattened by hail, but not plants leveled by rain.

Farmers, regardless of how many years they had under their belts, were humbled by the capsicum. There always seemed to be new revelations about when and with how much water to irrigate and new bouts of other plant diseases in addition to the wilt, each carrying long, scientific names and each resulting in a lowered cash yield. Farmer Alton Bailey of Anthony, a tall man with a slow, deliberate analytical bite to his speech, was philosophical about it all: "All farming is a gamble. A farmer gambles with the elements, the insects, the disease problems . . . He enjoys it or he wouldn't be there. But he is not necessarily making much money. For the most part, he's trying to make a living, it's a way of life for him. And [it's] contrary to many beliefs, [that] if you plant a crop, you make money. And that's not always the case. . . ."

What Bailey alluded to was the classic case of falling profits. In 1986, the typical net profit per acre of green chile in Doña Ana, Sierra, and Luna counties was estimated by the NMSU Agricultural Experiment Station to be about $717. Five years later, the net profit was around $600. The cost of growing chile outpaced by many times the price paid for it. In 1907 it cost about $26 to grow an acre of chile in Doña Ana County compared to $1,200 to $1,845 in 1992. In 1907, farmers were paid almost two cents a pound for green chile by the local cannery, a price that increased only about six times by 1992. Growers were kept afloat by improved irrigation techniques, higher yields from NMSU seed, and machinery that helped reduce labor costs from about 50 percent of the total expense to 27 to 35 percent between 1943 and 1992.

Chile enjoyed a profitable edge over other crops, though margins were slimming. All things considered, top-notch chile producers managed to keep their heads above water in the topsy-turvy world of U.S. agriculture in the 1980s. In contrast to the debt-burdened farmers of the Midwest, many New Mexico farmers managed to reduce their debt load and expand their crops. Statewide, a planter with a 500-acre farm could expect to earn about $50,000 in 1991. This was hardly a gold rush, but it was not too shabby, either.

A professional farmer was likely to have acreage devoted to chile, alfalfa, cotton, and vegetables, an inventory capable of balancing income through market vagaries, rotation requirements, and bouts with the dreaded chile wilt. The modern farmer, who is a far cry from the roadside seller of just a few decades ago, must make decisions in a market environment shaped by banks, processors, wholesalers, and of course, fickle consumer tastes. To flourish, he has foresworn a by-the-grace-of-God fatalism and replaced it with a no-nonsense business approach. Nowadays, fields are leveled for planting with laser-guided equipment, irrigation allotments are figured by computer data bases, and soil moisture is measured by a technometer. And already the next century is marked by genetically engineered crops and advanced drip irrigation awaiting their day in the field. The new chile farmer is a busy professional, juggling farming schedules with business planning and marketing. Hatch grower Silvino Ortiz explained: "We go see what needs fixing, take the water out of the fields if it's raining. It's hard for the farmer . . . we don't rest, there's no rest in chile. We finish with the green, continue with the red, and when the red is done we keep preparing the land for next year. There's no vacation here."

How the southern New Mexico chile farmer achieved a significant niche in the agricultural

Chile field in southern New Mexico.

world is the latest chapter in an almost 3,000-year history of farming in the Mesilla Valley and its environs. Blessed with fertile soil, a favorable climate, and a steady irrigation source, evidence shows Native American agricultural activity in the area as early as three millennia ago. In the 1830s and 1840s, the Mexican government awarded land grants and the communities of Doña Ana, Las Cruces, Mesilla, and La Union sprung up. Much of the region was acquired by the United States as part of the Gadsden purchase, and Anglo settlers trickled in. Like their Mexican neighbors, the newcomers planted grapes, wheat, beans, corn, and alfalfa and ran cattle and sheep. In 1880, there were 431 farms in Doña Ana county that averaged 107 acres. The dry, fertile land attracted people of all persuasions and backgrounds. They came in from Chihuahua, Santa Fe, Europe, Tennessee, Virginia, and New England. Freed African-American slaves found a home in Vado, and a

colony of South African white refugees from the Boer war with England sprung up in Chamberino, Berino, and La Mesa. Farther north in Doña Ana, the Shalam Colony was built by utopian socialists searching for a world of social justice, a dream many would argue has yet to be realized. Gradually, many of the earlier Mexican settlers lost much of their land, beginning with a land grab by Texans in the 1840s and culminating with the bit-by-bit sale of the grants in the 1900s.

In the tiny hamlet of Anthony at the turn of the century, a businessman named Charley Miller accepted land in lieu of payments for groceries and goods. Royal Jackman, who arrived in 1892 as a railroad clerk, concluded that by the time of his death, Miller was one of the "biggest landowners." Land prices were low in those days, ranging from $3 to $25 an acre, which according to Mary Coe Bevins of Anthony, "was a fancy price." But agriculture was hamstrung by the raging and unpredictable waters of the Rio Grande. Gushing waters roared down the Valley, flooding Hatch and Rincon several times and completely submerging the towns of La Union and Berino in the early twentieth century.

The newly arrived Jackman was puzzled at the midday siestas of Mexican tenant farmers who rented from them and one day approached the resting group.

"Why don't you fellows work like Americans?" quipped the New Englander.

"Yacky, the more you have the more you lose," replied one of the farmers. A short while later, Jackman understood completely the man's words when his farm was destroyed in the flood of 1905. The wrathful river wreaked a great deal of havoc in people's lives. Jackman's future wife, May Bailey, was sent away by her parents for two years of her childhood to escape the "freakish river," as she termed it. "Following a flood the water would stand in the sloughs, draw mosquitoes and start an epidemic of malaria, or as it was commonly called in the old days, chills and fever. . . ."

Nemecio Provencio of Anthony described the river as the central force in the people's lives: "We worked from early morning till dark, days, weeks, and months, cutting down trees, clearing the ground, building our homes, plowing, planting and fighting the Rio Grande," she said in an interview with Depression era writer Marie Carter. "It had a voice, Señora, that we grew to hate—a voice that struck terror in our hearts and souls. It was there in the rising river, increasing in volume as the water rose, submerging our land, stealing our seed, quite often our homes, leaving us nothing, nothing."

Toward the end of the last century, agricultural and business interests in the Mesilla Valley and in El Paso, Texas, stepped up their efforts to have the river dammed. A power struggle ensued, enveloping European capitalists, U.S. government agencies, and the Mexican government in a drawn-out conflict over the fortunes of the "American Nile." The U.S. Bureau of Reclamation emerged the winner, breaking ground at a mesa resembling an elephant north of the Hatch Valley. In 1915, Elephant Butte Dam and Reservoir were completed, creating a mammoth artificial lake with the necessary sustenance for the development of commercial agriculture from the Hatch Valley in the north to El Paso and Juárez in the south. "Before the dam was built, this was a wild arroyo," commented Gary Esslinger, the treasurer and manager of the Elephant Butte Irrigation District. "Elephant Butte Dam was built for one purpose, and that's agriculture, and the farmers paid for it and everybody else is reaping the benefit from it."

The Elephant Butte and Caballo projects put an end to the watery oppressor and triggered heightened settlement. New Mexico A&M President H. L. Kent reported the upsurge in a letter in 1925 to former student Fannie French. "The valley is certainly booming," he said. "It is surprising such a number of farms are being bought and cleared. Many of them are small tracts of 10 to 30 acres."

After 1920 cotton glistened in the fields sown on either side of the Rio Grande from the Hatch Valley to El Paso County. As a cash crop, the fluffy white stuff had historic significance. Government subsidies boosted the industry and Las Cruces university researchers dedicated their talents toward improved yields. Founded in 1917 and headquartered at the Temple of Agriculture in Las Cruces, the New Mexico Farm and Livestock Bureau grew into a major political force, uplifted by the wonders of King Cotton.

Farmer-labor relationships, which would prove so rocky in the later chile industry, evolved in the cotton-growing epoch of the 1920s to the 1960s. Pre-harvest meetings at the Temple of Agriculture to set a picking rate were attended by a few laborers, generally without representation, and by cotton farmers who complained about the prices offered by the ginners. New Mexico's cotton heyday lasted from the 1940s to the 1960s and gradually receded from the pest-borne effects of monoculture, international competition, and the appearance of synthetic fabrics. Farmers sniffed about for better-paying crops, lettuce and chile among them.

Commercially, chile made a splash nationwide as far back as 1904 when the Las Cruces-based Mesilla Valley Canning Company, known for its slogan "Chile: the Finest Condiment on Earth," won a prize for its canned chile at the Louisiana Purchase Exhibition in St. Louis. The cannery was run by Frenchman Theodore Rouault, who came to the Mesilla Valley in 1872. In 1893 the local newspaper commented that, "few of our people even now know what a valuable industry Mr. Rouault has inaugurated here."

Rouault grew his own vegetables and chile at a farm north of Las Cruces and employed hundreds to can the produce for shipment throughout the Southwest. Rouault's son, who was later employed by the First National Bank of Doña Ana, married Vivian O'Dell, a cousin of the Governor of New York, in 1904. A contemporary was Francis Barker, an Englishman who founded a farm in 1888 that became the first large-scale chile and vegetable enterprise in the Mesilla Valley. Barker's son, Percy, and grandson, Arthur, continued chile growing. In spite of the Europeans' probings of the market, chile in the Mesilla Valley remained a minor crop. Luis

Álvarez, "The Enemy of Weeds," remembered when locals sun-dried the fruit on the dirt roofs of their adobe homes. "Everybody had a little patch of chile," he said, "just for home use."

A second chile use was as a mash ingredient fed to chickens for better egg production. A 1936 agricultural college experiment disproved the old wives' tale that the egg yolks produced by chile-fed chickens became imparted with a reddish color "which in some instances gave a bloody appearance," lowering their value.

Early chile statistics for the Mesilla Valley and El Paso County are generally sketchy, though an Extension report estimated 2 to 3,000 acres in all of New Mexico in 1930. In 1927 a committee of growers, canners, and academics recommended expanding the chile crop. "We believe that chile is one of our promising crops for the future," prophesied the authors. That same year 80 acres, mainly in *chile ancho*, were planted in the Vinton-Canutillo area just across the line in Texas and grown with the advice of Dr. García. Edwin Burt went to California, learned about artificial dehydrators, and returned to help set one up at Vinton. The farmer group, "with its up-to-date plant for drying chile, has established a new industry," commented the New Mexico Extension. A year later, aware of the kiln-dryer's flaws, the Extension contacted Californians who knew about better machines.

In 1940, before the concentration of New Mexico farm ownership, 1,805 New Mexico farmers reported growing chile to the U.S. Census of Agriculture. Their numbers fell as the next two decades decimated farmers' ranks. Wage-paying jobs drew northern and central small farmers to Los Alamos, Santa Fe, and Albuquerque; the introduction of synthetic pesticides and fertilizers drove up farming costs for small producers; and off-and-on drought years discouraged some from hopping aboard the tractor. Times were tough even in the Elephant Butte Irrigation District. It was in this period, somewhere in the early to mid-1950s, that southern New Mexico overtook north-central New Mexico as chile leader. There was a trend toward larger commercial farms. Through the chile-improving work of New Mexico State University and the contracting of packers and canners, chile acreage in the state steadily increased from 900 to 1200 acres in 1950 to 34,500 in 1992. During this time, both the nature of chile farming and related farming patterns changed. More and more chile was sold out of state and contracted to processors, as opposed to the fresh market.

Mountain Pass Canning Company of El Paso County was a contract leader and was expected to handle 200 acres in 1959. Nine years later Bob Dorbandt and Ernest Riggs contracted 600 acres of Mesilla Valley chile for their new New Mexico Chili Company. Shortly thereafter, the Dreher Pickle Company of Denver began purchasing cherry peppers from Berino growers, and the Biad Chili Company was the customer for 80 acres of peppers raised in the Las Uvas Valley. They were joined by firms like San Juanito Chili Products, Universal Foods, La Victoria, Ashley's, Fiesta Foods, the Santa Cruz Chili and Spice Company, and others. The impact of the New Mexico Chili Company, in particular, cannot be understated. Mountain Pass was the green chile leader; New Mexico Chili Company became the red one. At the beginning in 1968 the latter was a fifty-fifty partnership between local investors and Beatrice's Cal-Compack.

A group of 10 to 12 New Mexicans, including members of the Riggs, Gary, and Gillis Hatch farming families and businessmen like A. Antweil, the principal owner of the predecessor to the Western Bank, teamed up to convince farmers to grow large amounts of red chiles for the powdered market. New Mexico Chili Company President Bob Dorbandt, a realtor, had visited the West Coast numerous times to prick Cal-Compack's ear and "convinced them that New Mexico was a good place to grow chile." Dorbandt's excursions bore fruit, since they came when the Disneyland-like sprawl of Orange County, the headquarters of Cal-Compack, was rapidly swallowing up adjacent chile fields. Dorbandt, Riggs, and company had to convince local farmers to plant more chile, not an easy task, because many were unfamiliar with Cal-Compack's contract specifications of planting and harvesting dates, field monitoring, and rotation requirements. The company favored 40-acre chile plots, a size that was bigger than usual in those days.

Working with NMSU professor Roy Nakayama, the company developed seed plots and perfected its relationship with Mesilla Valley farmers. In 1970 the New Mexico partners sold their interest to Cal-Compack because "the growth was faster than their financial capabilities at the time," added Dorbandt. Ernest Riggs remained plant manager and Cal-Compack one of the pillars of the southern New Mexico chile empire.

The 1960s introduced more southern New Mexico farmers to the chile contract system. A former engineer, Orlando Cervantes, decided to enter farming and became a contract farmer for Mountain Pass. Originally a manager for the J. F. Apodaca Farm south of Las Cruces, Cervantes dabbled in the open market before approaching a Louisiana hot sauce manufacturer and offering to grow the famed Tabasco pepper in New Mexico. In 1973 he counted 100 acres of Tabasco chiles in addition to his New

Before the Chile Empire, King Cotton reigned supreme.

Mexican variety. Incidentally, Las Cruces, New Mexico, cemented a sister city relationship with Tabasco, Mexico, at the time. In a 1976 interview, Cervantes pointed out that many lenders favored contracts, knowing the farmer had a certain sale. "With contracts, I know exactly what my market will be before the seed goes into the ground. I can plan a budget and I know exactly what I have to do to make money," he was quoted as saying.

In subsequent years, the contract system was institutionalized to the extent that local banks refused to give farmers loans unless they walked through the door with a signed contract. The 1959 U.S. Census of Agriculture listed a total of 506 chile farmers in the Rio Grande Valley statewide, with most harvesting less than 10 acres. The only place where growers harvested more than that amount was in southern New Mexico, and even there the number was minimal. A mid-1960s report listed seven growers in 1962 harvesting between 11 and 25 acres and only five bringing in more than 50. In 1960 Arthur Barker was rated one of the biggest growers, harvesting an astounding 95 acres. As late as 1969, the Farm Bureau magazine featured a photo of a deep-lined, brown-faced Garfield farmer standing next to the classic *ristra* and stating, "[chile] is grown all along the Rio Grande Valley in New Mexico, mostly by small farmers who produce it on limited acreage."

By 1994 chile farming had changed dramatically. The NMDA Agricultural Statistics Service estimated about 350 chile farmers in all of New Mexico. Farm size got bigger and farmers fewer. A 1934 Extension report listed more than one thousand growers in Doña Ana County, with most farming less than 200 acres; 20- to 100-acre units were typical. Sixty years later 1,500 to 2,000 acre farms were not unusual.

Several farmers, including members of the Franzoy family, Loyad Anderson, David Holguín, James Lack, Nick Carson, and the Cervantes family, cultivated tracts either individually or with other relatives that ranged between 500 and 2,300 acres.

Roswell farmer and Republican Party stalwart Colin McMillan epitomized the changing character of the typical chile farmer from a Spanish-speaking or Indian New Mexico native to a commercially oriented grower seeking a trendy investment. The Texan, who moved to New Mexico in 1961, achieved fame and fortune as both a state legislator and Bush administration Defense Department official as well as a farmer and rancher. His 700-acre Roswell Vegetable Farms, which grew chile as one of its products, was just one investment among many, including cattle and a majority ownership of the First Federal Savings Bank of New Mexico.

Whereas at one time chile growing had a definite egalitarian aspect to it and involved many farmers who tilled a few acres for local or regional consumption, now it was increasingly stratified. Land was at a premium, too, unlike the days when Joseph Franzoy and his neighbors bought it practically for the asking. In 1957, farm land in the Hatch Valley was selling for around $425 per acre. Thirty-five years later, in 1992, it averaged $2,500 to $5,000 per acre. "There's not much land, there's lots of demands for rent, for selling, for everything," explained Silvino Ortiz.

One characteristic of the bigger chile growers was their ownership of dehydrating equipment, an asset that allowed them to become primary processors of red chile. Costing up to one million dollars for a full-blown plant, dehydrating is not a cheap investment. But it can give a 15 to 20 percent profit edge to those farmers with the 100 or more acres needed to pay for the machines and buildings. In the early 1960s there were only a handful of farmers who ran dehydrators in New Mexico. Years later there were more than two dozen from Hatch to Artesia to Deming.

A few farmers took their operations beyond the dehydrating stage, signaling another step up in the world of chile farming. In 1992, Louis Biad, in conjunction with Loyad Anderson, announced the formation of a new corporation, Rezolex, dedicated to the extraction of oleoresins from chile for use in food coloring and cosmetics. And in early 1993, the Berridge family of Garfield exhibited a new product: Old Gringo enchilada sauce.

For farmers, the chile business was a far cry from the past. Crusty Luis Álvarez, still selling chiles from atop a car parked beneath the mulberry shade of his Mesilla farm, witnessed the complete transformation of the industry. When he was a boy, the Valley was *bosque*, horses plodded the fields, and chemical fertilizers were still in the future. Land was dirt cheap. Dairy herds consisted of 15 to 20 cows instead of the 3,000-plus milkers of today. He grew up with his father planting chile for the dinner table, later sold on the market in El Paso, contracted a bit for Mountain Pass, and finally produced cayenne for Louisiana hot sauce. What struck Álvarez was the change in seed procurement. "Back when I was young nobody was selling chile seed," he said. "Gimme some chile seed," he recalled people saying. Seed was saved from one harvest and used for the next. "Pretty soon it degenerated, it didn't make much, but we didn't know any bet-ter," laughed Álvarez. The better part of a century later, Álvarez spent cash for his cayenne seed, stating in slight amazement that he "paid (the seller) $1,000" for his last batch. Once a

source of nourishment shared among friends and family, who also took on the task of collective sun-drying preparation, chile had become such a valuable commodity that even the seed fetched a handsome price.

Notes

1. Robert Cosimati, interviews by author, Las Cruces, NM, February 1992 and July 1992.

2. "Disease May Wilt Chile Industry," *Albuquerque Journal*, 26 January 1992.

3. Sherry Robinson, "Agriculture: Economic Comeback," *New Mexico Progress Economic Review* 59 (1991): 2-3, 6.

4. Bryan Sims, interview by author, Hatch, NM, September 1992.

5. Alton Bailey, interview by author, Anthony, NM, June 1993.

6. *Crop Cost and Return Estimates in New Mexico by County and by Crop*, NMSU Agricultural Experiment Station, 1986, 25.

7. Bill Cox, crop consultant, untitled presentation to New Mexico Chile Conference, Las Cruces, NM, February 1992; *Fifty-Fifth Annual Report of the New Mexico Agricultural Experiment Station 1943-44*, 10-11; Ivan A. Reinoso R. and Wilmer M. Harper, *Production Constraints and Financial Evaluation of Mechanized Chile Harvesting, Staff Report #65*, Department of Agricultural Economics and Agricultural Business, NMSU, June 1991, Annex 4; Russell Matthews, Acting Division Director, New Mexico Department of Agriculture, written statement to the U.S. Commission on Agricultural Workers, Las Cruces, NM, 23 October 1991, *Hearings and Workshops before the Commission on Agricultural Workers 1989 to 1993*, Washington, DC, 819.

8. Fabián García, *Chile Culture*, New Mexico College of Agriculture and Mechanic Arts Bulletin #124, 1908.

9. *50 Years of Progress with the Cooperative Extension Service NMSU 1914-64*, NMSU Cooperative Extension Service, n.d.

10. Eldon Marr, "Agriculture in New Mexico," *New Mexico Business*, October 1967, 10-12.

11. *Agricultural Research at NMSU since 1889*, NMSU Department of Agriculture and Home Economics, March 1969.

12. Silvino Ortiz, interview by author, Derry, NM, September 1992.

13. Mindy McAbee, "PGEL: Biotechnology Engineers Future Farm Profits," *New Mexico Resources* (NMSU), Winter 1989, 8.

14. "New Electronic Data Logger Gives Accurate Water Measure," *The Courier*, 18 March 1993.

15. *Inventory of the County Archives of Doña Ana County, New Mexico, No. 7*, University of New Mexico, New Mexico Historical Records Survey, Works Progress Administration Project, November 1940, NMSRCA, 5, 8; Charles F. Coan, *History of New Mexico*, Vol. 3 (Chicago and New York: American Historical Society, 1925); Maude McFie Bloom, "A History of the Mesilla Valley" (bachelor's thesis, New Mexico College of A&M, June 1903); *New Mexico Farm and Ranch*, April 1971.

16. Hubert Howe Bancroft, *History of Arizona and New Mexico, 1530-1888, Bancroft's Works*, Vol. 18 (San Francisco: The History Company, 1889), 800.

17. "Old Timer Stories," Marie Carter interviews with Royal Jackman, 6 May 1937; Mary Coe Bevins, 8 March 1937; May Bailey Jackman, 30 May 1937; Nemecio Provincio, 9 May 1937; Works Progress Administration File #197, NMSRCA.

18. Gary Esslinger, Elephant Butte Irrigation District manager, telephone conversation with author, November 1992.

19. Frances French Papers, Ms. 6, Box 1, Folders 3 and 11, RGHC.

20. *Rio Grande Farmer*, 23 August 1934 and 30 August 1934.

21. George B. Anderson, *History of New Mexico: Its Resources and People*, Vol. 2 (Los Angeles: Pacific States Publishing, 1907), 1028-29 and 1045; *New Mexico Business Directory 1906*, 346.

22. Catalogue and Premium List, Doña Ana County Fair, 6-9 October 1926, Consolidated Collections, RGHC.

23. *Rio Grande Republican*, September 1893, 26 August 1904, 4 November 1904; *Las Cruces Sun-News*, 10 April 1940; "Better Farming, T. Rouault and Son, Las Cruces," Amador Trade Catalogs, RGHC; Leon C. Metz, *Southern New Mexico Empire* (El Paso, TX: Mangan Books, 1991).

24. *Historical Encyclopedia of New Mexico* (Albuquerque: New Mexico Historical Association, 1945); *New Mexico Farm and Ranch*, October 1960, 8.

25. Luis Álvarez, interview by author, Mesilla, NM, August 1993.

26. L. N. Berry, "A Test of the Value of Ground Chile Pepper in the Laying Ration," New Mexico College of A&M Press Bulletin #785, 12 June 1936.

27. *Recommendations of Committees, Economic Conference, EBID* (Elephant Butte Irrigation District), *State College, NM, Feb. 15-16, 1927, El Paso, TX, Feb. 18-19, 1927*, 20.

28. *New Mexico Extension Service Annual Report 1933, Extension Project No. 8, Horticulture*, H. C. Stewart, Extension Horticulturist.

29. *13th Annual Report of Cooperative Extension Work in Agriculture and Home Economics, For the Year Ending June 30th, 1927*, W. L. Elser, Director, 106-8; *15th Annual Report of the Cooperative Extension Work in Agriculture and Home Economics, June 30th, 1929*, W. L. Elser, Director, 68.

30. Margaret Meaders, "The Economy of Rio Arriba County," *New Mexico Business*, May 1965, 4, 8.

31. Craig L. Mapel, "The New Mexico Chile Industry 1991-92," New Mexico Department of Agriculture, 1993, 3; *1950 U.S. Census of Agriculture*, U.S. Department of Commerce, Vol. 1, Part 30 (Washington, DC: U.S. Government Printing Office, 1952), 15.

32. "New Mexico Chile Production," *New Mexico Agricultural Statistics* (Las Cruces, NM: New Mexico Agricultural Statistics Service, NMDA/USDA, 1990, 1991, 1992).

33. *New Mexico Farm and Ranch*, April 1970, 13; May 1970, 6.

34. Bob Dorbandt, telephone conversation with author, June 1993; Alan Antweil, telephone conversation with author, July 1993; Ernest Riggs, interview by author, Las Cruces, NM, September 1993; Carl Nakayama, interview by author, Doña Ana County, NM, November 1993.

35. Jeanne Gleason, "Tabasco Peppers in New Mexico," *New Mexico Farm and Ranch*, May 1976, 27.

36. *New Mexico Farm and Ranch*, September 1969, 2.

37. Gerald M. Burke, *Research Report 98*, NMSU Agricultural Experiment Station, August 1964, 2.

38. *New Mexico Farm and Ranch*, May 1975, 22. According to the Farm Bureau publication, 95% of chile was already sold by contract, in comparison to 5% on the open market. Twenty years later the estimates remained unchanged.

39. Larry Domínguez, NMDA/USDA Agricultural Statistics Service, telephone conversation with author, August 1991. One important question that remained was the preciseness of reported crop acreage. After all, farmers might have an incentive to underreport acres planted in order to increase prices for their crops. Some observers speculated that the amount of chile acreage reported to NMDA/USDA in the early 1990s might have been less than what really existed. Whatever the case, the statistics are useful for gauging trends.

40. "Voices of Experience," *Albuquerque Journal*, 18 September 1994; advertisements for land sales, *Hatch Reporter*, 1957 issues.

41. David Holguín, interview by author, Hatch Valley, NM, June 1993.

42. *1934 Report, R. E. Stockdale, Doña Ana County Agent*, Governor Hockenhull Papers, NMSRCA.

43. Bill Armstrong, "New Life on the Old Pecos," *New Mexico Resources*, Spring 1994, 6.

44. "Plant to Turn Chile into Coloring," *Las Cruces Sun-News*, 5 September 1992.

45. Louis Biad, telephone conversation with author, March 1993.

46. Luis Álvarez, interview by author, Mesilla, NM, August 1993.

From Derry to Deming

10

MARCHES ON THE CHILE EMPIRE

Owl Chile ▪ The Famous Chile Roaster ▪ Sexy Salsa ▪ Farewell to the Chili Line ▪ Luna's Lords of Chile

South of the town of Socorro proper, in the tiny hamlet of San Antonio, exists a chile oasis of sorts. Displaying a painting of a huge hooting owl on the west wall, the Owl Cafe is hard to miss. Owned by Fred and Rowena Baca, community activists and Republican Party stalwarts, the 1950s style soda fountain and diner is almost a mandatory stop on the itinerary of bird-watchers returning from the nearby Bosque del Apache National Wildlife Refuge, an item in European travel guides, and a place for a quick bite for motorists traveling between Albuquerque and Roswell.

The small diner is frequently as or more crowded than the trendiest of joints in Albuquerque or Santa Fe. Inside it is a beehive of activity. Paper money is tacked to the ceiling, ceramic and wooden owls perch on shelves, decals and business cards scream from the walls, miniatures ogle the scene from behind a perpetually uncleaned bar, and a bartender's paddle warns "For obnoxious drunks and loud punks." The Owl proudly serves Hatch chile on its green chile cheeseburgers, according to waitresses, which, upon further investigation, seems a bit strange since chile is grown right at the eatery's backyard in Socorro County.

On the north end of the county, the San Acacia Dam spews roaring cascades of water into an irrigation canal and over the ghosts of drowning victims who dared the treacherous waters for a farewell dip. A beaver paddles the width of the canal while a hawk soars overhead. Bird songs emanate from telephone poles, enlivening the slow pace of a hot midsummer day. In winter, the skies are filled with the honks of snow geese and sandhill cranes migrating south for winter warmth.

Down a nearby dirt road, Clemente Bustamante glides his pickup over bumps and past arching sunflower plants, braking the truck to a halt at a partially shaded field of chile where a dozen Mexican men and women are cutting weeds with a methodical rhythm, chopping the plants in unison up and down a row before moving on to the next one. The chubby farmer exchanges a few words in Chihuahua slang with the fieldhands and heads toward those chiles that show signs of ripening. At this stage of the season, weeds are his biggest headache, and he will send workers to the fields to hand chop with a hoe four or five times before the harvest is over. "If you don't control [a weed], it wraps around the vine of the chile plant and halts it from growing." The field and an adjacent one are reserved for the truly fiery New Mexican chiles, the Sandia and Barker's Extra Hot. As a rule, Bustamante keeps chiles of radically different heat strength separated in order to prevent a cross-pollination which might play tricks with the pungency. "My mild chile is about four miles from here," he explains.

In New Mexico, those in each growing region brag that they grow the best pepper. Hatch chile, of course, probably has the best known reputation, but chile growers from Chimayo or Santa Cruz or Deming or Roswell also proclaim theirs as the finest. So do Middle Rio Grande farmers like Bustamante. Born to a farm family, he followed his parents from their home in the lower Pecos River Valley and west to the Mesilla Valley before eventually settling in Socorro County in 1953 because of cheaper land. Bustamante started farming chile on a two-acre plot in 1968, saying he found the climate ideal because it was not as hot as the Hatch Valley nor as cold as northern New Mexico. Over the years Bustamante expanded his crop to about 60 acres, placing him among a handful of chile planters in Socorro County. He farms 300 acres, including hay and oats, but always has had to work another job, first for Safeway and then as an Albuquerque insurance agent, to keep the farm alive. He estimates that it takes about 400 acres to keep a grower in the business full time. "You always have to subsidize a farm," contends the grower.

Many of Bustamante's annual tasks and worries are familiar to southern New Mexico growers. He plants a little later than his southern colleagues but gets his seed from a feed store in Mesquite where many of the southerners purchase theirs, too. The store offers commercially bred, certified seed, which Bustamante prefers over stock from his own field. "Some people have their own seed and plant it, but I have found out that if you buy certified seed, you know what you're buying, and if you plant your own seeds back, the pods don't grow as big." The harvest on Bustamante's farm runs from mid-August through November, terminating a red chile season that ends a month or so earlier than in the south.

In the crisp days of autumn, Bustamante continues an age-old tradition by setting his freshly picked red chiles out in the sun to dry. "Chile is more meaty if you pick it and sun dry it, than if you leave it on the plant and pick it from the plant when it is dry. . . ." After the last red has departed the field, Bustamante keeps the land busy by renting it to cattle ranchers, a practice he has discovered leaves good fertilizer for the upcoming crop. In contrast to the Hatch Valley, however, he employs less chemical fertilizer, a decision which helps explain why his yield of green chile per acre—about 250 to 300 sacks, weighing 36 to 38 pounds—is about half that of the Hatch acreage. What Bustamante loses in yield, he tries to make up for in direct sales. He's opted for a one-on-one relationship with retail outlets in Albuquerque, repeat customers, and itinerant, out-of-state wholesalers. Every year, sacks of Bustamante's green head for California, Colorado, and the propane-powered roasters of Albuquerque.

A few years back, Bustamante remembers, a major Albuquerque processor sought contracts with Socorro growers, proposing to pay about $2.75 per sack of fresh green. Though it is not easy to turn down a guaranteed market, Bustamante earns more for his product by taking risks on the open market, where a sack can net between $8 and $10. It is a product that has been good to him. "Chile is one of the best-paying crops compared to hay and corn," concludes Bustamante. "It's a little more expensive to raise chile than any other crop, yet it's one of a [few] good-paying crops."

The region between Socorro County and Sandoval County, cut by the remaining stands of Rio Grande woodland and besieged by the sprawling, Los Angeles-like creep of Albuquerque, is one of the oldest chile growing regions of New Mexico. In 1992, probably no more than 1,150 acres were harvested here, rendering it but a patch within the huge capsicum quilt blanketing other parts of the state. Still, Middle Rio Grande chile, as it's called by aficionados, has its own reputation. And it was here in the shady river plain of the Manzano Mountains where chile history was made in 1981 by two Belén brothers, Clyde and Albert Sánchez. One was a nurse and the other a welder and heavy equipment operator. It was a New Mexican tradition, and still is for some, to roast chiles on a backyard grill while sipping beer and dodging exploding pods. The Sánchez brothers are behind the portable roaster boom that swept Albuquerque and Santa Fe and made chile roasting a potentially less painful, eye-stinging ordeal. They don't claim to be the first to develop the machine, but they have managed to make it a must for the chile seller.

Albert, the welder, had observed a commercial chile roaster in use and was aware of one makeshift, portable unit in the valley. Clyde, who was finishing his doctorate in health education, remembers that his family challenged Albert the tinkerer to build one of his own. The younger brother took up the dare and came up with a model: a wire metal basket heated by a propane torch and later improved with a chute and motor. Cleverly, Albert designed the machines so the chile would be downloaded from the chute and into a steaming plastic bag, making the pods easier to peel at home. Clyde and Albert introduced their innovation during the 1981 season, and they received an initial response similar to ancient thinkers who declared the world was round.

Clyde went to the biggest chile-selling store on Albuquerque's Fourth Street and tried to convince the owner he could roast a sack of chiles with the machine in five minutes. "Get out of here," retorted the storekeeper, who turned to a customer and said sarcastically, "This guy would roast his chiles in five minutes." Clyde then dutifully roasted the customer's chile in five minutes. The roaster was a hit with the media, and five machines were up and cranking in a matter of weeks. To keep the business going, Clyde and Albert hit the chile trail all the way from Roswell to Hatch. "We borrowed a truck from a guy and blew the engine in Vaughn," chuckles Albert. A bazaar-like scene developed in supermarket parking lots where the brothers Sánchez installed their portables.

On one occasion, a supermarket offered sacks of chile to the public for one dollar less than the brothers had sold it to the store, but wound up making a profit anyway because of the large number of plastic bags sold. People approached the machines, trying to hide their sketch pads and cameras. The brothers were amused and "drew out pictures of the machines and passed them out to people," according to Clyde. The men investigated patents for the machine but were told by a Sandia Labs acquaintance that the design was too generic in nature. After 1983, the Sánchezes called it quits, though their machines remain to this day. Albert is nostalgic about a time he now considers to be public service. "We had a blast. We were helping people. . . . for every sack of chile someone is roasting, that's one you won't have to roast on a grill."

Throughout New Mexico, the new chile roasters drew loads of customers to a new kind of social hour, some willing to wait hours in line for their turn at the revolving metal bucket when the next chile truck chugged up the highway from the farm. For years, natives had suckled the sweetness of wood-roasted chile, but now they tasted the propane-roasted chile that was striking with a vengeance. Which version tasted better was a matter of opinion, but soon dozens of roaster stands crowded the supermarket parking lots and street corners of every sizeable New Mexican town, their owners calling out greetings with the flair of carnival barkers. Signs such as "Chile Addict" or "We Roast Chile: Jesus is Lord" invited the autumn onlooker.

Once, when an Albuquerque-area roasting outlet offered a no-charge-for-the-roasting Labor Day special, dozens of cars jammed the road and 250 sacks were unloaded in a matter of hours. Customers sat and chatted. "You're lucky you came when you did, I've been waiting three hours," said a woman late in the day, still smiling underneath a shade tree and eating watermelon in timeless anticipation of her chile.

The technology popularized by the Sánchez brothers multiplied the fresh green chile market ten-fold or more in spots. At the Farmer's Market stores in Albuquerque, 38- to 40-pound sack sales shot up from 7,000 to 16,000 between 1990 and 1991 alone. "Now it takes five minutes in the roaster and you take it home and put it in the freezer," remarked Lance Browne, the son of the owner of Farmer's Market. "It's made it easier. Business has exploded in 10 years." A Roswell, New Mexico company, New Mexico Brands, later developed a smaller version of the Sánchez machine. "Next thing you know, we sold 42 states, Puerto Rico, and North Pole Alaska," said the company's James Cook. "That's New Mexicans. We get creative, we get everywhere." Giadone Farms, a Colorado business, claimed to have improved upon the original roaster, which still required users to "sit for hours, pulling the skins off." The Coloradans sold "Chile Master" roasters for a hefty $3,800 to $5,500, promising a "peel-free" model that separated 95 percent of the skins from the pods.

North of the Middle Rio Grande, picturesquely resting in the foothills of the Sangre de Cristo Mountains, is the "City Different," Santa Fe, New Mexico. The long-standing capital of New Mexico, Santa Fe is at once colonial, chic, and chile-caked. Known as a hangout of artists, crystal healers, and trust-fund soothsayers of all stripes, it is also chile heaven. The city's world-renowned restaurants utilize the capsicum as the basis of what's become the Santa Fe style of cooking; the old pueblo's food manufacturers dish out sexy-sounding, if pricey, salsas with names like Salsa de Juan, Pico de Santa Fe, and Santa Fe Exotic. The Santa Fe style, projecting an image of a silver- and turquoise-gowned Southwestern princess presiding over howling coyotes on a crimson horizon, is one of the promotional successes of the century. On a popular level, it has been commercialized in a Pizza Hut television ad featuring plump green chiles, rosy red *ristras*, and ruby-complexioned women.

This combination of Indian jewelry, landscape art, and chile peppers created a Santa Fe myth, celebrated by the legions of tourists drawn to the Plaza and, as was deftly reported in a U.S. Department of Commerce study, the attraction of the city's indigenous Indian and Chicano cultures. Unfortunately, few of Santa Fe's native inhabitants could afford to buy a home in the gentrified place of their birth during the 1990s. At one time, before the ascent of the contract industry in southern New Mexico, Santa Fe was at the doorstep of the original stronghold of the chile empire. From the early 1930s to the early 1940s, at least 700 to 900 acres of chile annually were planted in the villages between the Rio Grande and the Sangre de Cristos.

The 1930s, however, were the beginning of the end for the northern dominance of the New Mexico chile industry. The Great Depression hurt northern agriculture, and an act of the Colorado legislature virtually eliminated the brisk independent Colorado-New Mexico truck trade in one fell swoop when new transportation fees and mandatory insurance requirements proved financially burdensome for the small farmers who trucked their produce across state lines. Local Colorado ordinances also prohibited door-to-door produce sales, making lawbreakers out of small farmers trying to earn a buck. Symbolically, the "Chili Line" closed down in 1941, drawing the curtain on an era.

Also contributing to the decline of the northern industry was the failure of a canning or processing facility to take root nearby, an important facet of any market expansion. Southern New Mexican farmers also acquired a technological edge, introducing labor-saving tractors at a greater rate while the northerners still struggled with horse-drawn plows. In the wake of the Second World War, many Upper Rio Grande Valley villagers landed steady employment in the government jobs of Los Alamos and Santa Fe, putting a crunch on the time-consuming tasks necessary for chile production. Contemporary production in the north is but a fraction of what is grown in the south. Whereas chile fields were once an economic linchpin of San Juan Pueblo, one of the hottest moneymakers in the 1990s was the tribe's Las Vegas-style gaming business, which winsomely featured a slot machine called "Wild Chile." Nonetheless, the region retains an important niche in the annals of chile history.

Chimayo, a historic village on the high road between Santa Fe and Taos, is known for its rebellious episodes against both the Mexican and

U.S. authorities, its sacred shrine, and its deli-
cious chile (which has such a reputation that one
New Mexico processor added "Chimayo" chile
to its distribution line, even though the crop is
actually grown elsewhere). Chimayo special has
even been shipped to Guam.

A few hardy souls hang on under the
clouds. Chile is still hand-planted, hoed, and
picked by some farmers and their relatives or
neighbors. Northerners find it hard to compete
against the mass-produced chile from the south.
In what was once the center of New Mexico
chile growing, trucks from Las Cruces deliver
the hot pepper to a region that today cannot
produce enough to satisfy the chile-cherishing
population. Michael Martínez, a resident of the
village of La Puebla near Chimayo, gathers
home-grown chile from his own family, relatives, and friends and sells it at a stand down the
highway from Chimayo. One summer morning
he peddled sacks of Chimayo chile for $21
alongside sacks of Hatch for $12. The local
variety, he asserted, was smaller with a thinner
skin but had a better *sabor*, or taste, because it
was "mountain chile." As threatening, gray,
billowing banks of clouds crept in overhead
from the Jemez Mountains to the northwest,
Martínez waxed philosophical about chile
growing in this battered but still proud and
standing corner of the empire. "It's nice to plant
a seed and see something," he said. "When you
can grow out of the dirt, when you first plant it,
it seems like it's not gonna' come out nothing.
And it produces a lot." His words barely cusped
the wind when the Rain Gods spoke. The
clouds cracked and soaked the canopy shielding
Martínez's chile, sending the farmer for cover
before making another jab at the highway wan-
derers who had smelled out his Chimayo chile.
Both in Hatch and Chimayo, sudden, angry

tantrums of rain are a seasonal occurrence, scattering people from the fields and stands with
fingers crossed that the deluge doesn't demolish
King Chile.

Chile-growing in the north naturally is different than in the past. Old traditions such as the
drying of green chile are practiced less and less
by the inhabitants. And more northern growers
hire Mexican national laborers to pick the pepper and tie the eye-grabbing *ristras*. Gone too
are many of the community and family social
festivities that accompanied the harvest work.
When roasted chile can be quickly purchased
from a corner and zipped into the freezer, there
is less incentive to tolerate the hard work that
precedes the fun. As Ted Salazar, a school
teacher and part-time farmer from Velarde, flat-
ly put it, "Not too many people get together any
more and tie *ristras*."

While native chile seed (much of it undoubtedly crossed with No. 9 or other hybrids at one
time or another) passed down through family
hands is still a tradition, modern seed is a
resource for the grower as well. In recent years,
attempts have been made to revive the northern
chile industry. The non-profit Santa Fe Area
Farmer's Market exists for small growers to
directly market their chile and other produce to
customers, avoiding the middlemen who skim
the lion's share of agricultural profits. Visiting
the Santa Fe Market is akin to indulging in a carnival, food bazaar, intercultural trade exchange,
and family reunion all at the same time.
Serenaded by strumming guitar and fiddle, newcomers converse with old-time traditional
growers, nibble cookies, and chat with growers
who display blue corn, squash, apples, and of
course, plenty of chile. A social atmosphere per-
vades this and similar markets in the state,
perhaps in a time-compressed capsule of the *ris-*

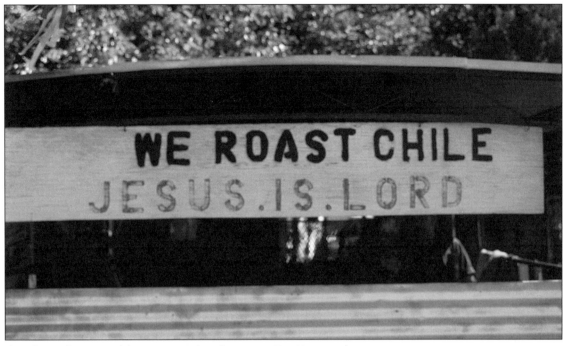

The Religion of Roasting: Chile roasting stand in Albuquerque, New Mexico.

tra-tying reunions of yore, where people can swap chile recipes, tell chile jokes, recount chile stories, and see again the *"gente* you grew up with," as Ron Romero did while hawking his wife's cookies and hot Sandia chile powder.

The markets, and even to some degree the corner roaster stands, are arenas in which Spanish-speaking New Mexicans, Native Americans, and Anglo newcomers interact with a common interest in mind—chile. If freeways, workplaces, and housing developments sometimes separate rural farmers and barrio residents from suburban transplants, a mutual visit to the roaster or grower's stand brings them together, if only a for a few fleeting moments.

At the Santa Fe market the old and modern chile traditions blend together in a uniquely New Mexican style. *Ristras* remain a favorite, and the small, distinctive-tasting northern, native chile is a hot seller, as are the NMSU-bred varieties. Grower Amadeo Trujillo of Nambé Pueblo cultivates both the old and the new varieties. "We're introducing this to a lot of people that are not familiar with the product. It also enhances the Farmer's Market, just the smell, and it's harvest time . . . and chile, it all kind of goes together," said Trujillo. "One of the other things that helps the chile market here is the newer varieties . . . they're meatier, they're fleshier, easier to peel, and they're not twisted or wrinkled and they don't wilt as easy."

Climate and economics work against a chile renaissance in the north. The northern growing season is short—from May to October—and higher-yielding NMSU chile varieties, which could make expanded production feasible, have a difficult time in the cool climate of the high country. Well-adapted to the valley of southern New Mexico, these are not as easy to grow in the north. NMSU experimented with varieties tailored for the upper elevations, especially the Española Improved cultivar, and was a recipient of a Kellogg Foundation grant in the early 1990s to research sustainable agriculture in the north.

Controversy surfaced in the early 1990s around the Kellogg-funded, NMSU Alcalde Experimental Station's sustainable agricultural project north of Española. Some growers were dissatisfied with the decision-making process, which they accused NMSU of dominating. It was just the latest chapter in a recurrent and sometimes explosive debate over the ultimate beneficiaries of NMSU's services, a long-running issue that once had Dr. Fabián García himself hustling up to Española to satisfy farmers' demands for an experimental station in their neck of the woods.

In the meantime, the main march of the chile empire lay far to the south in the Pecos River Valley and in Luna and Hidalgo counties. Along the waters of the Pecos River, the subject of long-running disputes between Texas and New Mexico, 10 national companies contracted for chile in the early 1990s. Acreage between Roswell and Artesia shot up 10-fold in the 1980s, from about 700 at the start of the decade to 7,000 at the end. Chile was so trendy it even popped up on the eastern plains of Hobbs, in the unlikely domain of New Mexico's "Little Texas" country. Hatch farmer Fred Riggs joined locals in turning the Pecos Valley into an up-and-coming production center, where dehydrators joined the competition and specialized in red chile for coloring. To the west, on the other side of the Mesilla Valley and toward the Arizona border, the expansion was even greater in the Deming

and Lordsburg areas. Headquartered in the county seat of Deming were a number of chile-processing companies, including Amigos' Foods, Trason Chile Products, Sun Products, and Border Foods.

Deming, a growing town of some 17,000 with about a 17 percent unemployment rate in 1992, one of the highest in New Mexico, sits off the highway one hour west of Las Cruces, graced with a desert greenery that nurtures yellow flowers and yucca plants brought to life by the desert rains. Over the city, a silvery U.S. Border Patrol radar blimp hangs suspended in the sky, acting as a guard-post against small planes flying north from Mexico with drug cargo. On the surface a placid town, Deming in recent years has acquired a reputation as a transshipment point for large quantities of illegal drugs. From time to time, the authorities stage high-profile raids and round up alleged dealers.

But in general, Deming attracts two distinct law-abiding groups of residents, a mix of Anglo retirees from the frost belt and Mexican laborers from the migrant belt. The town plays up its history, most notably the 1916 raid by Mexican revolutionary Pancho Villa's forces on the neighboring Luna County border town of Columbus. A hero in Mexico, Villa is reviled in Deming tourist brochures that denigrate him as a bandit. In the early part of the century several dozen Czech families arrived in Luna County to use their green thumbs in irrigated agriculture. Their legacy is celebrated every fall at the Klobase, a Catholic Church fundraiser that offers Bohemian sausage on the same plate as pinto beans while chile *ristras* hang in the background as the crowds enjoy the barbecue and accordion music.

Agriculture in Deming followed a pattern repeated throughout southern New Mexico.

After the 1920s, cotton was prominent, though growers utilized braceros to pick tomatoes for the Mountain Pass and Ashley canneries in El Paso County. Land ownership changed greatly between 1910 and 1987, resulting in a reduction in the number of farms from 340 in 1910 to 207 in 1987. During the intervening years, the size of units increased while their absolute numbers dropped. In the 1980s, Deming and Luna County accomplished a milestone when the area surpassed the legendary Hatch Valley in terms of actual chile acreage harvested, reaching an estimated 12,500 acres in 1992. Deming produced so much chile in 1992 that it could not sell it all, and unpicked red fields, their pods wilting on sun-browned stalks, remained well into the following spring. That was the year of "wildcats," uncontracted acreage sown by farmers in a gamble wagered on the upward spiral in chile sales. But they hadn't counted on a market glut, and they lost their bet accordingly.

Unlike Hatch, Deming did not go all out to promote its chile and won notoriety instead for the annual Deming Duck Race, an event, as the name suggests, that starred the frantic dashes of web-footed quackers. South of Deming proper, on the Columbus highway headed for the Mexican border, vast fields of the pepper stretch almost to the horizon, broken up here and there by the scattered vineyards. Deming has no river to speak of, except for the Mimbres arroyo that hosts stormy rains; as a result, growers must pump water from the ground to satisfy the chile. It is more costly than the Rio Grande-supplied irrigation of Doña Ana and Sierra counties, but Deming farmers have other advantages that put them in the current first place among New Mexico chile producers, as Javier Díaz can attest. Born in Deming into a Mexican family from the state of Jalisco, Díaz ventured into chile growing

about 1981 out of "necessity," as he describes it. "Cotton prices, milo prices all went down, and we had to look for something else that would pay the bills and [chile] was just another commodity that was accessible to us."

The young boot-wearing farmer considers himself lucky to have groundwater underneath his soles. On a trip to visit family members in Mexico, he learned how they endured "hardships" to raise corn and onions. "It's hill country and in hill country you don't get good wells, very few good wells." Díaz compares chile-growing in Luna and Doña Ana counties, regarding it as a trade-off between the cheaper water of the Rio Grande and the cheaper land of the Mimbres Valley. Nevertheless, Deming producers make more on the books, he adds, because they pay 25 to 33 percent less for land. Exhibiting the business savvy of the contemporary farmer, Díaz's family entered the dehydrating business. Landing a $660,000 loan through the offices of the U.S. Small Business Administration and the First New Mexico State Bank, the Díaz's New Mexico Chili Products became another entry onto the modern red chile drying scene.

Although many Deming chile producers only entered the business in the 1980s, they rapidly became sophisticated at the science of capsicum cultivation. There were growers in the Hatch Valley who watched with envy as Luna's new lords of chile avoided plant disease disasters and slid into first place without fanfare. Ed Goodbrake first went into chile in 1988, around the same time as many neighbors, finding himself in the same straits as Javier Díaz because of the economic "desperation" caused by falling milo prices. A red chile grower, Goodbrake cultivates heatless peppers, developed by the processor Cal-Compack, that have numbers instead of names like Big Jim or Sandia. The mild chile is used in sandwich sauces for children. Goodbrake never lost a crop to the weather; hails have come close but "seemed to stop at the fence."

Often, wind is a worry since "it can come in and cut off a small chile plant in a number of minutes." Because of the limited water supply in Luna County, Goodbrake and fellow farmers are careful about how they irrigate, taking up to seven to eight hours to fill a field as opposed to one hour in the Rio Grande Valley. They employ different methods, building a slight slope into the field in order to facilitate the drainage of water so an excess amount does not encourage the wilt like it has in Doña Ana County. The biggest advantage to Luna County, as both Díaz and Goodbrake articulate it, is in the relatively undiseased soil, so far free from major chile wilt outbreaks. The large amounts of available Luna land, says Díaz, makes rotation easier. "Rarely do you see chile going in the same ground for more than two years."

Forward-looking farmers to the east in Doña Ana County admired the successful practices in Luna County, and some initiated operations themselves in Luna to outwit the troublesome wilt. Virgin land, pure of the wilt, was the watchword for the southern New Mexico farmer of the 1990s. New lands opened up an hour to the west of Deming in Hidalgo County, and even in southeastern Arizona, where an estimated 3,000 acres of peppers grew in 1992. "We're now in eastern Arizona and west Texas growing chiles that come to the Rio Grande Valley here to be processed," said Dr. Paul Bosland. "So it's like ripples on a pond. We started here and kind of just expanded to Arizona (and) Texas."

New Mexico's chile-growing boom of the 1970s and 1980s inevitably led its growers to seek more of a voice. While chile growing in New Mexico had long exceeded the importance of California's crop, New Mexican farmers lagged behind their fellows in the Golden State in organizational cohesion. For example, in California's Salinas Valley, farmers under contract for 2,500 acres in the mid-1980s had the Independent Growers Bargaining Association to negotiate joint deals with processors and earn a few extra dollars as a result. And the Golden Staters had the California Pepper Foundation to channel money for variety breeding and virus vanquishing. In contrast, New Mexico farmers were out on their own, striking up individual deals for their chile. The signing of contracts was a personal matter between a grower and a processing company. Highly individualistic, the commercial New Mexico chile grower was prone to grumble about this or that farmer undercutting the others by selling his chile for bargain-basement prices.

One reported incident illustrates how the competitiveness could undermine farmers' interests as a whole. In 1992 a grower walked into the offices of a dehydrating company to see if he could unload a crop of chile.

"How much are you paying for red chile?" he asked the manager.

"63¢ (per pound)."

"I'll sell it to you for 40¢ a pound, and deliver it," replied the farmer.

It was an offer the company could not turn down.

Eventually, though, New Mexico chile farmers created their own specific organizational voice to better their growing conditions, although they still shied away from a collective front at contract time. The New Mexico Chile Improvement Foundation, headed by farmer Mike McNamee, distributed grants for breeding and plant virus work.

In 1988, growers proposed the formation of a state-recognized New Mexico Chile Commodities Commission, a group interested in seeking collective solutions to common problems such as the wilt. Another agenda item was monetary support for a machine-harvestable chile. Vado grower Orlando Cervantes presented the New Mexico Department of Agriculture with a petition signed by 95 farmers, whom he said controlled 85 percent of the more than 23,000-acre crop statewide, requesting approval as a state-recognized chile commission.

An election was held by 100 participating growers. Ninety-three percent of those casting ballots voted aye. The Commission was born, made up of anyone having 10 acres or more of chile for processing. Fees were collected based on tonnage sold to the processors and earmarked for improvement purposes. The money was principally donated to New Mexico State and Texas A&M in an effort to outfox the wilt and conjure up commercially viable cultivars.

"The chile industry at one time was a mom-and-pop type of industry growing small plots and marketing it themselves," said Cervantes, prior to the election. "That has grown into what is now a major industry in New Mexico." Cervantes's words ring true, stamped on the receipts for pods destined for the unlikeliest corners of the globe. But, as a big enterprise, chile needed stable and large-scale processing outlets. Several companies, many owned by out-of-staters, grew up hand-in-hand with the New Mexico farmers. The most important included Old El Paso Foods (Pet, Inc.), Anthony, Texas; Ashley's Foods (Bruce Foods of New Iberia, Louisiana), El Paso, Texas; Paso Pack (McCormick Co.), Fabens, Texas; Cal-Compack (Beatrice), Las Cruces, New Mexico; Biad Chile Company, Las Cruces, New Mexico; Joy Canning (Basic American Foods), Las Cruces, New Mexico; Border Foods, Deming, New Mexico; Fiesta Canning Company, McNeal, Arizona; and Bueno Foods, Albuquerque, New Mexico.

The stories of these border-belt processors are crucial for understanding how acreage and prices were determined, what type of chile seed was sown, how they shaped and reacted to consumer taste, and who raked in the receipts during the Great Chile Boom.

Notes

1. Silvino Ortiz, interview by author, Derry, NM, September 1992.

2. Clemente Bustamante, interview by author, Socorro County, NM, July 1992.

3. "New Mexico Chile Production 1992," New Mexico Agricultural Statistics Service, 1993.

4. Albert Sánchez, telephone conversation with author, August 1992; Clyde Sánchez, telephone conversation with author, September 1992.

5. Lance Browne, interview by author, Albuquerque, NM, August 1992.

6. Giadone Farms display and brochure, Fiery Foods Show, Albuquerque, NM, February 1994.

7. James Cook, interview by author, Las Cruces, NM, February 1992.

8. John Sichler, interview by author, Albuquerque, NM, August 1992.

9. U.S. Department of Commerce, Bureau of the Census, *1959 U.S. Census of Agriculture, New Mexico Counties*, Vol. 1, Part 42, New Mexico (Washington, DC: U.S. Government Printing Office, 1961), 155-57.

10. "Land Costs Rise in Valencia County," *New Mexico Farm and Ranch*, December 1975, 23.

11. "New Mexico Praised as Minority Tourist Site," *Albuquerque Journal*, 13 April 1991.

12. "Santa Fe Marketing More Substance than Style," *Albuquerque Journal*, 12 November 1991.

13. "Everyone Knows the Way to Santa Fe," *Santa Fe Reporter*, 22-28 May 1991.

14. Marta Weigle, *Hispanic Villages of Northern New Mexico* (Santa Fe, NM: Lightning Tree, 1975), 70, 81, 86-87.

15. H. E. Dregne, "Fertilizer Consumption Trends in New Mexico," Press Bulletin 1086, New Mexico College of Agriculture and Mechanic Arts, State College, NM, August 1953.

16. P. W. Cockerill, *Economics of the Production and Marketing of Chile, Bulletin No. 314*, Agricultural Experiment Station, New Mexico College of Agriculture and Mechanic Arts, 1944, 3-4, 11, 12-13.

17. John A. Gjerve, *Chili Line: The Narrow Rail Trail to Santa Fe* (Española, NM: Rio Grande Sun Press, 1969); John Stewart, "Chile for the Nation," *New Mexico Magazine*, May 1935, 26-27.

18. Vicente Ximenes, "Highlights of the Farm Census in New Mexico," *New Mexico Business*, October 1955.

19. Eldon Marr, "Technological Change: Agriculture in New Mexico," *New Mexico Business*, October 1967, 7, 10.

20. Margaret Meaders, "The Economy of Rio Arriba County," *New Mexico Business*, May 1965, 4, 8.

21. Brent Jones, "Rio Arriba County History," Works Progress Administration File #220, 30 April 1936, NMSRCA.

22. Longhino Vigil, interview by author, Cundiyo, NM, February 1994.

23. Michael Martínez, interview by author, Pojoaque, NM, September 1992.

24. Ted Salazar, interview by author, Velarde, NM, September 1994.

25. Ron Romero, interview by author, Santa Fe, NM, September 1993.

26. Amadeo Trujillo, interview by author, Santa Fe, NM, October 1993.

27. Dr. Paul Bosland, interview by author, Hatch, NM, August 1991.

28. Stan Crawford, Dixon farmer and board member, Santa Fe Farmer's Market, telephone conversation with author, January 1993. Crawford wrote a critical letter to NMDA Secretary Frank DuBois questioning decision-making procedures around the Kellogg grant.

29. H. Milton to New Mexico Gov. John Miles, 29 January 1941. Milton, then New Mexico A&M president, informed the governor of Dr. García's trouble-shooting in the Española Valley. Governor Miles Papers, Correspondence, NM State College A&M 1939-1942, NMSRCA.

30. Harold Hobson, presentation to New Mexico Chile Conference, Las Cruces, NM, February 1992; "New Mexico Chile Production 1992," New Mexico Agricultural Statistics Service.

31. "Unemployment 17.5 Percent in June," *Deming Headlight*, 18 August 1992.

32. *History of Luna County*, Luna County Historical Society, 1978.

33. Isabel Hooten and Geraldine Kretek, interviews by author, Deming, NM, October 1994. Ms. Kretek's family was among early Czech settlers of Luna County.

34. *New Mexico Farm and Ranch*, February 1968, 29.

35. *Proceedings of the 6th Annual Fruit and Vegetable Short Course, January 18 and 19, 1962*, Cooperative Extension Service, New Mexico State University, Las Cruces, NM, 8-11.

36. *New Mexico Farm and Ranch*, February 1959, 14.

37. "New Mexico Chile Production 1992," op. cit.

38. "Luna still sets chili pace," Associated Press wire story, *Deming Headlight*, 29 January 1992.

39. Javier Díaz, interview by author, Las Cruces, NM, February 1993.

40. "Deming business deal catches eye, interest of Federal Reserve," *Deming Headlight*, 22 August 1994.

41. Ed Goodbrake, interview by author, Deming, NM, September 1993.

42. Belaquín Gómez, "Chile Market Situation," *Proceedings of the 1985 Chile Conference*, New Mexico State University, Las Cruces, NM, 24.

43. *Albuquerque Journal*, 9 February 1989.

44. "The Humble Chile Gets a Commission," *Santa Fe Reporter*, 9-15 November 1988.

45. "Chile Farmer Urges State to Establish Commission," *Albuquerque Journal*, 22 June 1988.

The King of the Pass

11

OLD EL PASO AND THE CHILE CONTRACT SYSTEM

Jalapeño Fever ▪ The El Paso Chile Connection ▪ Labor Troubles at Mountain Pass ▪ A New Pet Prince Eyes the Throne

On the Texas-New Mexico border lies the dusty town of Anthony, an old railroad center that is now a burgeoning *colonia* pockmarked with unusual sights like the decaying, screaming black cat sign imprisoned behind a barbed-wire fence on the Doniphan Drive main drag. Just off Interstate 10, three Anthony landmarks are visible to the eye, forming a triangular monument to human pleasures and temptations. The closest is the Screamer, a six-story waterslide where inner-tube toting youngsters from Mexico and the United States find thrills. The next is La Tuna Federal Penitentiary, a bleach-white, storybook-like fortress whose walls have processed inmates such as Reies López Tijerina, the famed land grant activist. Across the street is the king of the border-belt chile pod processors, Old El Paso Foods. A tad across the state line from New Mexico, Old El Paso cranks out a huge volume of salsas, sauces, powders, and taco shells for cus-

tomers as far afield as Australia. An enormous, sprawling food factory where entire truckloads of chile are dumped onto conveyor lines, at the plant's guarded entrance flutter three flags: the Texas flag, the U.S. flag, and the Old El Paso flag. Missing, to the presumed annoyance of neighbors, is the New Mexican flag, because in 1988 alone Mountain Pass (as the company continues to be called) purchased 40 million pounds of New Mexican chile, about 30 percent of the harvested state crop.

The growers' plantings of the mild Tam jalapeño, developed by Dr. Ben Villalón of Texas A&M in Weslaco, boosted Old El Paso's fortunes as it cashed in on the smash-hit jalapeño fever. Bred to gringos' timid tastes, the pepper was something that could easily sell at a baseball game where "people could eat it on hot dogs," according to retired Old El Paso field man Joe Parker.

Registering over $400 million in sales by 1992, Old El Paso is the leader in the Mexican

> *"We had to do a lot of production, and the supervisors had to make quota."*
>
> —JACINTO SOSA, INJURED OLD EL PASO FOODS WORKER

foods industry, specializing in canned and packaged goods. The company is reputed to be responsible for separate Mexican food sections on grocery-store shelves, an idea that eased the acceptance of the hot diet into the mainstream of U.S. cuisine. One of the "Big Three" processors (the other two are Cal-Compack and the Biad Chili Company) credited by grower Alton Bailey for spurring the growth of the New Mexico chile industry in the 1970s, Old El Paso's financial support of the NMSU breeding program and its contracts with farmers have been instrumental in making New Mexico the head chile producer.

The contemporary company is the direct descendent of a lively El Paso canning industry that gave birth to Mountain Pass and a number of other outfits in the early 1900s, turning the city and supplier rural areas in Texas and New Mexico into a big center of the early Mexican foods business. The Pass on the Rio Grande first hosted the Christie Canning Company in 1908, a firm that offered stock for $10 per share and planned chile as its premier product in a splashy unveiling aimed at "developing the fertile land adjacent to El Paso." A decade later, the Powell family relocated their tomato canning specialty from a farm in Deming, New Mexico, to Canutillo, Texas, on the outskirts of El Paso and opened the doors of the Mountain Pass plant, producing around 20,000 cases of the red juicy cousin to capsicum and contracting chile, pinto

beans, and other vegetables from New Mexico and Texas.

At first the contract system was informal, according to former owner Les Dodson, who started at the cannery in the 1930s with El Paso wholesale grocer James Dick. Mountain Pass "knew all the farmers" and invited them to bring in their chile during the harvest, said Dodson.

More canneries soon broke ground so that by 1935 an estimated 100,000 four-ounce cans of green chile were prepared for the mouths of hungry El Pasoans. This figure barely tapped the vast possibilities of the underdeveloped chile industry, and California chile canners flooded El Paso supermarkets with their own wares. Not to be outdone, J. I. and R. B. Domínguez founded Tru-Mex the next year and purchased chile from New Mexico, Mexico, California, and El Paso County for their pickled jalapeños, canned chili sauce, and spiced yellows. In 1936, Idus T. Gillette, president of the El Paso-Hudspeth County Farm Bureau and co-operator of another cannery in Canutillo, actively promoted the four Elephant Butte project canneries from Hatch to Canutillo, telling a reporter that "not the best comes from California." As the reporter described it, Gillette claimed the plants were capable of packing enough "garden truck" to supply vegetable stew for Sheriff Chris Fox's jamboree and have leftovers for six months afterward. Local farmer Warder Wallace understood this, and he earned $900 from just three acres of green chile in 1936, a large profit for the time.

The World War II era was a crossroads for the local canners. Tin shortages forced manufacturers to abandon the use of smaller containers and temporarily replace them with green chile and chile sauce sold in bottles or glass jars. Canned chile from Mexico also became popular. Technological and promotional innovations followed suit. In Canutillo, the Valley Canning Company used sterilized cookers and modern machinery to stamp the "Valley Brand" on its enchilada sauce, a creation manager Idus Gillette claimed as a "culinary masterpiece." Even then, Southwestern images were used to evoke the desires of the buying public, a technique utilized in Valley Canning's portrayals of smiling señoritas, chile pods, and pueblo-style buildings on the cans. Mass-produced canned chile grew more popular, signifying a change in both the Southwestern food tradition and the broader American kitchen culture. Whereas drying green chile was once a widespread New Mexican practice, canning influenced the decline of this ritual in favor of easy convenience. Gillette boasted that besides being attractive, tasty and inexpensive, his products rescued housewives from "endless hours of kitchen drudgery."

Another individual, restaurateur George Ashley, figured prominently in the growth of the El Paso-New Mexico chile business during the war era and even more so in the years to follow. After Pearl Harbor got things hopping at El Paso's Fort Bliss, Ashley was there to serve the soldiers heapings of Mexican food he simmered up from local recipes he'd collected. In all likelihood, he was responsible for exposing soldiers from isolated rural corners and distant strange cities outside the Southwest to a kind of cuisine

they would not have experienced if it had not been for Adolf Hitler and George Ashley. It was a forced dinner date that nudged Mexican foods toward national acceptance. While the war trudged forward, Ashley was dreaming of opening a food manufacturing plant. One possible future competitor was eliminated in an accidental 1943 fire when the Downey Canning Company, which canned chile in beer bottles, suffered a blaze that scorched its adobe walls. As smoke filtered into the sky, hundreds of neighbors gathered to sniff $10,000 worth of canned chile roasted in the flames.

Ashley's dream came true when he was the first to win a government military contract for Mexican foods. Building his plant after the defeat of the Axis powers, he had a nearly million-dollar-a-year establishment by the middle of the 1950s, capable of sealing 250 cans of enchilada sauce a minute. Ashley's Mexican foods were sold internationally, and the family's two trucks burned tires hauling chile from as far as California and cans and cardboard cases back from Dallas and Houston. Warehouses in Portland, New York, and Baltimore stored the products of El Paso's up-and-coming Mexican food czar.

Although Ashley's food factory was within miles of New Mexico, chile farmers in the neighboring state initially did not reap the full potential of the growing market. Unlike the green chile market, Ashley's was limited in buying dried red chile from the New Mexicans because of the absence at the time of the dehydrating machines necessary to bring the product into compliance with FDA standards. But the Mexican food leader handled tomatoes from southern New Mexico and the company signed strict contracts with growers similar to those of the subsequent chile contract era, reserving rights to exclusive first purchases, setting the harvest date, and other conditions.

Meanwhile, down the arroyos from Ashley's plant on the Carlsbad Highway, Mountain Pass was embarking on a venture which ultimately led it to surpass the chefs in the heights and become the king canner of the Pass. A blend of business acumen and good timing lay behind the triumph. A series of crucial events for the company's success began unfolding in 1943 when the Powell family sold off Mountain Pass for a mere $6,000, a deal that, in hindsight, was the chile industry's equivalent to the purchase of Manhattan Island for a few wampum.

Mountain Pass's owners made another shrewd move in the mid-1950s, when they purchased the Valley Canning Company and the rival canner's Old El Paso label, a name that was already gaining a national market. And in this period, Mountain Pass's canned bean product showcasing an "Indio" on the label was a favored buy of the cotton-working Mexican braceros.

In 1958 another momentous decision was finalized. That is when the company planned the move to Anthony, setting its sights on a half-completed plant built by bankrupt Frio Frozen Foods, a firm that lost the empty building for its 800 shareholders. The stillborn frozen foods giant had been Mesilla Valley investors' vision of a vegetable kingdom on the Rio Grande. Construction began in 1955 and picked up steam as 250 local farmers and businessmen pledged $200,000 in backing and expanded the ownership circle. The owners anticipated employing 300 people to process 10 million pounds of frozen food grown on 5,000 acres. Optimism was strong, and contracts were signed with 360 growers to supply the produce. Frio proposed to turn farmers into processors and thus maximize crop values. But then the bottom fell out of the business when creditors demanded loan repayments. A 1958 "Save Frio" campaign fizzled and the project was history. "So ends the Frio Frozen Foods Inc. dream of a bustling, modern plant which was to be the nerve center of a giant new agricultural industry in the Mesilla Valley," stated the Farm Bureau publication in an obituary.

Yet where one dream disintegrated another was realized. The Frio Frozen Foods site did indeed become a "nerve center" of a giant agricultural business, the fiasco coming at an opportune time for Old El Paso/Mountain Pass, whose owners were considering a new plant site. According to Les Dodson, the relocation was precipitated by a flood that "came in one day and ran through the little ol' cannery in Canutillo and covered half the chile in mud." Paused at another fateful intersection, Old El Paso/Mountain Pass paid $50,000 for a building that now earns hundreds of millions of dollars.

Nowadays, Old El Paso is part of a club that gives a guaranteed market to the New Mexico chile farmer. The border-belt companies provide an outlet for powdered, dried, canned, and frozen forms of the pepper. In the words of one plant manager, it is an arrangement beneficial to both parties. "We're in this together," he said. "We're all in it for the long haul. What's good for them is good for us."

In their negotiations with farmers, the processors specify not only the price they will pay, but also the seed, the amount, and the quality. "We have to grow what the processors want and can sell," notes Hatch Valley farmer David Holguín, Jr. Processors are picky, mulling over the crop to ensure a superior grade, size, and heat strength. Holguín grows for one company that has a modern quality control operation and laboratory to check for the preferred "fluorescent green" color, forcing him to be exact about the shade he puts on the truck. "It's more work, but I get compensated for it. You know, you wouldn't want to buy junk," said Holguín.

Planting dates are set so the processors can have a crop in their hands by a certain date, delivered within hours of picking. Bigger firms employ a "field man" to inspect the crop and give growing suggestions. This yearly business cycle typically begins in the slow season of December or January when contracts with growers are signed. Favored contract farmers have good rotation practices, proper pesticide usage, and a good track record. The proximity of Old El Paso and a few other major processors to the chile fields allows freshly picked chiles to be delivered straight to the plant gate within hours or even minutes. Once the green chile is let through, it is washed and then steamed or roasted, depending upon a particular company's process. Then it is sent through several processing lines where workers destem, peel, and chop the chile in the manner of methodical surgeons before the ready product is packed into cans, some as large as barrels and weighing 200 pounds, and shipped to other processors, who prepare the final meal in a restaurant or mass-market foods plant.

For red chile, the pods are also washed but then they are packed into dryers for a number of hours before being unloaded onto the assembly line and sorted by grade into boxes for customers. Delivery time from the field to the factory can be a tense period. Field supervisors might berate pickers and drivers if a shipment were behind schedule. And at the plant, a quality control inspection awaits. Samples are lifted from each load to check for a number of potential defects. Are there any bugs stuck in the chile? Are the pods too small or sunburned? Are the pods "pinto," half-red and half-green? Are broken or complete plant stems too numerous? If

there is a high percentage of these defects, the processor can reject the shipment, which results in the grower's loss.

Over the decades the processing companies became extremely sophisticated in their business plans. Growing seasons, pest problems, irrigation sources, local labor costs, transportation, weather, and climate were all weighed in deciding when, where, and how to contract. The biggest contract chiles came from not only a wide area in New Mexico, but from the Southwest, Mexico, other Third World nations, or even the paprika regions of Europe. The reason was simple: to guard against losses from hail or flood, chile wilt, insect plague, or contract failure. If Field A was ravaged in Hatch, New Mexico, perhaps Field X in Cochise County, Arizona, could be salvaged.

One observer likened the contract system to a "big chess game" in which the players made every move as part of a grand strategy. In the long run, the contract system, intentionally or not, powered the drive toward larger chile farms. As sales boomed, larger acreage was needed. If rotation formulas were held to, a farmer with a 100-acre chile contract would require another 300 to 400 acres of other crops to stay healthy. The industry created a multi-tiered system of farming, especially boosting those farmers who were primary processors of red or cayenne, since they accepted product from other growers, dehydrated or mashed it, and then turned it around to sauce or spice makers. A few even acted as middlemen, subcontracting acreage from other planters for the processor.

Thus, chile went through numerous stages from the farm to the plate. The crop was grown by a farmer, maybe passed by a dehydrator or subcontractor, sold to a main processor, brokered by a distributor, and sometimes sold to a

A Hot Time: Women processing chile at Old El Paso Foods.

third processor who included the chile in, say, a restaurant serving of red enchiladas.

An enormous mark-up spiraled up the chain. Laborers picked green chile for around 3¢ a pound for a farmer who received about 12 or 13¢ for the same pound that was ultimately sold frozen in the grocery for $2.44. For red, pickers received between 15 and 20¢ a pound from a farmer who could be paid as low as 50¢ a pound for a commodity that might fetch almost $30.00 a pound on the stand as ground paprika. Dried jalapeño retailed for as much as $51.09 a pound at the store. The essence of the contractor-

farmer relationship revolved around price. Red fetched one price, green another, cayenne yet another, and jalapeño still another. There were bonuses for superior grade chile and penalties for a surplus, because when an extra amount was harvested, processors could pay below the contract price.

One study by NMSU Professor Constance Falk reported that processors used a variety of criteria in deciding what price to pay. These included cost of production, going market rates, intervals between price increases, and company financial health. For much of the 1980s processor prices to farmers were flat. In 1981, growers received an average $237 per ton for green chile, a price that fell the next year, inched up to $246 in 1985, dipped again the following year, and stayed at $245 for the next four years. By 1992, green got an average of $254 per ton. Red chile prices nose-dived from $1,083 per ton in 1981 and remained in the $850 to $900 range for the remainder of the decade. In 1991 farmers saw a raise to about $1,030 per ton, but they lost it the next year when the famous red market flood of 1992 resulted in about a 10 percent drop to $935.

A degree of discord and tension existed between farmers and processors. Disputes sometimes broke out over a company's refusal to accept a shipment because of alleged defects in quality; complaints were registered about farmers' growing practices; Chile Commission head Don Hackey threatened in 1993 to sue some processors for not collecting fees assessed on each ton of produced chile earmarked for the commission's efforts to eradicate chile wilt; and resentments surfaced over stagnating prices paid to farmers.

One farmer called the contract system "a racket," adding that, "when (processors) get products they sell them for more money, but they don't pay the farmer enough. They'll get a contract for the cheapest they can." Farmer Alton Bailey was more sympathetic, noting that processors had lenders and investors to pay off. Nevertheless, he remarked that a price lag existed between production costs and contract prices. "As a grower, I'm not ever satisfied with the prices that are paid . . . I think the buyers would like to pay more, it's a competitive . . . market."

For a long time, Old El Paso was the king of that market. After a decade in Anthony, the locally owned Mountain Pass sold out in 1969 to Pet Inc. of St. Louis. Dodson, who raised the

"damn business" and "never had a day off," said the sale to Pet was a good deal for both parties. "We knew we had a good business there and it kept getting bigger and bigger and we let it go," he said. Pet hardly had time to adjust the time clocks as the early 1970s saw green chile production grow three-fold. On busy days, upwards of 60 trucks loaded down with Mexican food departed the gates.

But inside, discontent was simmering. In 1977, a bitter two-month-long strike rocked Old El Paso as hundreds of workers walked the picket lines to protest arbitrary management and low wages. The walkout began the morning of April 1 when employees ground the processing lines to a halt, demanding a 40¢ an hour raise, cost-of-living increases, better insurance, and improved working conditions.

Challenging an El Paso County Sheriff's ban on more than six pickets, 200 strikers gathered outside the plant gate on April 11. Deputies arrested leader Armando Curiel and hauled him to the El Paso hoosegow, at which point 100 strikers staged a demonstration calling for Curiel's release. The activist was let go and the strikers promptly returned to the cannery, this time enduring 34 arrests for mass picketing. Among the arrested were members of "Los Tres del Barrio," well-known El Paso Chicano movement activists. The strike was punctuated by other incidents. María Álvarez, an Anthony worker who crossed the picket line, reported that her mobile home was mysteriously destroyed by fire the first week of the walkout.

Before the stoppage, hundreds of grievances were pending against management. Two months later, the strike was settled, the United Food and Commercial Workers Union (UFCW) had a new contract, and labor-management relations took a turn for the better, according to Ramón

Corral, president of the new UFCW local. Under union contract, Old El Paso paid its workforce more than other chile processing plants. Wages for year-round employees ranged from $7.00 to $11.41 per hour in 1993, considerably higher than the starting pay of $4.25 to $4.50 an hour at other border plants. Workers also received insurance benefits, training, vacations, holidays, and English classes.

One year after the strike, IC Industries (ICI) Inc. (later, the Whitman group), a conglomerate with railroad interests, embarked on a hostile takeover of Pet, drawing lawsuits by Pet management and counter lawsuits by opposing shareholders who favored the sale. And, if a courtroom battle between rival company factions was not enough, Pet management was simultaneously embroiled in yet another labor dispute, this time involving the United Steelworkers over replacement workers at a struck company subsidiary. ICI won approval for its purchase, and Pet underwent a series of company-wide restructurings. Periodically, officials were diverted here and there by legal troubles. In 1991 the corporation agreed to pay a $3.5 million fine for fixing milk prices in southern schools during the mid-1980s. Also, the Justice Department probed overtime violations at Pet subsidiary Stuckey's.

But on the border and beyond, the company forged ahead. Pet's Mexican foods became the undisputed leading brands in the United Kingdom, Canada, and Australia, and were sold in Scandinavia and the Far East. In the late 1980s, Pet's Old El Paso management embarked on a drive to modernize the plant and fine-tune its labor-management philosophy. The Kearney consultant group was brought in, the workforce trimmed, and shop-level employees given more job responsibility. One company bulletin urged workers to be diligent, reminding them that every wasted chile was "23 Cents in the Trash Can."

Not everyone was happy about the new Old El Paso. Current and former workers complained of speed-ups, injuries, and firings. Furthermore, gripes surfaced from time to time about not getting paid for overtime, for downtime when machines broke down, and for lock-outs from the floor when bosses decided who could work and who could not.

Employment at the huge plant skyrockets each year between July and October when chiles arrive from Mexico and the Southwestern states. Although factory automation has reduced the number of seasonal processing workers needed to can the chiles over the year, hundreds are still recruited to get the chile off the truck and into the supermarket stands. Seasonal helpers are divided into sections of a half-dozen or more workers, generally women, who are assigned a daily quota of 30,000 cans or so and then thrust into competition against the other sections. Winners are given soda and pizza. One employee, who labored for several seasons in a row, worked for a minimum wage that only changed from $3.80 to $4.25 with the 1990 federally mandated hike. The worker recalled being eyed by observers who timed how fast the line employees stuffed chiles into cans and then turned the information over to supervisors.

The task of chile processing requires a strong back and an arrow-straight stare at the thousands upon thousands of pods, green or red, wrinkled or firm, tumbling by in spicy succession. One worker at another plant entered the job already savoring chile in her food but never sampled the employer's specimen. "I've only seen it and not tried it," she swore. She still got all the chile she bargained for and then some. In her first year, she could not forget the peppers and felt the stuff 24 hours a day, even in her deepest sleep. "I dream I'm going with the lines full of chile. *Ay, Dios mío*, I don't rest either at night or in the day, because during the day I go to work and at night I sleep working," she exclaimed. On the plant floor, the tears of chile initiated her into the workforce. "At the beginning, it made me cry . . . now I put on my [face] mask and it seems now I can take it," she said.

Occasionally, processing workers suffer downtime when the plant cannot can or dry because of a poor quality of chile delivered, flies that need plucking, or in the case of one factory, when a stray snake roasted with the chile needed to be recovered. Working in a chile plant has its own occupational hazards, namely the burning sensation of capsaicin in the throat, eyes, and skin. A safety-conscious plant provides gowns, gloves, and masks to workers. As Anthony, New Mexico, resident Diana Sosa experienced at Old El Paso/Mountain Pass in the mid-1980s, a few holes in the gloves could mean burns on the skin. Her husband, Jacinto Sosa, worked for Old El Paso for 15 years, advancing to machine operator. In 1990, he injured his knee and waist in an accident and was forced to go on workman's compensation. Sosa once liked the way the company was run, but the atmosphere changed as management, using the argument of competition, expected greater output. "All the responsibility fell on me," said Sosa, "if I made an error they were going to fire me or write me up." Line employees were told that "we had to do a lot of production, and the supervisors had to make quota. They were pressured and they pressured the workers." Sosa was compensated for his accident for three years but was left with nothing when the coverage expired. He did not share in the basket of goodies passed around in

the offices of a Pet/Old El Paso whose fortunes were peaking.

In April of 1991, Pet Inc. spun off from the Whitman Corporation, and shareholders named Miles Marsh, a native South African, as company chairman. Pet's respectability within the financial establishment soared, highlighted in part by the nomination of former Delaware Governor Pierre S. Du Pont, IV, to the board. Other noteworthy directors included former Oklahoma federal judge and Baltimore Orioles director Molly Shi Boren and Richard Battram, a director of both May's Department Stores and Boatmen's Bancshares Inc. For the privilege of serving on the board, each was entitled to a yearly retainer of $20,000. Pet's main owners included the New York investment firm Gabelli and Company; The Prudential Insurance Company of America; Gamco Investors; TCW Management; Hong Kong and Shanghai Banking; and Boatmen's Bancshares of St. Louis, which, conveniently, is also the owner of Sunwest Bank, the largest in New Mexico. In addition to Old El Paso, Pet owned Pancho Villa Mexican Foods and the Ramírez and Feraud Chili Company.

The spin-off boosted shareholder's profits by 50 percent in one year. Aggressively pursuing a new public profile, Pet doubled the company's annual advertising budget to $40 million in 1991. The new Pet was saddled with a $609 million long-term debt but managed to pay off more than one-third of it in just two years. Pet experienced a 26 percent gain in per-share earnings for fiscal year 1992, earning a net income of $103 million on $1.8 billion in sales. Although sales were slightly down in 1993, stockholders saw another hike in profits from 98¢ per share in 1992 to $1.06 per share in 1993. Marsh himself reaped a sizable reward, getting an estimated three-year compensation of $1.7 million from 1990 to 1992, according to *Business Week*. Four other top company executives garnered annual compensations of between $301,926 and $422,835. Pet's Old El Paso division, called by one writer the "jewel" of the company, contributed 30 percent of the company's earnings. Old El Paso's profit margins hovered around 20 percent, higher than Pet's

other grocery items like Progresso soups. Wall Street was enamored and rated Pet in the same category as food industry titans Campbell's and Con-Agra. The border-belt gem shined brightly from the Texas-New Mexico border, leading one analyst to suggest that Pet was ripe for yet another takeover.

Notes

1. *Albuquerque Journal*, 16 July 1989.

2. Joe Parker, telephone conversation with author, March 1993.

3. "Pet to expand Old El Paso to put offensive to work," *St. Louis Business Journal*, 5 April 1993.

4. Information on the history of the El Paso canning industry: Dena Hirsch, "The Bean That Made El Paso Famous," *El Paso Today*, August 1981; *El Paso Herald*, 30 October 1907 and 9 June 1908; *El Paso Times*, 27 September 1936, 23 January 1941, 14 August 1943, 25 April 1954; *El Paso Herald Post*, 24 April 1954.

5. Alton Bailey, telephone conversation with author, February 1993.

6. David Holguín, interview by author, Hatch Valley, NM, June 1993.

7. Belaquín Gómez, "Chile Market Situation," *Proceedings of the 1985 Chile Conference*, NMSU, 23.

8. *New Mexico Farm and Ranch*, February 1959, 17.

9. Constance L. Falk, "Contractual Relations between New Mexico Producers and Food Processors," paper presented at 1993 New Mexico Governor's Conference on Food Production and Processing, Albuquerque, NM, 29 April 1993, 6.

10. Don Hackey, interview by author, Las Cruces, NM, February 1993.

11. Dena Hirsch, *Union of Eagles: El Paso/Juárez* (El Paso, TX: Rainbow in a Tree, 1987), 102.

12. Les Dodson, telephone conversation with author, September 1993.

13. "Chile Outlook Appears Bright," *Las Cruces Sun News*, 9 January 1977.

14. For the fate of Frio Frozen Foods, see *New Mexico Farm and Ranch*, September 1955, 22, and December 1958, 6, 13.

15. Tom Barry and Jim Frazin, "New Mexico Agriculture and Ranching: Its Present and Future," *Who Runs New Mexico?: NMPE Power Structure Report* (Albuquerque: New Mexico People and Energy, 1980).

16. Newspaper accounts of the 1977 strike: "Lid Is Closed Tight on Mtn. Pass Co.," *El Paso Herald-Post*, 2 April 1977; "Mountain Pass Pickets Limited," 7 April 1977; "Strikers Protest Jailing of Leader," 12 April 1977; *Las Cruces Sun News*, 7 April 1977.

17. Ramón Corral, telephone conversation with author, February 1993.

18. Pet Transition Report, Securities and Exchange Commission File 1-10672, 23 September 1991, 59; 1978 Annual Report, SEC File 1-242-14-03, 3-4; 1993 Annual Report, SEC File 1-10672, 2.

19. *Daily Report Card*, American Political Network, Inc., 2 March 1992; Antitrust and Trade Regulation Report, Bureau of National Affairs, Inc., 29 August 1991, 290.

20. "Firm rigged milk bids: Pet to admit guilt in Hall school deal," *Atlanta Constitution*, 27 August 1991.

21. James Ferguson, Old El Paso/Pet Anthony manager, memorandum to plant employees, 26 October 1990.

22. Diana Sosa, interview by author, Anthony, NM, September 1993.

23. Jacinto Sosa, interviews by author, Anthony, NM, July 1992 and September 1993.

24. Kathleen Morris, "Pet: How About Some Mexican Food?" *Financial World*, 10 November 1992, 20.

25. Securities and Exchange Commission, Complete Company Records, Pet, Ownership and Subsidiaries, Section 1 of 1, Directors and Officers.

26. *Business Week*, 26 April 1993, 70.

27. *Media Week*, 6 May 1991.

28. Seth Lubove, "On Their Own," *Forbes*, 16 March 1992, 68-69.

29. Reuters news service, 4 March 1993.

Golden Pods

BORDER-BELT PROCESSORS

Hatch Name Hassles ▪ Frozen Chile Queen ▪ Maryland's Manor of Spices ▪
Mexican Foods Explosion ▪ Pepper Merger Mania

Old El Paso once called itself "The Big Enchilada in Mexican Foods," and it was the leader in the canned end of the New Mexico chile business, enjoying the same position in that category as Cal-Compack did in powders. Soon enough, however, claimants to the Enchilada Grande title appeared.

Over in the small Arizona town of McNeal, Fiesta Canning Company processed more than 35 million pounds of New Mexican, Arizonan, and Mexican chiles, selling its Macayo and Fiesta del Sol brands to eateries, dicing chile for McDonald's breakfast burritos, and packing private labels for Hormel and Carnation. Fiesta's chile, grown both in the New Mexico chile belt and at the doorstep of its Arizona plant, tested tongues in Canada, Australia, Germany, Hong Kong, and Korea.

Another canner, Border Foods, surfaced in the west and played a role in Luna County similar to Old El Paso's in Doña Ana County,

pushing the production of chile to new heights. Bringing an old World War II military warehouse to life in 1973, the company treaded the hot pepper waters slowly at first, contracting with three Hatch growers. Fifteen years later it employed 300 people and bought 90 percent of its chile from about 20 Luna County growers. Under the stewardship of the late Martin Steinman, the former president of Uncle Ben's Rice who acquired a majority share of Border Foods in 1983, the chile processor expanded by leaps and bounds. "Prior to the company there was virtually no chile in the area," stated Steinman. During the next five years, Border Foods automated its production and quadrupled its output. In 1990, Steinman's company built a new production facility, and it grew in the course of the decade to include about 1,500 full-time and seasonal employees. Steinman had plans for better productivity. "[I] would like to see the activities in chile grow around this area

117

because we're the leading producer. We certainly have what I consider the best chile in the area," he said.

Border Foods' rise was due to the financial backing of United New Mexico Bank, a highly profitable banking operation that boasted a strong profit margin in the early 1990s. An attractive plum itself, United New Mexico was acquired in 1993 by Norwest Bank of Minnesota. By 1999 Border Foods claimed to be the biggest processor of green chile in the nation, though at an estimated $50 to $100 million in sales it still lagged behind Old El Paso's more varied product line. The company sold small and large cans of chiles bearing the Rio Luna label and customized for other processors and restaurants, and it also packed for Hatch Farms, Inc.

Hatch Farms was launched in 1987 by Steve Dawson, a seventeen-year veteran of the food brokerage business and a former Old El Paso employee. Hip to the Hatch chile name, Dawson told a reporter in 1989 that he got the idea for his company's name while sitting in a restaurant and studying a Hatch advertisement.

With the assistance of a business plan written by a University of New Mexico professor, Dawson hit the production line. His new company quickly proved a formidable competitor for Old El Paso and by 1988 was closing in on the company in canned chile sales in the Southwest. "I don't know how we could have had the colossal conceit to believe we could compete with them. But we felt that we could, and it's been the truth. Going against the big boys like that is a dare." In 1991, Hatch Farms reported a gross profit of $524,174 on $1.5 million in sales. "Demand is going up more and more every year. Demand surpasses expectations. It's been a real juggling act to keep up with demand," said Director of Operations Tom Beck.

Hatch Farms' journey to the chile kingdom was not without controversy, however. In 1988, Dawson was sued by his former bosses for using the Mountain Pass name on one of his canned chile products. A judge ordered him to drop the name and he complied by replacing the brand with the name "MP." Controversy also erupted over the use of the Hatch name itself. The Hatch label had been trademarked in the 1980s by a group of local businessmen. The trademark was titled to the Hatch Chile Association, an early attempt to organize area farmers that was later eclipsed by the New Mexico Chile Commission. "We never did police the trademark, we didn't have the money," admitted 77-year-old Adrián Ogaz, a one-time Doña Ana County politician and prominent Hatch Valley stalwart.

While Biad and Cal-Compack oversaw the red chile business and Old El Paso battled it out with the canned product upstarts, Albuquerque's El Encanto, Inc. swept the frozen market. The maker of Bueno Foods, it was founded in 1951 as a small tortilla manufacturer by three brothers, Raymond, August, and Joseph ("I was born on red and weaned on green") Baca. Fiercely independent and willing to combat giants like Mission Foods and McCormick and Company, Bueno became a genuine Albuquerque landmark, encircling the Duke city with its ubiquitous billboards that left no doubt in the mind of any passerby that she was in chile territory.

The death of company founder Joseph left two of his children in command: MBA Jackie Baca as president and Harvard Law School graduate Gene as vice-president. Together, they represented the modern entrepreneurial ethic, imbued with a sense of Japanese-style management, "quality" circles of worker-manager coordination, outreach to the no-preservatives buying sector of the public, and the ability to

CHAPTER 5　The Old Method of Drying: Chile blankets a southern New Mexican hill.

CHAPTER 6　Protestor José Socorro Coronado in Hatch, New Mexico, 1990.

CHAPTER 10   The Chile Social Hour: Chile roasting stands replaced the old harvests and *ristra*-tying get-togethers.

CHAPTER 12   The King of the Can: Old El Paso Foods.

CHAPTER 14   Red Flags and Hot Green Peppers: UTAF strike on the Anderson Farm, 1992.

CHAPTER 14   Jalapeño Power! Farmworkers outside the old Kansas Street UTAF offices in El Paso, early 1990s.

CHAPTER 16   Fearless Flyboys: Crop dusting a chile field, Luna County, New Mexico, 1998.

CHAPTER 19   Organizing the New Burg: Margarita Luján (center) and other *colonia* residents, Columbus, New Mexico, 1998.

capitalize on the development of microwave cooking by customizing their food products to fit the desire for an instant palate fix for harried times. Rounding out Bueno's product line, in addition to frozen green chile, were tortillas, spices, and dried chiles, the last of which Bueno found harder to sell as national companies flooded the New Mexican market with red chiles grown in New Mexico but processed or labeled elsewhere. Bueno engaged the services of several food distributors to deliver its products in the Southwest and beyond, netting $10 million in sales in 1990, a figure company head Jackie Baca overambitiously planned to double by 1995. Nevertheless, the company scored a marketing coup by having Pepsico's Pizza Hut advertise the use of Bueno's green chile on its pies.

Although smaller producers of frozen green handed some challenges to Bueno, the company viewed its real competition as being the habits of the New Mexico buying public, many of whom preferred to drive down to that corner chile stand, have a sack or two roasted underneath their noses, and then take the steaming pods back home where they were frozen and stored until the next chile urge screamed to be satisfied. Realizing the dent this practice was making in sales, the company developed an ad campaign on billboards and in the Sunday Albuquerque newspaper. Bueno appealed to tradition-loving New

The New King of the Can: Border Foods, Deming, New Mexico.

Mexicans to "relax and enjoy," while still having "Do-your-own chile . . . It's done" prepared, frozen, and sold by the Bacas.

Ultimately, though, the family of frozen green chile fortune reached its position by using public subsidies to its own benefit. In the 1980s, El Encanto received two Housing and Urban Development (HUD) Action grants to help build a new plant and install refrigeration equipment, permitting Bueno to dominate the frozen chile business. Totaling about $1 million, the grants were actually low-interest loans, paid back to municipal accounts for economic development activities in low-income communities. Sensing a winner, the city of Albuquerque, in conjunction with the HUD grants, issued a series of industrial revenue bonds worth more than $7.5 million to El Encanto for facilities expansion in 1983 and 1989. A subsequent $5 million bond was issued in 1996. The first bonds were bought by private investors who used the First Interstate Bank of Albuquerque and later the United New Mexico Trust Company, which was affiliated with the United New Mexico Bank of Border Foods history, as trustees. City of Albuquerque records indicated that the bond deals exempted El Encanto from paying property taxes until at least 2011. During the approval of the bonds, Jackie and Gene's uncle, Pat Baca, sat on the Albuquerque City Council, the body responsible for okaying the deals.

However, Pat Baca, invoking a possible conflict of interest, abstained from the discussion and voting during the November 1989 city council meeting that gave the go-ahead for the third and latest bond. Councilor Steve Gallegos carried the ball for El Encanto, winning a 7–0 yes vote with Pat Baca abstaining and a ninth representative absent. Legally, the measure was passed under an emergency provision of the city charter that permits such financial breaks to private companies as necessary "to alleviate an immediate danger to the city." Apparently, there were some who felt that Albuquerque without a viable Bueno Foods was akin to New York without its delicatessens or San Francisco without its wax museum.

In 1991, the Bacas were the recipients of a $400,000 Economic Development Administration (EDA) grant to improve sewer lines under their plant. The city of Albuquerque kicked in another $730,000, prompting a powerful friend, Republican Senator Pete Domenici, to comment, "I am very pleased that Bueno Foods will now be able to expand. Bueno continues to be a striving business from what started as a small family grocery store. Not only are they successfully marketing products that clearly represent New Mexico, but they are creating new jobs." Bueno continued to maneuver its way in a Mexican foods market in which, not too far in the past, it might have been proclaimed king because of its volume of sales. Now, however, it was only a growing yet still regional company competing with corporations of much bigger proportions.

Sitting quietly at the top of the global chile business totem pole was Bueno's archrival, spice manufacturer McCormick & Company of Baltimore. Politely known for going after what is called "sole-source" positioning on supermarket shelves, McCormick operates 14 spice extraction plants in as many countries, including joint ventures in India and China. The spice giant started modestly in 1889 through the efforts of Willoughby McCormick, a 35-year-old door-to-door root beer and flavoring extracts salesman. Gradually the company came to dominate the spice market in the United States, achieving a 40 percent market share in 1992, trailed by Durkee-

French with 11 percent and Spice Islands with three percent. "McCormick has ground down the competition," punned Richard Davis, a financial broker.

Though McCormick concentrates on powdered chiles in addition to a full range of spice items, it has dabbled in the Mexican food market (Tío Sancho, later sold) and the salsa trade, signing a distribution agreement with Herdez of Mexico in 1988. McCormick's products are sold to more than 80 of the top 100 U.S. food processors and are found in U.S. Armed Forces commissary shelves abroad. After a stagnant performance in the early 1980s, McCormick reached for the stars with the unveiling of the "Buzz and Bailey" show, made up of CEO Charles "Buzz" McCormick, Jr. and COO Bailey Thomas. From 1987 to 1992, the company grew at a stellar 13 percent a year. The year after "Buzz and Bailey" took the helm, company profits soared with the sale of $500 million in prime Baltimore real estate. 1988 also witnessed the Federal Trade Commission's blocking of McCormick's attempt to acquire Spice Islands, citing the move as anti-competitive. McCormick did not lose any sleep over that one. In 1990, it had an estimated $1.3 billion in spice sales and profits of $65 million, more than a doubling of profits over 1986. A 1992 company report stated that dividends almost doubled in the two year period between 1990 and 1992 from $18.7 million to $30.4 million, attributing the three percentage point increase in profit margins to "high quality raw materials, grown to specifications at the lowest possible cost and partially cleaned at the source." Under mixed ownership, McCormick was controlled by individuals closely connected to the firm and investors who ran the gamut from the Rocky Mountain telecommunications company U.S. West to Citicorp

bank to public employee retirement funds in Colorado and California.

The biggest institutional owner was State Farm Mutual Insurance, which was the target of a prolonged AFL-CIO union boycott in the 1990s for its connections to a long-running and raucous labor dispute in the town of Decatur, Illinois. Having financial ties to the British-owned A. E. Staley Manufacturing firm and its Decatur paper plant, State Farm earned the wrath of striking A. E. Staley employees who protested against incidents such as the pepper-gassing of striker Vic Pickle. But, seemingly removed from the financial entanglements of its big investor, peace and prosperity reigned in the Maryland suites where "Buzz and Bailey" were paid well for their performance. Together, the two earned almost $2.7 million in compensation between 1990 and 1992.

From its home office on Chesapeake Bay, McCormick & Company cast a golden net across distant shores. *Forbes* magazine noted that the spice maker, as a supplier of McDonald's and Burger King, was poised to embark on a new Third World expansion, reselling processed product to the same countries the manufacturer bought them from in raw form, just as it did in New Mexico with dehydrated red chiles. At the same time, the corporation was hoping to "improve [profit] margins by pursuing new, low-cost sources for spices." Centuries after Western merchants scoured the East for the serenade of spices, the search was still on for that lucrative venture promising unequalled rewards.

In a broader sense, the fortunes of the border-belt processors were ultimately bound up with far-reaching changes in the North American diet, ushered in by a series of deep-cutting sociological transformations including the massive immigration from Third World countries such as Mexico, India, and Korea, where hot foods were prevalent, and an ethnic revival within the United States that, on the culinary side, resulted in a popular embrace of New Mexican, Tex-Mex, and Cajun dishes, all cuisines that had long utilized the chile pepper in one manner or another.

The legendary out-migration of New Mexicans carried the chile pepper into new territory, building on an epoch when New Mexicans wrote home from places like California in order to get their chile. In Seattle, Dan Gómez sold Amalia Gómez salsa stirred from his grandmother's Spanish-Pueblo recipe. In Ohio, Michael Zakany did a jumping business in José Madrid Salsa. And in the little town of Phoenixville, Pennsylvania, close to both the rusting steel centers and the leisure spreads of "old money," former Albuquerquean Julienne Browne used imported New Mexican chile in her Brown Adobe brand, catering to a clientele that pronounced the word salsa as "Sal-Suh."

Was chilemania a fad or a trend? Dave DeWitt, the publisher of the *Chile Pepper* magazine, thought most definitely that chiles were here to stay. "We've seen steady, steady growth in the chile pepper industry in New Mexico," he observed in 1991. "And the chile pepper industry in the U.S., including all hot sauces, all products, all powders, all pods, is well over $2 billion on the wholesale level now. And you don't see too many people who eat chile peppers who become interested in giving them up."

The chile market exploded in the 1980s, and profits were potentially enormous. Take, for example, the Mexican restaurant end of the business, in which the chile pepper provided the spicy and flavorful base. While fast food giant Taco Bell invited customers to "run for the border," its ledgers took a sprint of their own as corporate operating profits jumped 140 percent between 1988 and 1991. Two years later, a cocky Taco Bell acquired the upscale Chevy's restaurant chain of San Francisco, an establishment that offered grilled salmon fajitas and earned $70 million from 34 stores in 1991. That figure was small peppers for Taco Bell, which planned 300 Chevy's. The number of Mexican restaurants in the United States increased 40 percent between 1985 and 1991, jumping from 13,304 to 18,339. At the forefront were chains like Pepsico's Taco Bell (4,000 units and $3.2 billion in 1992 sales), Chi Chi's ($423.7 million in 1992 sales), El Torito ($349.6 million in 1992 sales), Del Taco ($195 million in 1992 sales), and Taco Time International, an Oregon-based firm that once had a partnership with Japan's Nissan Corporation and had holdings in Canada, Venezuela, and the United Arab Emirates. But there were also the quaint local outlets that diners could experience, ranging from the salt water fish tank of Baja Bay in inland Kentucky to Nacho Mama's in Texas, where tortilla chips were served in car hubcaps. Perhaps more significantly, chile and Mexican food went mainstream, and appeared on the menus of national chains and in grocery aisle refrigerators. Use of the chile extended far beyond the counters of Taco Bell or the tables of Chi Chi's restaurants. There appeared every imaginable concoction of the chile: jalapeño-flavored popcorn and ice-cream, chile-flavored pistachio nuts, green chile turkey sausage, chile-spiked Bloody Marys, chile pasta, and yes, even chile-hearted chocolates. "The number of product introductions is astounding in the United States, and literally there are hundreds of new hot sauces, new mustards, cookies with chile peppers in them," said DeWitt. "Every conceivable product you think of, people are putting chile peppers in them."

The explosion sparked a frenzied pace of activity on the part of companies who were cashing in. During the 1970s, 1980s, and well into the 1990s, the big corporate end of the business was characterized by mergers, buy-outs, and advertising wars. A definite pattern of national companies absorbing local processors predominated, as first witnessed by Pet Incorporated's purchase of the home-grown Mountain Pass Canning Company in El Paso County and soon followed by the Beatrice Company's acquisition of the New Mexico Chili Company and the Valley Chili Company in the Mesilla Valley. Ashley's cannery in El Paso was then snatched up by the Brown brothers from Louisiana; Central Soya of Indiana bought Caribe Food Products of Albuquerque and ignominiously renamed it Fred's Frozen Foods; and Joy Canning Company in Las Cruces was sold to Basic American Foods of San Francisco. A similar outcome was experienced by a group of El Paso area farmers in Texas who began the Paso Pack Chili Company in Fabens as a red chile processor. Up against a tough market, the partners sold their business to McCormick & Company at the end of the 1980s and went back to what they knew best: acting as contracted growers, this time for the Maryland-based spice giant. "I lost my ass dehydrating," stated farmer Charles Ivey. Nationally the bigger players also carried the ball. McIlhenny finally bought Trappey's; Pepsico swallowed Frito-Lay; Durkee Famous Foods merged with R. T. French (mustard) to become Durkee French, which was later sold by its English owners Reckitt-Colman to Burns-Phillip; Campbell's Soup absorbed Vlasic; Pace Foods acquired New Mexico's Territorial House Salsa; the ketchup king Heinz courted Pace but was rejected in favor of Campbell's; and an investment group known as KKR went to work dismantling both Beatrice Companies, owner of Cal-Compack, Rosarita, and Gebhardt's, and RJR-Nabisco, owner of Ortega and Del Monte.

KKR won notoriety in the HBO movie "Barbarians at the Gate" for its leveraged buy-outs involving enormous borrowing to finance an acquisition, a practice that resulted in companies' cutting costs, reducing overhead, and keeping profits high. In 1990 what remained of the once powerful, global Beatrice Company, along with its chile and Mexican food fiefdoms, was sold off by its financial whiz kid directors from the East Coast to Con-Agra for $626 million in cash and additional shares of stock. An international powerhouse in aquaculture, agro-chemicals, and processed food, Con-Agra stepped up its practice of acquiring whatever profitable food-related concern appeared on the horizon, and the Nebraska-based agribusiness goliath did not miss seeing the opportunity that lay in the Mexican market now heated up with chile. In 1996, Ortega's new owner, Nestle USA, closed the historic Oxnard plant, leaving 550 workers jobless; part of the production was shifted to Border Foods.

The modern chile trade was a dynamic and expansive system, overseen not only by regional firms but, increasingly, by big corporations with portfolios full of other interests and a bottom-line commitment to shareholders. The chile business was eons away from the days of the New Mexican past when *ristras* were loaded on the "Chili Line" or when a few truckloads were brought to the El Paso market. And, not unexpectedly, it was ripe for more than a few rivalries and conflicts.

Notes

1. Kate Walter, "The Border Gets Bigger," *Restaurant Business*, 10 August 1993, 155.

2. Vince Maietta, "Red-Hot Chile Peppers: Southwestern Food Staple Is Big Business in Arizona," *The Business Journal* (Phoenix, AZ), 7 October 1991.

3. *Albuquerque Journal*, 20 March 1988.

4. Martin Steinman, telephone conversation with author, August 1992.

5. *Crosswinds*, February 1999.

6. *Deming Headlight*, 7 July 1993.

7. "The New Mexico Private 100," *New Mexico Business Journal*, November 1992, 12; *New Mexico Private 100 Companies* (Albuquerque, NM: Sierra Publishing, 1999).

8. *Albuquerque Journal*, 28 January 1992.

9. *Las Cruces Bulletin*, 29 July 1993.

10. *Albuquerque Tribune*, 27 October 1989.

11. *Albuquerque Journal*, 5 November 1991.

12. Tom Beck, telephone conversation with author, August 1991.

13. Adrián Ogaz, telephone conversation with author, August 1991. Ogaz is a longtime Hatch Valley farmer and political leader. In an October 1994 interview with the author in Garfield, NM, Ogaz opined that the controversy benefited the chile industry through increased publicity.

14. *Background Memorandum on Bueno Foods and the Baca Family: 40 Years As a New Mexican Food Company*, July 1991.

15. *Albuquerque Journal*, 22 April 1990.

16. *Albuquerque Journal*, Business Outlook, 29 October 1990.

17. Eric Pfeiffer, City of Albuquerque planner, interview with author, Albuquerque, NM, August 1991; *Journal of the City Council of the City of Albuquerque*, minutes of the council meeting of 20 November 1989 and exhibit 43 to Council Bill No. 0170, 11, 157, 158-60, 169.

18. *Albuquerque Tribune*, 6 September 1990.

19. *Albuquerque Journal*, 17 September 1991.

20. Sherry Robinson, "Agriculture: Economic Comeback," *New Mexico Progress*, September 1993, 6.

21. New Mexico's Own, Inc., board list, New Mexico Economic Development Department, Santa Fe, 1994.

22. *Albuquerque Journal*, 9 September 1994.

23. Reed Abelson, "Spicy Days at McCormick," *Fortune*, 15 January 1990, 97.

24. Overseas Private Investment Corporation, 1987 and 1988 annual reports.

25. "McCormick and Co. Piquancy Play," *Financial World*, August 1992, 13-14.

26. Dan Wechsler Linden, "Hot Stuff," *Forbes*, November 1990, 164-66.

27. Janet Novack, "A Close Call," *Forbes*, 26 January 1987, 38.

28. Strongin Dobbs, "Well-Seasoned," *Financial World*, 2 September 1986, 114-15.

29. Local 7837 Allied Industrial Workers of America, AFL-CIO, Decatur, Illinois, letters and pamphlets, 1993, 1994.

30. Securities and Exchange Commission, Complete Company Records, 1992 and 1993, McCormick & Co., Proxy Statement, 17 February 1993; Annual Shareholders' Meeting Minutes and President's letter, 18 March 1993; Management Discussion: Discussion and Analysis, 18 March 1992.

31. Dan Gómez, interview by author, Albuquerque, NM, February 1993.

32. Michael Zakany, interview by author, Albuquerque, NM, February 1993.

33. Julienne Browne, telephone conversation with author, June 1992.

34. Dave DeWitt, telephone conversation with author, August 1991.

35. James Scarla, "Mexican Market Segment Report," *Restaurant Business*, 10 April 1992.

36. *Albuquerque Journal*, 9 June 1993.

37. "South-of-the-Border Showdown; Supermarket Business," *Food and Beverage Marketing*, May 1993, 16.

38. *Restaurant Business*, op. cit.

39. David Wellman, "Spice Skirmish," *Food and Beverage Marketing*, May 1993, 60.

40. Mike McNamee, formerly of Valley Chili Co., telephone conversation with author, September 1993.

41. Mitchell DeWitt, Walker Foods, telephone conversation with author, January 1993.

42. Barry and Frazin, "New Mexico Agriculture and Ranching: Its Present and Future," 6.

43. Tim Vaughn, Joy Canning Co./BAF, telephone conversation with author, August 1991.

44. Charles Ivey, telephone conversation with author, April 1994.

45. Securities and Exchange Commission, ConAgra, 10-K Report, 26 May 1991.

46. Standard Corporation Descriptions, Index and Section C-E, *Standard and Poor's*, January 1994, 6707-10.

47. Neil R. Gazel, *Beatrice: From Buildup through Breakup* (Chicago: University of Illinois Press, 1990), 215-16.

Fire on the Furrow 13

Chile Addicts ▪ Salsa Shootouts ▪ Plant Raids ▪ Texas-New Mexico War ▪ Pickers Picket

Held every February in an echoey ballroom in Albuquerque's Convention Center, the Fiery Foods extravaganza sets ablaze the drab interior of the downtown hall. On stage is a cast of salsa wizards, chile picklers, *mole* manufacturers, and anyone else inclined to tickle the taste buds of spice seekers. The show is *the* place to grab a look at—and a hot bite of—the latest trends in the industry.

Behind a booth, a large man puts bottles of Louisiana hot sauce in paper bags for customers. "It is so wonderful, it is so good, that I have oldtime Cajuns write me letters and say it's a lot easier to buy from you in the bottle than have my wife try to make it . . . *Playboy* picked that as the best picante in the world, they tested over 300," he bellows. Dick Chileen and sister-in-law Maria give samples of their chile beer. Residents of tiny Cave Creek, Arizona, they hatched the brew in 1991 at Ed and Maria Chileens's restaurant The

Satisfied Frog. Asked about the name, Maria, cracking a smile, replies that there was already a restaurant down the road called the Horny Toad, and the Chileens decided they would rather be a "satisfied frog than a horny toad." The beer, which is topped with a serrano chile, was originally meant for the restaurant, but news spread, and by 1993 the Chileens were shipping 25,000 cases a month including 2,000 to Japan and England. They had orders waiting to be filled for the Caribbean and Europe. "It's going like gangbusters," remarks Ed.

In 1993, the biggest hit at the show was the habanero pepper, the world's hottest, or the "real McCoy" as one professor—turned Virgin Islands sauce seller—put it. That was good news to one man decked out in an old green army jacket and sweating profusely in the face. "I'm a habanero buff," he brags. "That's probably the hottest pepper there is and I'm addicted to

> *"Texans are the world's greatest bullhorns, they claim they can grow crawdads better than the Louisianans, chile better than the New Mexicans."*

—GORDON BROWN, BRUCE FOODS CO-OWNER

these, so I keep coming back to the habanero tables time and time again."

To prove the versatility of chile and its use in many other products besides food, Robert Schneider of Southwest Ventures had a display featuring "Body Guard," a cayenne-based self-defense spray effective in warding off attackers, animal or human. On the display table were testimonials from SWAT team members, harried drivers, and pitbull-dogged joggers swearing to the utility of the spray. A Californian, Schneider himself keeps a canister on the right-turn signal of his truck. "With all the car-jackings going on, I try to keep it handy there." The "Body Guard" product is a good illustration of how the chile business touches many facets of life, as a food, a condiment, a food-coloring agent, a cosmetic ingredient, a medicine, and a weapon. Brave, new industrial uses await the chile producer.

Keeping a close tab on these trends was Dave DeWitt, the brains behind the Fiery Foods shindig and editor of a magazine dedicated to the capsicum appropriately titled *Chile Pepper*, the bible of the hard-core chilehead. Before it was sold off to a publishing group in Texas, the magazine kept watch on the ups and downs (mostly ups) of the industry from an Albuquerque office. Reaching a circulation of 70,000 within just a few years, the publication began by a fluke in 1987.

DeWitt, a New Mexico chile lore author, approached publisher Robert Siegel with the idea of putting out a one-time catalog of chile products. Buyers assumed the catalog was a magazine and sent blank checks to the publisher. "And it just sort of took off," recalled DeWitt. "It was just one of those weird things, without any organization, without a business plan, with a very small office, without any backers, without any operating stock, without a fleet of cars or anything, we started a magazine." Five years and dozens of issues later, *Chile Pepper* boasted fans worldwide and cosponsored California rock concerts headlined by luminaries such as Carlos Santana and Sammy Hagar, an achievement realized by the luck of the pepper. The most visible boom was in hot sauces, salsas, and picante sauces. By 1990, hot sauce sales in U.S. supermarkets nudged $60 million, not counting restaurants and processing uses in popular foods like the Buffalo Wing. The chile was mainly produced in New Mexico and Latin America, but was made into hot sauce in the old Louisiana market corner. Of course, McIlhenny Co. was at the pinnacle of the hot sauce phenomenon.

In its early years, the Louisiana hot sauce business was highly competitive, hosting a line-up of companies such as B. F. Trappey's, which gave the Tabasco-mashing McIlhennys a serious knockdown challenge for the championship. The McIlhenny Company jabbed back by embarking on a relentless campaign to claim the trademark for the Tabasco pepper and pursued decades of court battles that paid off in 1948 when a Louisiana court ruled that the family-run business had a proprietary right to the Tabasco name. The zealousness with which the hot sauce maker has guarded the label is well documented in Amal Naj's book *Peppers: A Story of Hot Pursuits.* After the court win, McIlhenny Company and chief rival Trappey's duked it out in the stores for years, only ending the slugfest when Trappey's called it quits and sold off its gloves to the opponent.

A family enterprise of about 60 shareholders, McIlhenny pours out its sauce in the idyllic surroundings of Avery Island, Louisiana, amid the flight of egrets, the grunt of alligators, and the stony silence of a Buddhist shrine once given to a Chinese emperor. Enjoying more than $50 million in annual sales of merchandise encompassing pepper-flavored jellies, jalapeños, and "Cajun Chic" novelties, McIlhenny Company is perpetually on the make for new markets and has penetrated former Eastern Bloc countries like the Baltic States. "Sales have grown compoundly," says Paul McIlhenny, the company's vice-president, matter-of-factly.

In 1990 the contest was virtually over. McIlhenny had 33 percent of the hot sauce market, 11 points over its nearest competitor, Durkee French Foods; it sold its products in more than 100 countries; it was the semiofficial hot sauce of U.S. troops, and it won grander conquests as a condiment to astronauts' rations in outer space. These facts prompted one Cincinnati businessman to exclaim, "McIlhenny is laughing all the way to the bank."

The sales surge was even greater in the salsa and picante sauce business. Old El Paso, La

Victoria, and Pace, the traditional royalty of the market, got some new competition from both expected and unexpected sources in the 1980s. Borden, Hormel, Frito-Lay, and Anheuser-Busch waded into the waters with their own sauces. Even the actor Paul Newman got into the act with his Newman's Own brand. Surely the only salsa company to donate all its profits to charities, Newman's Own touted its salsa in a poster showing the actor sitting in a jail cell in a scene harking back to *Butch Cassidy and the Sundance Kid.*

Salsa sales soared in the 1980s and 1990s, jumping from about $245 million in 1984 to about $700 million in 1993; by 1999 sales had reached $1.4 billion. Displays in supermarket aisles were often combined with tortilla chips, a marketing device that proved beneficial to both salsa and chips. More than 300 salsa and picante sauce brands were available in the U.S. market, running the gamut from handmade recipes to mass-produced household names.

Symbolizing the change in Americans' dietary preferences, salsa surpassed ketchup in sales in 1991. Recognizing the historic milestone, Heinz Company entered the salsa business in 1993, with a cross between salsa and ketchup. Michael Zakany of Zanesville, Ohio, was an example of the new small salsa entrepreneur. He ran José Madrid Products, named after his grandfather from Lincoln County, New Mexico. His original creations like Clovis Red sold in gourmet shops in the Midwest and other regions. "In a lot of areas, the grocery stores will only carry the national brands and the salsa consumer out there just wants something different, and therefore they will go to specialty stores and find my product," he explained. Nevertheless, the die was cast early on in the salsa world. "When this market matures, there will be no room for mediocre sauce makers or companies with small budgets," predicted Frank Smith of the Sami market research firm.

In 1989 several companies already had the bulk of the business. Vying for the championship were Old El Paso and Pace, both Texas-located companies using New Mexico chile and doling out a huge amount of picante sauce. Pace, the San Antonio giant, had a modest beginning in the 1940s in the rear of David Pace's liquor store, where the upstart chile blender bottled syrups, jellies, peppers, and pickles with the aid of his wife and a pair of employees.

In the days after sugar-starved World War II, Pace decided that the true future lay with his onion-tomato-jalapeño picante sauce, hardly a new creation but novel enough for the gringo taste to launch him onto the road to success. According to spokesman Matt Mohr, one early company oversight was the failure to trademark the word "picante sauce," a legality that could have done for Pace what the word "Tabasco" did for McIlhenny. No matter. Pace became a common shelf item in the 50 states, Canada, and Mexico, utilizing chile purchased on a "trail" that extended from New Mexico to the Yucatan Peninsula and from Florida to California. In 1989, Pace was the spicy condiment of choice at President Bush's inauguration. Pace workers were referred to as "associates," a term flowing from the company's philosophy of worker-management cooperation. Guiding the team were a powerhouse of food industry veterans, drawn from the likes of Uncle Ben's Rice, Anderson-Clayton, Kraft Foods, General Mills, and Church's Fried Chicken. Pace and chief rival Old El Paso succeeded in controlling about 50 percent of the salsa-picante market in 1991. Three years later Pace surpassed Old El Paso, gobbling up 26 percent of salsa sales versus 21 percent for the

Mexican foods kingpin. Competitors such as Pepsico's Frito-Lay, La Victoria, RJR-Nabisco's Ortega, and Hormel's Chi Chi's lagged behind but were making strenuous efforts to catch up or at least make a respectable showing at the finish line. The corporations spent generous sums on advertising, reaching more than $20 million in 1986, with three of the contenders for the salsa crown, Pace, Old El Paso, and Ortega, equaling that amount in 1991. Pace engaged La Victoria in an advertising war on La Victoria's home turf in California, which was conducted in an almost gentlemanly way compared with the truly nasty rivalry that broke out between Pace and Old El Paso. Like two crusty old gunslingers facing off at high noon for the fifteenth time, the companies waged a no-holds-barred shootout as they fired away at each other with an arsenal of insulting television ads and lawsuits.

Mythical western imagery was included in the firms' ads, associating salsa with the old Wild West. Oddly, a Pace product, Territorial House Salsa, had a history that was really related to the new violent West. A New Mexico favorite, Territorial House was first made by a family that ran the old Territorial House restaurant in Corrales, New Mexico, situated in a building where hangings were reputed to have occurred in the last century. The "T-House's" owner, a former New Mexico state policeman, went down in a blaze of gunfire in the mid-1970s. In a still mysterious shooting incident, the ex-cop confronted two men in the bar's parking lot and let loose a staccato of rifle fire at them, killing the two and then breaking the butt of his rifle on their bodies. The man walked back into the bar-restaurant and collapsed 45 minutes later. He was dead of a heart attack.

In 1986, Pace, upset at an Old El Paso ad resembling a Pace jingle and infuriated at an Old

El Paso salsa jar seemingly copied from Pace's, filed against the St. Louis-based company in San Antonio's U.S. District Court, requesting that Old El Paso cease using the bottle. Pace President Kit Goldsbury charged that his longstanding rival had implemented a secret plan called "Project Pace-Like," a clandestine operation allegedly involving attempts to pry information from Pace employees and from the San Antonio company's garbage. The two salsa makers settled out of court in 1987, Old El Paso scuttled the bottle, and the contenders returned to their television jousts. One Old El Paso ad, for instance, implied that Pace's sauce was akin to a watery soup and upheld Old El Paso as the "taste that runs wild," while Pace simply "just runs."

Eventually, the stakes were raised to a possibly deciding hand in the Pace/Old El Paso rivalry. Late in 1994, Campbell's Soups, a company with a sales base about six times that of Pet's, trumpeted the deal of the century in the salsa-chile business. After three years of secret negotiations, Campbell's announced it was purchasing Pace for a whopping $1.1 billion. For Pace, the sale closed the book on what was once a penny-ante, back-room kitchen concoction whipped into a billion-dollar bonanza. Pace head Kit Goldsbury, who had risen to the top through marriage to David Pace's daughter and the earlier buyout of both his former father-in-law and spouse, was vaulted into the Fortune 500 list. In the wake of the Pace sell-off, the business magazine estimated Goldsbury's personal fortune at around $900 million.

The buyout added Pace products to Campbell's growing line of chile-related foods: Vlasic peppers, chile poblano soup, and Fiesta tomato soup. While the Pace buyout was admittedly an expensive splurge on the part of a company with a relatively conservative record of business prac-

tices, it forced the main players in the salsa race, especially Old El Paso, into a do-or-die position considering Campbell's name recognition in supermarkets and the firm's access to the global consumer.

The Pace-Campbell's deal foretold a redoubled scramble for markets, leaner production methods, and cheaper-source chile. By entering a business in the throes of a contest for monopoly champion, and by doing it with a sweepstakes ticket bought at scalper's rates, Campbell's was certainly engaging in a daring risk. But by using an arguably strange accounting loophole that granted tax breaks for acquisitions on the basis of a name's "value," which in this case corresponded to Pace's reputation in the dip 'n' chip realm, Campbell's stood to gain a $200 million tax deduction for the deal. Certainly the soup and salsa chefs were putting their bets on Pace's familiarity and favorable consumer trends. As the company's own ad boasted, "Never underestimate the power of Campbell's."

Apparently, Pet was not minimizing Campbell's. Under the new economic circumstances, it was inevitable that the St. Louis-based food company would once again fall to the global tidal wave of corporate buyouts. After a winter of courting from the likes of England's Grand Metropolitan, ConAgra, and H. J. Heinz, Pet and its Old El Paso Foods division were sold to the British company in early 1995 for the staggering sum of $2.65 billion. The sale represented the fourth instance since the 1960s that the onetime El Paso-owned company was put on the auction block. Old El Paso was next put under the management of Grand Metropolitan's Pillsbury foods, which itself had been acquired by the conglomerate in 1988 in a deal that landed one Minnesota lawyer in court for earning a $4 million profit from insider trading. Grand

Metropolitan, which later signed a $15.8 billion merger with the brewing company Guinness to form the seventh largest food and beverage company in the world (Diageo, Inc.), now counted Burger King, Häagen-Dazs, Green Giant, and Pillsbury among its holdings. The conglomerate was boycotted by labor unions and sympathizers in the early 1990s when its Green Giant division shut down a Watsonville, California, broccoli-processing plant and moved it to the cheaper labor quarters of Irapuato, Mexico. Unconcerned, Grand Metropolitan ran a food empire based on the trendiest delectables of the times: fast, frozen, sweet, and spicy. Henceforth, the Pace-Old El Paso salsa wars would strictly be the business of global titans.

True to form, Old El Paso performed for Pillsbury much as it had for Pet. One year after the acquisition, Old El Paso was contributing nicely to Pillsbury's profits, taking in $353 million from salsa sales in 1996 alone. In other categories, Old El Paso could boast at being *Número Uno* in the nation's rising Mexican foods business. The firm held the lead in seasoning mix and dinner kit sales, inventing the one-skillet Mexican dinner that delivered a meal to hungry customers in a quick 20 minutes. Old El Paso's flag touched the shores of Europe, Australia, Canada, South America, and Asia. A character, "Nacho Man," was created to ensure consumer identification with both a popular product and an individual company.

But Old El Paso's future was being shaped far from its original home on the Rio Grande. From the Twin Cities, a 20-person Pillsbury team coordinated company strategies. None of the team members was Mexican or Latino. One culinary observer noted an iconization in progress. "The food that is being manufactured by Pillsbury and Hormel is not really Mexican food," said Food

Processing magazine editor Bob Messenger. "We basically shook the culture out of pasta. We're doing the same to Mexican food."

Grand Metropolitan's Pillsbury, reflecting the lean and mean ethos of the times, then devised a clever way to squeeze even greater profit out of Old El Paso Foods. In June 1997, the company announced the sale of its Anthony factory for an undisclosed price to a group of Denver-based investors including businessman Jim Lewis. Despite the sale, Grand Met/Pillsbury wasn't willing to part completely with a bulging cash cow. As part of the agreement, Pillsbury retained the trademark rights to Old El Paso for seven years. The name was so valuable that Pillsbury could contract out production while reaping dividends from the actual store sales. In explaining the deal, Pillsbury officials described the sale as "consistent with an ongoing strategy to reduce fixed assets and to lower costs." Ultimately, the innovation added another link in the payoff chain from producer to distributor. The new plant owner named itself Anthony Foods, a division of Santa Fe Ingredients, which itself was under the JELTEX umbrella formed to leverage agribusiness companies. While producing for Pillsbury, Anthony Foods also custom packed for labels such as Clover Club and Dillon Foods. In serving its clients, Anthony Foods was able to make far more product with far fewer people. From a figure of 800 full-time and 1,200 to 1,300 seasonal (chile pack) employees in about 1977, the number of workers dipped to 250 full-time and 400 to 600 seasonal employees twenty years later. Although ownership changed numerous times and automation slashed the workforce, the historic Mountain Pass cannery continued shipping massive amounts of chile-based Mexican foods the world over.

Whether as a condiment or as cayenne spray, chile was a much coveted commodity. Per capita use of chile peppers in the United States nearly doubled from 3.5 pounds per person a year in 1980 to 6.5 pounds per person by the early 1990s. An herb industry trade publication pointed to the shifting preference for ethnic foods such as Mexican as being responsible for the surge. In a milestone of sorts, retail sales of Mexican foods almost hit the $3 billion mark in 1999, portending a brisk business in the coming century.

As sales skyrocketed, technological innovations were introduced, always with the same goal of eliminating extra labor and increasing profits. Companies thought of using electrical energy to peel chile more efficiently and reduce the amount of lost, exploded pods wasted in the steam-roasting method, and processes were developed to rapidly remove red chile stems. Rudderless after the Cold War, even New Mexico's Los Alamos National Laboratories (LANL) got involved. The mission: to automate the troublesome business of picking out the teeny-weeny pieces of chile skin stuck to peeled, roasted pods. LANL scientists investigated ways of using laser scanners to identify the remaining bits of peel on chiles rolling down the canning line. A successful device would rid a cannery's owners of the need to employ 40 people to inspect each pod by hand. Of course, not every breakthrough needed to be as high tech, and NMSU researchers tried finding ways of packaging fresh New Mexican green chiles for a longer shelf life and export to new markets. New Mexican chile, indeed, was almost everywhere in the heyday of the chile bonanza. What was troubling to some New Mexicans was that the state was not reaping the full benefits. The main processors—Pet's Old El Paso, Beatrice's Cal-

Compack, Basic American Foods' Joy Canning, and others—were all owned by out-of-staters. Profits flowed to St. Louis, San Francisco, Chicago, and Baltimore. NMSU economist Robert Coppedge compared New Mexico's chile economy to a colonial one in which a raw product is extracted, processed elsewhere, and even sold back to the source country in a finished form—of course at a very high price. Furthermore, it was difficult for small New Mexican processors to get onto the grocery shelves of stores in their own state. Up-front payments were sometimes required. Several out-of-state chains—Albertson's, Smith's, Furr's, and others—crowded the landscape. They serviced large numbers of customers, were supplied by big distributors, and dealt in nationally recognized products. On occasion, outright conflict broke out between local and national processors. When McCormick's Mojave Foods bid for exclusive space in Furr's Supermarkets in 1993, Bueno Food's Jackie Baca went to war to keep her company's chile on sale at the chain.

Consequently, one NMSU study claimed the absurd statistic that 95 percent of the processed Mexican food purchased in New Mexico, the country's largest chile producer and per capita consumer, was imported from out of state. A diner could stumble into a Las Cruces barbecue joint and find a bottle of Louisiana-bottled hot sauce that was most likely heated with Mesilla Valley chiles. It was in the "value-added" segment of the chile industry that the most money was earned. For example, the farm-gate value of New Mexico chile (the amount sold by the farmers) was about $88 million in 1991 compared to the value-added amount of between $230 and $300 million that same year.

New Mexico's neighbor to the east and the south, Texas, noticed the vibrant chile industry

up the Rio Grande and decided to give the Land of Enchantment a run for its chile, setting off the "Texas-New Mexico Chile War," surely one of the most ingenious marketing schemes of the modern U.S. food industry. In 1992 Texas's 5,000 acres of hot peppers put the Lone Star State far behind New Mexico, but Texas had lots of potential. For one thing, the Texas Department of Agriculture aggressively promoted its producers and processors in a "Taste of Texas" campaign that matched interested buyers with a computer database of sellers. Two growing seasons, in contrast to New Mexico's one, blessed the Rio Grande Valley of south Texas, where a jalapeño industry took shape. Other production areas included the Texas Panhandle, the "Hill Country" between San Antonio and Austin, and, of course, El Paso County just south of the New Mexico chile belt. Texas also had a chile-breeding research program second only to New Mexico's at the Texas A&M agricultural experiment station in Weslaco—the laboratory of Dr. Ben Villalón. Favored with fertile soils, varying climates, and, in some areas, virgin lands unspoiled by the chile wilt disease, Texas farmers planted more than 100 varieties, ranging from hot Thai to jalapeño varieties.

Jeff Campbell, a Hill Country farmer and the owner of the Stonewall Chili Pepper Company, grew 40 acres of many different peppers. His most popular was the habanero, the world's hottest, and he doubled his plantings between 1992 and 1993. "Everybody's habanero crazy," he asserted. "Certain chiles, like the habanero . . . like a higher humidity; it's a very tropical chile, that's why I think it grows well here."

The opening shot of the "Texas-New Mexico Chile War" was fired in August 1992 by Hill Rylander, the proprietor of the Austin Farmer's Market. In a brazen challenge, Rylander told the press he was "tired" of New Mexico's claim to be the chile leader, and he proceeded to sponsor the first annual Texas Chile Festival in Austin on the same weekend as the Hatch Chile Festival. The Texas event drew thousands and featured the christening of a Texas chile capital statue. Rylander's bold challenge aroused old New Mexican fears of Texan colonization, which dated back to the 1800s. Then a would-be Texan conquering force got lost in the desert and was rounded up by Mexican soldiers. The fears survived into the present century and are exemplified by a Santa Fe County bumper sticker that reads "Welcome to Aztlán: Now Go Home." New Mexican reactions to the Texas festival were amusing. "Texans are the world's greatest bullhorns, they claim they can grow crawdads better than the Louisianans, chile better than the New Mexicans," chortled Gordon Brown, the co-owner of Bruce Foods. "Texas is my neighbor," said farmer Robert Cosimati. "They grow everything big in Texas, including their mouths."

In response, the City Council of El Paso declared the first chile war cookoff for El Paso in 1993 and promised to storm Santa Fe if New Mexico did not cease its rhetoric about being the world's chile capital. In turn, New Mexico set its own chile war cookoff for Las Cruces, inviting the Texans in for a match on the New Mexican turf, and when New Mexico Speaker of the House Raymond Sánchez appeared before legislators in Santa Fe at the 1993 session, he crowned a pepper and proclaimed the Land of Enchantment's chile supremacy. It was all in jest, of course—at least most of it.

On a truly competitive note, Texas, New Mexico, and other states vied with each other for new processing facilities, offering tax breaks and other incentives for plants to relocate. Wes

Grable, owner of the popular Southwestern Piada brand of picante sauce, got calls from the New Mexico Department of Economic Development, which tried to lure him away from his home base in rural Texas. Over in Deming, Arnold Orquiz, the proprietor of Amigo's Foods, received similar queries from at least eight states but decided to stay in New Mexico after the state government stepped in to rescue his business. Apparently, Orquiz's arguments about saving jobs for the Deming community and the future potential of his growing business with Mexico convinced the state to make a direct investment in his food-processing firm. "There's a giant on the other side of the border and you guys are sleeping," Orquiz told officials including Governor King. Competition in the chile business from other states and countries prodded New Mexico officials to take a long, strategic look at not only preserving the industry, but making sure it stayed number one as well. The involvement of NMSU was critical to achieving this goal, and the school made plans to assume an even bigger role in chile. Dr. Bosland teamed up with Dave DeWitt of *Chile Pepper* magazine to launch the Chile Institute, headquartered at NMSU. The Institute declared ambitious goals: its intent was to keep New Mexico the *chile grande* through enhanced pepper breeding, education, and even the opening of a museum dedicated to chile peppers.

Bosland also conceived of the Institute as the main international depository of chile germplasm, a responsibility he regarded as vital in light of the disappearance of chile species caused by the destruction of the tropical rainforests. One of those species, he pointed out, might have been the successful cross-breed of a wilt-resistant variety, or even an invaluable aid in fighting cancer and other diseases.

The NMSU-based Chile Institute drew financial support from both the State of New Mexico and private food-processing corporations. Five of those companies—Bueno, Border Foods, Biad, Cervantes Enterprises, and Pet/Old El Paso—were represented on the Institute's Board of Directors. The Chile Institute was officially announced at the NMSU-sponsored 1992 Chile Conference at Las Cruces Hilton Hotel, where hundreds of growers and processors from as far away as Wisconsin hobnobbed in the hallways and lobby and heard presentations about free trade, fungus control, and opportunities in paprika.

Inside the hotel, attendees lunched with staff members from Senator Domenici and Senator Binghaman's offices, who were present to show their bosses' unyielding support for the New Mexico chile industry. Outside, it was an entirely different scene altogether. About 50 pickets from the Border Agricultural Workers Union stood on a sidewalk in front of the Hilton and conducted a loud, vocal demonstration for higher wages and improved working conditions. "We want them to pay us more, to pay us better," commented one picket, who described his picking job as *agachado*, or bent over, all day long. "If you work seven to eight hours they'll [labor contractors] put down three to four hours. They pay you for four hours," he charged.

After chanting slogans for a good spell, the workers huddled together to wait for union director Carlos Marentes to return from the hotel. Marentes entered the conference in an attempt to address the farmers who employed the labor contractors. He was out of luck: the agenda already had been set, he was told. Marentes walked back to the picket line and told the workers he would not be speaking to the growers. But he was not surprised at the rebuff: "The role of the university here in Las Cruces is to support the production, to help them find ways to make the chile farm productive every time. But see, the only way they can make more profits from chile is to pay less to the workers and [by] avoiding benefits other workers enjoy. Now we hear about all this money from the federal government and the State of New Mexico going into the pockets of farmers, and basically the chile industry, and not a single penny for the benefit of the farmworkers, or not a single penny to alleviate the situation [farmworkers] are facing."

In front of the Hilton, with the volcano-coned Picacho Peak lording over the morning haze of the Valley, stood Gloria Escovedo. She was hurting, but she felt compelled to be on the picket line that day. "I'm a farmworker, I was a farmworker, and I support the union for better wages, so that there will be justice," said Escovedo. "It's an injustice that [farmworkers] don't get paid what they should earn. They should put bathrooms [in the fields], have better salaries, and be fair to us farmworkers that make the least."

Undeterred, the protesting chile pickers wrapped up their red union flags and boarded their bus for El Paso. The 1992 harvest season had not yet started, and many workers faced several more months of unemployment or underemployment before the pickings would be good. The union temporarily settled back into its routine work, priming itself for the fall harvest when its demands would resurface. Once again, conflict was brewing in chile country.

Notes

1. Dick Chileen and Maria Chileen, interviews by author, Albuquerque, NM, February 1993.

2. Robert Schneider, interview by author, Albuquerque, NM, February 1993.

3. Dave DeWitt, telephone conversation with author, August 1991.

4. "Hot, hot, hot," *The Times-Picayune* (New Orleans), 24 June 1990.

5. Dana Wechsler Linden, "Hot Stuff," *Forbes*, 26 November 1990, 164-66.

6. Amal Naj, *Peppers: A Story of Hot Pursuits* (New York: Alfred A. Knopf, 1992).

7. For an overview of the McIlhenny Co., see Diane M. Moore, *The Treasures of Avery Island* (Lafayette, LA: Acadian House Publishing, 1990); "Tabasco-Sauce Maker Remains Hot after 125 Years," *The Wall Street Journal*, 11 May 1990; Patricia Mandell, "Louisiana Hot," *Americana*, February 1991, 26-31.

8. Paul McIlhenny, telephone conversation with author, August 1992.

9. William Updike, Eagle Salsa/Anheuser Busch, telephone conversation with author, June 1992.

10. Todd McKenzie, Frito Lay, telephone conversation with author, June 1992.

11. Mary Barinka and Richard Crane, Hormel, telephone conversations with author, July 1992.

12. Linda Rohr, Newman's Own, telephone conversations with author, June 1992.

13. "Food Industry's War of the Salsas is Getting Fierce," *Wall Street Journal*, 11 April 1989.

14. David Weiss, Packaged Facts, telephone conversation with author, July 1992.

15. *Fiery Foods and Barbeque Business Magazine*, July/August 1999.

16. Michael Zakany, interview by author, Albuquerque, NM, February 1993.

17. *Advertising Age*, 19 July 1993, 8.

18. "Pet Peeves Pace with Parallel Picante Packaging," *Albuquerque Journal*, 17 May 1987.

19. *Albuquerque Journal*, 29 December 1991.

20. "Campbell picks up Pace in hot market," *USA Today*, 29 November 1994; *Fiery Foods!*, March 1995, 5.

21. *Fortune* Web site.

22. *Minneapolis Star Tribune*, 21 February 1995; *Twin Cities Business Monthly*, July 1995; *St. Paul Pioneer Press*, 17 May 1996; *Minneapolis St. Paul City Business Journal*, 3 February 1997, 19 May 1997, 30 June 1997, 29 December 1997; Pillsbury/Old El Paso web site, Pillsbury press release, 25 June 1997; telephone conversations with Tom La Hut, Anthony Foods, 8 June 1998, and Ramón Coral, United Food and Commercial Workers Union, El Paso, TX, 1 June 1998.

23. *Fiery Foods and Barbeque Business Magazine* Web site.

24. Arlene Cinelli Odenwald, "Rural Economic Development: The Issues," *New Mexico Business Journal*, August 1992, 24.

25. *New Mexico Technology Enterprise Forum*, January-February 1994, 3.

26. Kip Smith, interview by author, Hatch, NM, September 1992.

27. *New Mexico Resources*, spring 1992; *Albuquerque Journal*, Business Outlook, 4 May 1992.

28. Valerie J. Gerard, "Technology Enterprise Division Helps Las Cruces Pasta Business," *New Mexico Technology Enterprise Forum*, September-October 1992, 2.

29. *New Mexico Business Journal*, October 1991.

30. "Taste of Texas Companies," Texas Department of Agriculture, 1992; Mark Ellison, TDA, telephone conversation with author, August 1992.

31. Jeff Campbell, interview by author, Albuquerque, NM, February 1993.

32. "Texas Growers Pepper N.M. with Insults," *Albuquerque Journal*, 21 July 1992.

33. Hill Rylander, telephone conversation with author, September 1992.

34. Gordon Brown, Bruce Foods, telephone conversation with author, August 1992.

35. Robert Cosimati, interview by author, Las Cruces, NM, July 1992.

36. "Texas Fires First Festive Salvo in Chile War with New Mexico," Associated Press wire story, 17 December 1992.

37. "State Accepts Chile Challenge," Associated Press wire story, n.d.

38. *Las Cruces Sun-News*, 16 March 1993.

39. Wes Grable, telephone conversation with author, June 1992.

40. Arnold Orquiz, interview by author, Deming, NM, July 1992.

41. Paul Bosland, interview by author, Hatch, NM, August 1991.

42. Chile Institute informational brochure, NMSU, 1993.

43. Unnamed chile picker, interview by author, Las Cruces, NM, February 1992.

44. Carlos Marentes, interview by author, Las Cruces, NM, February 1992.

45. Gloria Escovedo, interview by author, Las Cruces, NM, February 1992.

Huelga

14

STRIKES IN THE CHILE FIELDS

The Valley of Tears ▪ Amnesty and Activism ▪ Chile Pickers Pepper Gassed ▪ In César's Spirit

ate July is a hot time in the inner reaches of the Mesilla Valley, and in 1992 the heat emanated from more than just the sun. Before sunrise on July 31, a caravan of cars and vans left El Paso for the New Mexico border, exiting Interstate 10 at the Anthony exit and stopping at the Dairy Queen. Farmworkers, union activists, and legal observers disembarked for a strategy session illuminated by the lights of television cameras. Soon, they were back on the road, pushing north in a straight line past landmarks like the brushy river bottoms where one of the passengers said agents of "La Migra" once tossed rocks at him to flush him from hiding. The caravan turned on Snow Road between La Mesa and Mesquite where it made a sharp left over railroad tracks and reduced its speed on the narrow road running parallel to irrigation canals, corn and cabbage fields. Minutes later the caravan arrived at its destination: two chile fields ripe for plucking. Participants grabbed red union flags and a noisy bullhorn and entered the

dirt road that divided the two fields, marching past the parked cars of local pickers anticipating work. One man, a self-described evangelical Christian, snatched a Bible and sauntered off to the strike.

"Huelga, huelga!" "Strike, strike," commanded the forceful, foghornlike voice of union leader Gloria Salcedo. "Únense a la huelga." "Join the strike, you won't regret it." A few hundred yards down the rows, the strikers formed double columns and continued to shout slogans and plead their case to the 150 to 200 workers waiting for the picking to begin. A trio of teenage boys stood coolly in their midst, happy to have a day off from the sweat. Arms folded, some of the field hands appeared nervous and puzzled by the picket line, but a few flashed confident looks and walked over to the columns. A few more followed, then several more, and soon virtually the entire workforce. For the moment, no chile was leaving this field for the cans of Old El Paso. The strike was solid, galvanized by the

139

"We have a new type of farmworker who realizes that something is wrong with the agricultural industry in general, we have a new type of farmworker who realizes he has to fight."

—CARLOS MARENTES, LABOR ACTIVIST

union's demands for higher pay, drinking water, and bathrooms and for dismissal of a labor contractor accused of mistreating the workers.

The 1992 work stoppage at the Mesilla Valley jalapeño field was one of the strongest actions conducted by the El Paso-headquartered Border Agricultural Workers Union (Unión de Trabajadores Agrícolas Fronterizos), a militant, no-nonsense outfit dedicated to the complete transformation of the chile pickers' lot in life. Viewed by many farmers and labor contractors as the source of innumerable troubles, UTAF, as it is known by its Spanish acronym, had succeeded by the 1990s in building an impressive base among a labor force that had been regarded as next to impossible to organize. It had accomplished this in spite of nonexistent collective bargaining laws for farm laborers in New Mexico and Texas; in spite of lack of affiliation with the AFL-CIO; and in spite of a shoestring budget, which at the beginning of the 1992 strike amounted to $104 in the bank—a financial situation that any labor bureaucrat would have regarded as ludicrous in terms of even discussing a strike, much less actually starting one and ending up with some gains.

In many respects UTAF spearheaded the most dynamic labor movement to emerge in New Mexico and far west Texas since the 1970s. And the union led the most sustained New Mexico farmworker movement since the 1930s, when La Liga Obrera agitated among northern New Mexicans working the Colorado sugar beet fields, and the leftist Agricultural Workers Industrial Union (AWIU) mounted protests in the Roswell area for cash wages instead of food. In order to understand how UTAF's rise was possible, it is first necessary to review both the history of the old Texas Farmworkers Union (TFW) and that of a former editor of its newspaper, a quiet, introspective man named Carlos Marentes, who later became the coordinator of UTAF.

Headed by the charismatic Antonio Orendáin, the TFW was an offshoot of the California-based United Farmworkers Union (UFW). Striking out on its own in the mid-1970s, the TFW concentrated most of its efforts in the southern Rio Grande Valley of Texas, called the nation's winter vegetable garden and the "Valley of Tears" by workers there. From its office in Hidalgo, Texas, the TFW coordinated strikes in onion and cantaloupe fields, organized demonstrations at the state capital in Austin, and even conducted a 1977 march across the Deep South to Washington DC in order to build support for its cause. Those were turbulent years for the Texas group: its members were jailed, shot at, run over in fields, and spied on by the Federal Bureau of Investigation.

Marentes, then a cartoonist for a Juárez, Mexico, newspaper, had a proclivity for political satire that got him into trouble with his employer. He was told about the TFW and hooked up with the organization, becoming the editor of its newspaper, *El Cuhamil*. A young man who was influenced by the union activities of his father and the predicament of Mexican workers in the United States, Marentes was attracted to the TFW because of the union's uncompromising stance on organizing all workers, whether or not they had legal papers to work in the United States.

According to Marentes, Orendáin of the TFW and Lupe Sánchez, the chief of the closely allied Arizona Farmworkers Union, first checked out New Mexico in 1978. They were interested in the state because Texas workers traveled to New Mexico for the onion harvest. Two years later the TFW's efforts began in earnest when the union dispatched Marentes and Ron Fernández to organize in the Mesilla Valley. Fernández departed shortly after, leaving Marentes on his own. Marentes was a natural for the job. Born and reared in nearby Ciudad Juárez, he was familiar with the area and the agricultural work force. Still, his early years as a labor organizer were what could best be described as lonely. Many workers distrusted unions, an attitude fostered in part by experiences in California when César Chávez's UFW battled it out in the fields with the employer-encouraged Teamsters for the right to represent California's huge farm-

worker population. Marentes also found divisions among the workers themselves on the basis of legal status.

The workers in El Paso and southern New Mexico were a mixed bunch, categorized as citizens, legal residents, "green carders," and undocumenteds. The job of Marentes was, like a latter-day Wobbly, to organize them into one big union. It was not an easy job, and a primary goal sketched by Marentes was to overcome divisions based on national status.

Marentes held the first TFW meeting at the Sacred Heart Church in El Paso. Workers asked the organizers, "Are you going to pay us for the time?" "No, this meeting is for you," Marentes replied. Only eight farmworkers showed up at the first meeting, an encounter Marentes described as a "disaster" because the participants spent most of the time lambasting unions. A less dedicated organizer surely would have thrown up his or her hands in frustration, but Marentes persisted. One individual he credits with prodding him along is Lupe Sánchez, the former head of the once highly successful Arizona Farmworkers Union. Initially, it was crops other than chile that attracted Marentes's attention. He soon found a group of workers at the Stahmann Farms pecan orchard trying to organize a union. The men had contacted the Albuquerque office of the International Laborers Union but had no luck there, reported Marentes, since that union was not interested in pursuing a cause with a group that had no standing under the state collective bargaining law.

The first workers Marentes met were "old-time" farmworkers including ex-braceros like Raúl Granados, who arrived in New Mexico in 1948 from the Chihuahua countryside. Granados worked for the same Mesilla Valley grower for many years, eventually landing a job with an egg plant at Stahmann after the owner died and his sons sold off the old man's property. Charged with spraying the egg farm with pesticides such as Sevin, Granados became ill and filed a worker's compensation suit against his employer. He also accompanied Marentes to Santa Fe in the early 1980s to testify on behalf of farmworkers' rights. It was incidents such as the Stahmann episode that helped Marentes frame his views on the issues confronting southern New Mexico's farm labor force.

Once Marentes was in a blistering hot field conversing with a worker and wondering why the man would tolerate such an occupation at such low pay. "You know, when I'm in the field I'm happy," the worker said to Marentes. For that worker and others, wages and working conditions were a symptom of a larger wound closer to the heart. "It's about dignity," the man told Marentes.

Reminiscing about "the old days," Marentes considered older workers like Granados to be the pivotal force of the nascent movement he was building. Coming from a common geographic region of Coahuila, Durango, or Chihuahua, they were of a shared background, having been brought up on small farms, or *ejidos*. Many west Texas and southern New Mexico farmworkers also had a common sense of history dating from the times of Pancho Villa's northern revolution, the 1930s land battles in the La Laguna area from which many of them originated, and the bracero program. They also shared a common northern Mexican culture and dialect.

Slowly Marentes's contacts and efforts paid off: There were scattered work stoppages in tomato and onion fields, and the workers at the Santa Fe Bridge recruitment spot in El Paso were inundated with leaflets. One conversation that stuck in Marentes's mind is a talk he had with one of the workers who slept on a piece of cardboard near the bridge. "Carlos, are things going to change?" the man asked. "Yes, they will," Marentes replied. Marentes also recalled one individual who was convinced to join an early strike action, and who in turn was able to get "60 people to join."

In the meantime, the Texas Farmworkers Union broke apart due to internal problems, and it dissolved in 1983 at the very moment when Marentes was beginning to make headway in El Paso and southern New Mexico. Then in early 1984, 100 farmworkers from the United States and Mexico met in El Paso to establish La Unión de Trabajadores Agrícolas Fronterizos, the Border Agricultural Workers Union. The union went public late in the summer of 1984 when it organized a strike of 500 chile pickers against growers in the Mesilla Valley. The action began at a jalapeño chile field owned by farmer David Brown near Anthony, where UTAF established its first firm base. Brown was initially unresponsive, according to Marentes, declaring that he would rather leave the chiles in the field than pay more money. The next day, walkouts spread to farms in La Union and Mesquite. For a week, the strikers met at the Anthony Dairy Queen and from there headed out to the fields for picketing.

About 120 workers held a war council and resolved to organize the workforce at the Santa Fe Bridge. Until then, the workers in El Paso had not been involved. "Well, yes, we went to work on this farm and we knew that you people were on strike, but since we weren't part of the union, we didn't feel part of it [the strike]," Marentes recalled the El Paso workers saying. UTAF's first strike lasted three weeks and brought mixed results. The stoppages at the Mesquite and La Union farms were overcome by strike-breaking labor contractors as the fledgling union was hard-pressed to maintain pickets at three separate locations. Brown, however, raised piece rates from 5¢ to 10¢ per bucket, though some workers were afraid to return to work.

The mid to late 1980s were a period of consolidation, growth, and rethinking for UTAF. The ability to organize workers in El Paso was a boon to its campaign as it tapped into networks like the one at the Santa Fe Bridge formed by people who already knew each other and had a degree of social solidarity. Rather than continuing the narrow, business unionism practiced by most labor organizations in the United States since the 1940s, UTAF viewed its struggle as part of a larger worldwide fight waged by the dispossessed against the powerful.

UTAF networked with like-minded groups that included Lupe Sánchez's AFW, the International Union of Agricultural and Industrial Workers (IUAIW), and the Central Independiente de Obreros Agrícolas y Campesinos (CIOAC) in Mexico. The IUAIW, another TFW offshoot, led a 1985 strike of grape harvesters in west Texas, raising demands for better pay and treatment in an industry which, like chile, was growing in the hospitable climate of the Southwest. IUAIW leader Jesús Moya, who met the field hands camped out and eating rabbits

¡Huelga! A young Carlos Marentes (foreground) leads chile pickers in a 1984 Mesilla Valley strike.

El Paso riot squad at 1984 farmworker protest.

in the Texas countryside, summed up organizers' sentiments when he explained the nature of their struggle: "The struggle of the farmworkers is not just an economic struggle. It's trying to get the farmworkers to benefit from the fruits of their labor, and to demand better working conditions and better places to live. Every time a worker goes to a place he's many times denied food stamps. He's denied access to medical attention in the hospitals. His children are discriminated [against] in the schools because they speak Spanish or because they're migrants. The police constantly harass them. There's raids in the fields and in the labor camps. So the struggle of the farmworkers is not just a struggle for economic benefits, but more than that it's a struggle for economic and social equality."

Before UTAF could devote its full attention to the bread-and-butter issues in the chile fields, it was compelled to cope with a new law that changed forever its destiny—the 1986 Immigration Reform and Control Act (IRCA). Passed by Congress in the days before the Iran-Contra scandal rocked the Reagan administration, IRCA held out the promise of freedom to previously illegal workers and contained provisions for a massive guest worker program similar to the bracero program. The latter was a measure designed to ease the fears of farmers concerned that their newly legal workforce would flee the fields for better paying jobs in the cities. Alarmed by the guest worker provision and other sections it regarded as detrimental to worker interests, UTAF opposed IRCA, viewing it as a tool to drive down wages by pitting closely controlled contract guest workers from Mexico against their brethren in the chile fields. The majority of chile pickers at the time were undocumented and were eligible for legalization under the Special

Agricultural Workers (SAW) provision of the law. When workers realized this part of the law was in their interest and desired papers, UTAF decided to help.

Between 1987 and 1989, the union helped almost 2,000 farmworkers to obtain amnesty, an action that spurred the group's growth. By the 1989 chile harvest, farmworkers were again ready to take collective action, this time fortified by the security of amnesty. In September they conducted work stoppages at the Santa Fe Bridge. Around this time farmers in southern New Mexico were complaining of labor shortages. The discontent was a prelude to the 1990 strike, UTAF's biggest action so far. The strike movement got off the ground on August 6, 1990, when about 100 workers declared a labor stoppage in a Hatch Valley field operated by Loyad Anderson and demanded a 10¢ raise for each bucket of chile. Two nights later, between 500 and 700 pickers began a demonstration at the Santa Fe Bridge, refusing to board buses until wages were raised and labor laws respected.

About four a.m. on the morning of August 9, 1990, El Paso police arrived on the scene and forced the strikers, some of whom allegedly were throwing rocks, away from the buses and pushed the workers and legal observers into the streets. The police arrested two strikers, Luis Rivera and María Elena Navarro, on charges of inciting a riot. Union members accused the police of brutality and of pushing Navarro's 14-year-old daughter to the ground. "They should be looking for criminals," remarked worker Carlos Méndez. "Why are they trying to bring oppression to the people?" Police spokesperson Captain Louie Mier told an *El Paso Times* reporter that the police would not interfere with further demonstrations as long as the strikers complied with the law. "Yeah, there were some hostilities that erupted between police and demonstrators," conceded the captain.

During the next several weeks the protest movement spread to fields in southern New Mexico's chile belt. Workers picketed the U.S. Department of Labor offices in El Paso because of labor law violations and protested at the Hatch Chile Festival. Walkouts, some spontaneous, occurred in fields from the Hatch Valley in the north to Lordsburg in the west to Dell City, Texas, in the southeast. A small group of UTAF sympathizers marched on the U.S. Consulate in Ciudad Juárez demanding an end to what they said was the mistreatment of Mexican workers in the United States. On September 20, 1990, the Organización Popular Independiente (OPI) of Ciudad Juárez raised funds for the strikers in a citywide day of solidarity.

UTAF refined its strike strategy on a selective basis, targeting only those labor contractors who refused to raise wages. "The strategy has been to boycott some of those contractors and go to work with the people who are sympathetic to our demands," explained organizer Willivaldo Delgadillo. "What the workers have been doing is taking turns. Not all of them can go to work with these contractors every day, so what they do is several people go to work for one day and then they stop and the other group goes to work the following day."

According to UTAF, at its peak, before it ended in November, the protest involved 800 workers, a small percentage of the 5,000 or so chile pickers in New Mexico and west Texas, but enough to pressure some contractors into raising piece rates a few cents and installing bathrooms in fields. UTAF also pressured the U.S. Department of Labor, whose inspectors conducted a "chile strike force" and cited dozens of contractors for labor law violations.

Assessments of the strike were mixed, depending on whose side was voiced. Chile Commission head Don Hackey downplayed the protest, the largest of its kind in New Mexico in years, saying that only a handful of workers participated and did not affect the harvesting. But Sandy New, a UTAF staff person, had a different view of the strike's results, claiming that it increased worker involvement in the union and improved pay and field conditions. The 1990 strike also produced a historic first in the fields of New Mexico: a labor contract between UTAF and grower Loyad Anderson to cover the 1991 harvest.

Overall, the new decade saw an important change in the climate between labor and employer in the New Mexico fields, perhaps best symbolized by the 60 farmworkers who stormed Hatch farmer Eddie García's house in February 1991 to demand back wages they claimed he owed them. Emboldened by the amnesty law and motivated by falling wages, more workers spoke up, manned the picket line, and walked out. Commented Marentes: "We have a new type of farmworker who realizes that something is wrong with the agricultural industry in general; we have a new type of farmworker who realizes he has to fight." Of course, farmers and labor contractors were distressed by the escalating protests. The union "has hurt our industry tremendously," contended Mesilla Valley grower Dino Cervantes, who farmed about 500 acres of cayenne and green chile. "The first question I get when I go to a processors' convention is, 'Do you have labor problems?'"

But for UTAF, it was a time of growth. The union was run by a mainly female farmworker board and directed by a staff that included Marentes, his wife Alicia, Miguel Borunda, and Sandy New. The UTAF office routinely was packed with workers wanting help with everything from income tax returns to job grievances. The house newspaper, *El Bote sin Capote*, featured news of interest and appeals to collective action. Sandy New, a redheaded Anglo from a little East Texas town who was once half jokingly crowned the queen of UTAF by a group of women workers, had previously been an administrator with a Comprehensive Employment and Training Act (CETA) program that attempted to place farmworkers in jobs outside of agriculture. New came to disagree with that goal because she appreciated the dignity in farm work and understood that there was always another crop of workers to replace the ones who left. In her view, this only served to perpetuate a system of exploitation.

Ain't Gonna Work on Anderson's Farm No More: UTAF strikers in the Mesilla Valley, 1992.

UTAF was kept busy in 1991 administering the contract with Anderson, an agreement that was not renewed. Anderson later said the union did not abide by its promise to provide the same 150 workers throughout the period of the contract and claimed that he was overwhelmed with a thousand pickers, many of whom did not want to be paid on a weekly instead of a daily basis— a pay schedule stipulated by the union agreement. UTAF countered that Anderson did not follow all the provisions of the agreement and failed to return several calls and letters after the contract expired. Either way, the stage was set for another strike.

Meanwhile, far to the south, in Texas's "Valley of Tears," the expansion of the jalapeño chile industry provoked a worker movement of its own. Small and medium-sized farmers grew peppers for companies like Pace, contracting their fields to the burgeoning salsa business. One grower, perturbed by the militancy, suggested that the solution was to move the Texas jalapeño industry across the border to Mexico, hardly an idle threat in view of the already existing ties between food processors in the United States and growers south of the Río Bravo.

As they had in New Mexico, workers in the Rio Grande Valley complained of subminimum wages (paid in one case for destemmed jalapeños), and in January 1992 about 100 field hands struck the Santa Sarita Import and Export Company in Weslaco. Workers who picketed outside the plant held signs that read "We demand $4.25 an hour" and "We are humans, not slaves." Santa Sarita's owner disputed the strikers' claims of below-minimum earnings yet settled with the workers and promised to pay minimum wage.

UTAF on the March: El Paso, Texas, early 1990s.

tomato and pickle processors Heinz and Campbell's.

UTAF reemerged in the public spotlight following a July 26, 1992, mass meeting at an El Paso community center. Outside the stuffy hall, a huge mural portrait of Che Guevara stared from an opposite building. Inside, the more than 200 workers and their family members voted to strike the new chile harvest for higher wages and better conditions. Around midnight, a handful of women UTAF members pounded nails into picket signs in their cramped office. Twelve-year-old Martha Barrera had worked the fields since she was nine and said it was her first strike. "I think it's a lot of fun, to help the people how I can. It's my first time, I'm very excited." She was involved in order to "help the farmworkers with their rights . . . the contractors treat them very badly. Everyone is equal."

Before complying, however, Santa Sarita declared bankruptcy, leaving the pickers' pockets empty. Texas Rural Legal Aid (TRLA) represented the workers and investigated the contracting chain. They concluded that Pace Foods had ultimate control over the placing and paying of field labor. Lawyers for the agency negotiated with the San Antonio company but failed to come up with a satisfactory resolution. In July 1993, they sued Pace for back wages due the Santa Sarita workers. Pace, stating that the company wanted all workers in the industry to be treated fairly, settled out of court with TRLA.

In a similar vein, UTAF examined the chile production system and concluded that eventually the processing companies would have to be drawn into the wage issue. In the late 1980s this approach was successful in the Midwest when, after a lengthy boycott, the Farm Labor Organizing Committee signed contracts between the union, growers, and

Early the next morning, in the still darkness of the Segundo Barrio, about 30 UTAF members approached a vacant lot in front of a run-down apartment complex where several dozen farmworkers were sleeping in parked cars and in a labor contractors' bus. Packing a bullhorn and the red and black UTAF banner, the strikers got sympathetic workers to emerge from the bus and refuse to go out to the fields until wages were raised. Others, friendly to the contractor, melted into the darkness, while a few more, not unreceptive but who needed immediate work, were uneasy. One worker said he did not think the boycott would be effective because the labor contractors would simply recruit others from the Hatch and Mesilla Valleys to fill the strikers' shoes. "We're not gonna' work, we're gonna' lose a fucking day," he dissented. "The right thing to do is to go out there and stop everybody."

Here was UTAF's problem: Most workers did not argue with the need for better pay and treatment, but they were so financially strapped they could ill afford even one day without work. On the morning of July 29, 1992, the strike hit Loyad Anderson's fields near La Mesa south of Las Cruces in an event termed an "uprising" by the press. Hundreds walked out in support of UTAF, and, according to Anderson, slashed tractor tires and threw rocks at strike breakers, charges the union denied. The next day UTAF was back in full force, but so were contingents of the Doña Ana County Sheriff's Department and the U.S. Border Patrol.

The facts of what transpired that day are in dispute. According to some workers, the sheriffs attacked without provocation, spraying mace and sending seven people to El Paso for treatment. The Sheriff's Department accused the workers of not obeying an order to leave the field and said they had used pepper gas, not mace, certainly an ironic twist considering the object of the strike—chile. Striker Amparo Reyes was gassed, grew "nauseous" and "got blind." Her eyesight fully recovered and she later returned to the strike. "I remember eight years ago we worked in Garfield, New Mexico, and that's what they paid, $1.00 a bucket, and right now it's 85¢. I don't know what is the reason," questioned a defiant Reyes.

After the gassing, UTAF regrouped. On Friday, July 31, union members marched back into the field and shut it down completely for two hours before Anderson moved in about 30 to 50 strikebreakers, one of whom entered the field making an obscene gesture with his finger at the 200 or so strikers lining the field. Catcalls returned the greeting. "Here comes the *patrón*," somebody was heard to say, and sure enough, there appeared Loyad Anderson in his pickup truck, a mobile phone close to his hand. Wearing a gold Rolex watch and sunglasses that gave him more of a resemblance to a misplaced Jimmy Buffett than a New Mexico farmer or rancher, Anderson initially refused to comment on the strike. "Excuse me, I've got work to do," he said.

Thirty-nine-year-old Anderson, with his 1,000 acres or so of chile, was widely held to be the biggest chile grower in the southern Rio Grande Valley; he had been sending much of his crop to the Mountain Pass cannery for a long time. In addition to chile, his Anderson Enterprises cultivated 2,000 acres of other crops, and at the time of the strike he was preparing to open a potentially lucrative chile oleoresin extraction plant with Louis Biad. The chile business had been good to Anderson and he farmed fields that stretched from the Hatch Valley to the Mesilla Valley south of Las Cruces. In the middle of his far-flung farms, he lived in a pink, colonial-style ranch house between Las Cruces and Hatch, a chile field at his doorstep.

Cornered on a narrow dirt road that split the chile field in half, Anderson gave in to reporters' inquiries. He was unbudged. The strike had set him back two days, but production was picking up, he claimed, although most workers were still honoring the picket. No, he couldn't pay more money because he had negotiated a contract with the food processor the previous winter and he was receiving a set price for the chile. "These people don't intimidate me, I know what I'm doing is right," he said. "The only people I have to satisfy is the Department of Labor." Confronted by lawyers from Centro Legal Campesino and Texas Rural Legal Aid, Anderson promised to pay the difference in minimum wage shortfalls workers had claimed from previous days and said he would make sure his labor contractors obeyed the law. Then he drove off in his pickup, leaving the strike temporarily unsettled.

Unmoved, Carlos Marentes stood at the edge of the field and pronounced the strike a success. He conceded that the workers probably would not get everything they wanted, but he was confident that they would get something in a few days. During that time, UTAF members picketed the field even when the rains kept everyone else away, won endorsements from prominent El Paso political leaders, and organized a march through El Paso's Segundo Barrio. Voices calling for a boycott or picket of Old El Paso Foods, the purchaser of Anderson's chile, began to be heard. On August 3, Anderson and the union agreed to a temporary increase, subject to review at a later date, of five cents for each bucket picked. When the agreement expired, some UTAF members wanted to strike again but the overall situation was not deemed timely and the nickel hike stayed. Another chile season passed.

In March of 1993, UTAF and its friends, old and new, gathered at the Sacred Heart Gym in the heart of the Segundo Barrio to commemorate "Diez Años de Lucha," 10 years of struggle. It was in the same stuffy building where, more than a decade earlier, a younger Carlos Marentes had convened a disastrous meeting of eight disgruntled workers who were upset as much at unions as at bosses. Now, hundreds regularly attended UTAF meetings and workers deep in Mexico knew the organization. For many UTAF had produced tangible gains, the sort of things most people take for granted, but which are life

and death issues for field workers. For Jesús Placencia Hernández, a California migrant, it was UTAF that got him a sleeping space in the Sacred Heart church. For Ramón Valdez of El Paso, the union was a full-service social organization. "They've made many benefits for us . . . unemployment [benefits], they advocate for us, fill out papers, everything." And for 80-year-old José María Holguín of Nuevas Casas Grandes, Chihuahua, the union was a last ray of hope for his failing eyesight. The old bracero cotton worker, who had not set foot on a New Mexico farm in decades, walked into the UTAF office one day with his wife holding an ancient commendation card from the Doña Ana Farm Bureau, asking for help in finding a U.S. specialist to perform surgery.

Union activist Gloria Salcedo analyzed UTAF's record from the vantage point of a worker: "The union's been like the *paño de lágrimas* for the worker. Look, before the union existed, a worker never got his income tax. Every year, the union helps the worker do his income tax. The union searches everywhere when there's no work to find help. It obtains clothes, economic assistance, food stamps. They've helped the people from Mexico put our kids in school. When Esperanza Rodríguez died, the union asked for donations to help her family bury her. We didn't collect everything that was needed, but we walked around the bridges carrying buckets."

As the 1993 harvest drew to a close, UTAF's crowning accomplishment to date was almost ready for groundbreaking: a worker recruitment center built by the City of El Paso and managed by the farmworkers themselves, designed to keep the pickers in a nighttime shelter and off the streets. Seasoned by years of battles that had taken him from the "Valley of Tears" into the heart of Mexico, over to Europe and back to the bridges, farms, and makeshift camps of the New Mexico chile belt, Carlos Marentes took the long view. That year, as in others, there would be new challenges, new opportunities. There was a trip to a Farm Aid concert in the Midwest to support small family farmers; an upheaval at the agricultural college in Ciudad Juárez during which students were shot; and a crisis when pro-free trade President Clinton's "new" Border Patrol blocked off the El Paso-southern New Mexico border in a military-style operation that set off a counter-blockade of international bridges by infuriated Mexican protestors. In March, Marentes sat down at a joint press conference in El Paso with UFW head César Chávez just weeks before the legendary farm labor leader breathed his last breath, marking a recognition of mutual respect between two groups that had long maintained a distance from each other. A few weeks later, he was part of an estimated crowd of 35,000 who made the pilgrimage to bid Chávez farewell in Delano, California, the place where the son of Arizona migrants initiated the modern farmworker movement in the United States a seeming century ago, in 1965.

In El Paso, UTAF and its friends mounted one of the largest demonstrations the city had seen since the 1960s and early 1970s. For three miles, between 2,000 and 3,000 people—high school students, workers, and community members—trudged along barrio streets to the Chamizal National Monument for their tribute to Chávez. UTAF flags and giant portraits of UFW head Chávez rose alongside each other above the procession. "Viva César Chávez" chanted the throngs. "Se ve, se siente, la UTAF está presente." "You can see it, you can feel it, UTAF is here," clamored the 500 UTAF members leading the march.

Was Chávez's death an occasion for the rebirth of a national farmworker movement not only in west Texas and New Mexico, but in the rest of the nation as well? Only time would tell. Some weeks before the march, at the podium of the Sacred Heart Church before the eyes of hundreds of men, women, and children in their Sunday hats and dresses and in front of a giant UTAF birthday cake spiced with jalapeño chiles, Marentes strode forward and remembered that worker on the cardboard who had asked, "Carlos, are things going to change?" "Yes, they will, and they are," said Marentes.

Notes

1. Author's observation of the UTAF strike and interviews with strike participants, La Mesa, NM, July 1992.

2. E. E. Maes, "Labor Movement in New Mexico," *New Mexico Business Review*, April 1935, 139.

3. Accounts of the Pecos Valley strike: *Roswell Morning Dispatch*, 11, 20, 22, and 29 June 1933; 1 July 1933.

4. Texas Farm Workers Union, *The Struggle of the Texas Farm Workers Union* (Chicago: Vanguard Books, 1977).

5. *El Cuhamil* (newspaper of the Texas Farm Workers Union), various issues, 1975-82.

6. *The Texas Observer*, 13 March 1992.

7. Carlos Marentes, interviews by author, El Paso, TX, 1992-94.

8. Raúl Granados, interview by author, San Miguel, NM, March 1994.

9. Carlos Marentes, presentation at Sacred Heart Church, El Paso, TX, March 1993.

10. Jesús Moya, telephone conversation with author, September 1986.

11. Carlos Marentes, interview by author, El Paso, TX, September 1986.

12. *El Paso Times*, 10 August 1990.

13. *Norte de Ciudad Juárez*, 25 August 1990.

14. *Diez Años de Lucha*, UTAF publication, March 1993.

15. Willivaldo Delgadillo, interview by author, Hatch, NM, September 1990.

16. Sandy New, interview by author, El Paso, TX, October 1990.

17. Don Hackey, telephone conversation with author, October 1990.

18. *Albuquerque Journal*, 18 April 1991; *Albuquerque Journal*, 20 April 1991.

19. Dino Cervantes, telephone conversation with author, August 1991.

20. *The Monitor* (McAllen, TX), 8 January 1992.

21. *The Monitor*, 11 November 1992.

22. Jeff Levin, Texas Rural Legal Aid, telephone conversation with author, January 1993.

23. William Beardall, Texas Rural Legal Aid, telephone conversation with author, September 1993.

24. *Dallas Morning News*, 14 July 1993.

25. *Detroit Free Press*, 10 April 1987.

26. Martha Barrera, interview by author, El Paso, TX, July 1992.

27. Unnamed chile picker, interview by author, El Paso, TX, July 1992.

28. *Las Cruces Sun News*, 30 July 1992.

29. *El Paso Herald Post*, 31 July 1992.

30. James Hatch, Doña Ana County Sheriff's Department, interview by author, La Mesa, NM, July 1992.

31. Amparo Reyes, interview by author, La Mesa, NM, July 1992.

32. Loyad Anderson, interview by author, La Mesa, NM, July 1992.

33. Carlos Marentes, interview by author, La Mesa, NM, July 1992.

34. Sandy New, telephone conversation with author, August 1992.

35. Jesús Placencia Hernández, interview by author, El Paso, TX, March 1993.

36. Ramón Valdez, interview by author, El Paso, TX, March 1993.

37. José María Holguín, interview by author, El Paso, TX, September 1993.

38. Gloria Salcedo, interview by author, El Paso, TX, April 1992.

39. *San Francisco Chronicle*, 30 April 1993.

40. *El Paso Herald Post*, 24 May 1993.

Los Contratistas

LABOR LAW IN THE CHILE FIELDS

Deming Chile Picking King ▪ Dead Social Security Beneficiary ▪ Bathrooms and Blow-Ups ▪
Chile Roadblocks ▪ War of Lawyers and Farmers

For 16 years, John Gasper ran a labor empire from the Santa Fe Bridge. His half-dozen buses whisked upwards of 200 workers a day to the chile fields. In time he carved out a turf in the Deming area, netted more income than some farmers, dabbled in silver, went into debt at a Las Vegas casino, and involuntarily became the star attraction of a conflict between the New Mexico agricultural industry and government-funded legal agencies.

A Midwesterner of Italian descent, Gasper arrived in the New Mexico chile fields in the 1970s, starting as a picker before agreeing to help farmers acquire laborers. His service rapidly expanded and in almost no time he claimed to control 90 percent of the contract labor in Luna County and oversaw the picking at 27 farms. It was a hectic pace: "I was using a bottle of Excedrin a week. I was doing it, but I just couldn't keep doing it." Prior to the start of picking, Gasper negotiated the terms of his contract with

the farmers, basing his price on the dry-weight basis of chile. He was well acquainted with all the major Luna County growers, judging them variously as "cutthroat," "one of the nicest men I've ever known," "okay," or living by the motto "do unto others before they do unto you." Seated on a comfortable couch in his El Paso suburban home, Gasper regretted ever having entered the chile business, calling it an industry that set "brother against brother." In due time, Gasper made enemies among farmworkers, some of whom conducted work stoppages and sued him for such infractions as failure to pay the minimum wage, failure to disclose the conditions of their work, and bodily injury.

Although cited by the Department of Labor (DOL) for labor law violations as far back as 1979, Gasper's first serious trouble surfaced in 1983-84 when María Vega and coworkers sued him and Deming farmer Darrel McCauley (who later declared bankruptcy and was settled from

> *"They ain't gonna rest until they put me in jail . . .*
> *I don't believe what's happened. I should be on 60*
> *Minutes.*"

—JOHN GASPER, FORMER LABOR CONTRACTOR

the suit) on a number of counts, including failure to pay the minimum wage. In 1991, an El Paso judge issued a ruling in the suit against him, *Vega vs. Gasper*, that shook the New Mexico chile and agricultural industry. Deciding in favor of the plaintiffs, U.S. District Judge Lucius Bunton ordered payment of not only $35,000 in compensation for back wages owed but demanded payment as well for time spent traveling back and forth from the fields. "A picture of abject poverty emerges," said Bunton in favor of the plaintiffs, ". . . having to stoop and bend for long hours, and then having to get back on the bus and be transported back to the El Paso-Juárez area and not receiving one farthing for the time spent on the bus, is indeed a sad and pathetic situation." The decision was challenged by the New Mexico Farm and Livestock Bureau, which immediately protested that the extra transportation cost to farmers would financially impair them. Gasper and fellow labor contractors had thus become the center of a raging controversy that swept chile country and was as stormy as Hurricane Salem. Stuck squarely in the middle of an on-again, off-again war of words and legal skirmishes between the New Mexico Farm and Livestock Bureau and federally supported farmworker legal service groups, the contractors came to symbolize much more

than their seasonal business. They were cast in a drama involving the White House and Capitol Hill, multinational agribusiness corporations, shadowy contractors, big-time chile growers, high-stakes gamblers, and, of course, thousands of farmworkers.

Theoretically, disputes that revolved around farmworkers centered on the provisions of the Fair Labor Standards Act (minimum wage) and the Migrant and Seasonal Workers' Protection Act, a federal law that mandated posting and disclosure of pay rates, registration of labor contractors and their supervisors, and the maintenance of safe, insured transportation to the fields. In reality the issues were those of human rights, equal legal representation, and the balance between private profits and social responsibility, ideas rooted in one corner or another of the contradictory American political psyche.

No topic in chile country was as likely to spark fireworks as the contractor-busting activities of Texas Rural Legal Aid (TRLA) and the Centro Legal Campesino (CLC) of Las Cruces, New Mexico. For more than a decade, those two organizations have been at the heart of the sharpest controversies that have torn the chile empire.

In a modestly furnished office in downtown Las Cruces directly across from the chile-promoting headquarters of the Chamber of Commerce, CLC hosted a small staff that included managing attorney Olga Pedroza and paralegal Ismael Camacho. As a team Pedroza and Camacho were the Lois Lane and Clark Kent of the farmworkers, though to many farmers, they were akin to Bonnie and Clyde. Simply put, their job was to raise legal hell in order to assure farmworkers of equal protection under the law whether in a government entitlement case or a back wages claim against an employer. Conversely, as agricultural representatives viewed it, their role was to harass law-abiding farmers while being outrageously funded by those very farmers through their federal taxes.

In all his long years of involvement with agriculture, not much has changed, says Ismael "Smiley" Camacho. California-born, Camacho was raised in a farmworker family and entered the fields when he was a child younger than eight years old. "The only thing that changed for me, for example, was when I was in California. I was picking grapes. Here you just got a different situation where maybe the conditions are different. For example, picking grapes you're underneath the vines. It's very humid, very hot. And here, when you're picking chile, it's just pretty dry heat. Still, it's unbearable conditions. But things have not changed, it's amazing."

Camacho's colleague, CLC managing attorney Olga Pedroza, is a Mexico City native who got her legal feet wet in the rough, frosty hills of Mora County in northern New Mexico. In the two years after she came to Las Cruces, Pedroza handled about 170 separate cases in which individuals or groups sought back wages owed, mostly for working for less than the minimum wage in the chile harvest. During a visit, she reached into a file and sorted through time sheets from labor contractors to prove her point

that many pay below the federal minimum. "Six hours, $20, ten hours, $25," she read. "Most people come in not because of the minimum wage, or because of violations of the minimum wage or because of violations of the agricultural workers' protection act, or any of those things," added Pedroza. "They come in because so and so added insult to injury. 'He yelled at me, he called me this or that.' And then after you begin to find what went on: 'Oh, well, they changed the rate of pay during the day. They didn't pay minimum wage. There were no bathrooms, or there are very, very dirty bathrooms. There was no water.' All of these other things come up."

Pedroza and her associates at TRLA handled cases verging on the bizarre. They sued the New Mexico Department of Labor for denying farmworkers unemployment benefits because labor contractors did not report wages; threatened to haul the state of New Mexico into court for deducting workers' compensation administration fees from farmworkers every quarter, even though the majority of farmworkers were not covered by workers' comp; investigated a ranch hand's complaint that he was offered cowboy boots instead of money; and saw a law firm go after the nonexistent assets of penniless field hands because their employer declared bankruptcy. Camacho once represented a hapless couple who were claiming Social Security benefits because as farmworkers in New Mexico they were not covered by workers' compensation. "A lady client of mine was picking onions in the Hatch area, and while she was picking onions, unfortunately for her, she encountered a rattlesnake . . . as a result lost her eye," recalls Camacho. I represented her for her Social Security benefits for disability and now she's been on them for six or seven years. I also represented her husband who died of cancer shortly thereafter. He was denied benefits because he was not disabled. Once he died, they gave him his benefits."

Almost from its inception in 1978 and later reinforced by the El Paso office of TRLA, which opened its doors in 1983, CLC was on the opposite side of the fence from its chief nemesis, the New Mexico Farm and Livestock Bureau. The two groups drew swords over a variety of issues including workers' compensation, field sanitation regulations, the short-handled hoe, and responsibility for labor law violations.

Historically conservative, over the years the New Mexico Farm Bureau had, at various times, opposed mandatory workers' compensation, minimum wage, and collective bargaining for farmworkers; supported child labor in the fields; devoted great attention to countering the UFW grape boycott; and backed the curtailment of farmworker legal services activity, endorsing a complete termination of federal monies for the Legal Services Corporation, the parent agency of both CLC and TRLA. "It's always been amazing to us that these lawyers can sit behind a desk and file suit against our farmers and file suit against a certain regulation at the state level, funded by our tax dollars and basically attacking the industry," explained Farm Bureau spokesman Erik Ness.

After the ascension of Ronald Reagan to the presidency in 1981, the Republican administration tried to cut off all funding for farmworker legal services but was checked by Congress. Nevertheless, budget cuts, restrictions, audits, and even raiding of office files plagued Legal Aid offices from Maine to California. In its early years, the CLC engaged in impact legislation to change the laboring conditions of whole groups of farmworkers. Their attorneys filed suit against a Mesquite onion producer's cooperative

in the early 1980s in order to guarantee the minimum wage, pushed for New Mexico field sanitation regulations prior to the enactment of federal rules, and testified in 1986 in favor of banning the short-handled hoe, a field tool opponents contended ruined the backs of stooped-over hoers.

On this issue, as on countless others, the lawyers ran into opposition. Vado chile farmer Orlando Cervantes was exasperated at the activism of people he said were seeking to drive a wedge between farmers and farmworkers. He cited the June 1986 Environmental Improvement Division hearing in Las Cruces to gather testimony on the enactment of state standards for bathrooms, drinking water, sanitation, and the outlawing of the short-handled hoe. The event featured uninformed statements by people who had no knowledge of agriculture's reality, according to Cervantes. He concluded that they must have found their ideas in movies where "the farmer is a little less than a slave driver with a whip and what have you. That is what really griped me." Most crew leaders supplied water, he asserted, and besides, a good many pickers brought their own refreshments because it was a "picnic type of thing."

He recalled claims that working with a short-handled hoe was equivalent to carrying 600 pounds on the back, that field workers were getting feces on their hands from filthy portable toilets, and that pickers went to work sick. "If that is the case," said Cervantes, "then I'd say that there is obviously a problem, but I don't agree that's the case." In Cervantes's mind the only thing achieved at the hearings was to "lob stones at the farmer, which obviously the farmers did not appreciate." Why anyone would want to harass the farmers puzzled him: "We think that we are human beings just like anyone else . . . and that we do to the greatest extent have compassion on our workers. And I think sometimes they should have compassion on us, because we're not having it so easy ourselves, you know."

It was with the labor contract system that the CLC and TRLA had the biggest axe to grind. From the smoky corners of the Segundo Barrio and the placid little towns of southern New Mexico, a small group of men (and a few women) employed and transported human cargo to every nook and cranny of the chile belt. These are the labor contractors, or *contratistas*, as they are called, payrolled by chile farmers to supply a specified number of workers for a specified length of time at a specified price. To assist them, *contratistas* employed *choferes* to drive the buses, *soqueros* to monitor the fields, *ficheros* to hand workers tokens, and thousands of field hands to harvest the crop. In Mexico a *fichera* is a woman who frequents cantinas to inspire the men to buy drinks.

Most *contratistas* earn about $15,000 a year, though a handful have become big chiles, boasting a gross that tops $1 million, an amount that

A Token Economy: Farmworker piece rates sparked legal battles in the chile fields.

surpasses the earnings of many chile farmers. A few El Paso *contratistas* even ship workers as far east as Pennsylvania or North Carolina for jobs in mushrooms and tobacco. To the workers, *contratistas* are "good," "bad," "fair," or "unfair." On the street they are known by their nicknames: "El Jaiba" (the crab), "El Maloso" (the bad one), "El Botecitos" (little buckets), "El Mosco" (the fly), and so on. Most are ex-farmworkers or children of labor contractors, but some are interlopers that wandered into the chile fields. Camarina Ballarso, for instance, took to labor contracting after an unsuccessful stab at selling precious metals in Europe and the Juárez *maquiladora* industry. For two years, Ballarso searched for workers to pick chile, striking up deals with growers and bus owners. Never once did she encounter an inspector from state OSHA, USDOL, or NMDA investigating field conditions. She scoffed at the suggestion that farmers were not really netting large amounts from chile. In January 1992 she was contracting a farm for red chile. "[Workers] make 45¢ per bucket, and that's not enough. After [employers] have the bucket, they tell me, 'Tell them to put more chile on top because that's not enough.' "

Legal precedents, established in litigation, generally treated contractors as joint employers with farmers, but some growers treated the arrangement as if it were a buffer of sorts between agricultural employers and workers. Finger-pointing arose occasionally between contractors and farmers when federal enforcement officials poked their noses in, with one side either claiming the other responsible or professing ignorance of a particular law.

Farm labor activists and legal aid attorneys likened the labor contract system to an ongoing criminal enterprise. One TRLA lawyer, Debra Smith, filed a class action lawsuit on behalf of New Mexico lettuce harvest workers in 1986 under the RICO act, a law used against mobsters and later radical opponents of the U.S. government. From her out-of-the-way office in Hereford, Texas, Smith accused a group of growers and labor contractors of engaging in wire and transportation fraud, minimum wage violations, and illegal tax deductions in New Mexico and other Southwestern states during a 10-year period. One defendant, Presidio Valley Farms of Texas, was a beneficiary of a 1977 intervention by President Carter's Justice Department, which allowed onion growers to import hundreds of Mexican H-2 guest workers (a little-known descendant of the bracero program), in an action that overrode an earlier DOL decision to deny the request because of prior labor and guest worker law violations. The 1977 workers became dissatisfied with their wages and filed a suit of their own. In ruling on behalf of the plaintiffs, a federal court in Texas found that "many laborers earned less than one dollar an hour for their onerous, back-breaking labor." Labor contractors who operated in the chile fields were charged by TRLA and CLC with also systematically paying workers less than the minimum wage, transporting them in unsafe buses, failing to post the terms of work, neglecting to pay into the workers' social security and unemployment compensation funds, and not providing bathrooms, handwashing facilities or drinking water as prescribed by law. In addition, charged TRLA and CLC, they were permitted to continue because of lax enforcement by the DOL and other responsible agencies such as OSHA.

Though complaints arose about virtually all the contractors at one time or another, a few became high profile, including Gabriel Galarza and John Gasper. Galarza was one of the first targets of the budding UTAF. The group compiled an extensive list of allegations against Galarza dating back to 1979 and charged the contractor with not disclosing the terms of work to pickers, paying them below the minimum wage, and endangering lives in two separate bus accidents in 1983 and 1985. As ammunition, UTAF pointed to a 1983 U.S. Department of Labor investigation that determined that Galarza and Roswell-area farmer Frank Rhodes paid below the minimum wage to hundreds of red chile pickers.

The most serious accusation centered around a bus accident in July of 1985 that was captured for posterity in the pages of *Life* magazine. In the accident two farmworkers were killed and several others seriously hurt when the "ancient bus," which had defective brakes and horn and lacked passenger seats and a speedometer, slammed into a car on an El Paso street after returning from a day of onion picking at a Franzoy farm in Hatch. Sacks of onions piled in the back rolled forward, crushing Hilario Urrutia and Román González and injuring their coworkers. Galarza's driver, Zeferino Sánchez Rodríguez, was not licensed and had had beer to drink. Sánchez was briefly jailed, then released on probation, and he wound up in a cramped Segundo Barrio apartment, barely surviving on food stamps with his wife. Bárbara Urrutia was left a widow to care for the children of her husband Hilario. The accident didn't seem to shock her as much as it represented the sad culmination of what she had lived though in 14 years in the fields. "Most of the buses are in poor condition . . . all the drivers drink," she added. "I've come with drivers that were drinking on the road." Pending a license hearing, Galarza was free to work as a labor contractor but eventually had his authorization cancelled by DOL. In the interim his registration was renewed for two

years beginning in 1986. Still, as late as 1989, UTAF received reports that Galarza was contracting in the Roswell area.

UTAF presented a list of contractors to the DOL office in El Paso, charging them with multiple violations of the Migrant and Seasonal Workers Protection Act (MSWPA). The man who read the letter, inspector Ricardo Anaya, stated that he could not investigate the allegations because they were "nonspecific." Sitting in his downtown office one hot day in 1986, Anaya was visibly irked at mention of UTAF, pejoratively calling the group a "quasi-union." Yes, many labor contractors had violated the law in the past, he acknowledged, but conditions were improving. The biggest problem, he continued, was transportation insurance, since rates doubled in the past year.

Subsequent findings contradicted Anaya's rosy assessment. In August 1990, for instance, the DOL cited 16 contractors in southern New Mexico and west Texas for MSWPA violations. Three were on the 1985 UTAF list submitted to the DOL. Two months later, DOL inspectors fanned out across the west Texas-southern New Mexico chile belt, setting up roadblocks and handing out citations to 45 of the 51 contractors and farmers they inspected. Half of the vehicles checked lacked insurance and properly licensed drivers; there were safety infractions; and three housing providers were slapped with 52 citations. The year was capped off with a December 5 van accident near Las Cruces involving an unauthorized driver and resulting in serious injuries to several farmworkers.

The DOL issued hundreds of citations to 21 of the main chile labor contractors from 1986 to 1992. The charges were basically the same in many cases: not having a safe or inspected bus, employing nonregistered helpers, providing no work records, maintaining bad housing, or simply not possessing a license to operate as a federally registered labor contractor. One complaint, heard numerous times in additional instances, charged that the contractor did not "furnish each worker a written statement of payroll information which included the basis on which wages were paid; the number of piecework units earned if applicable; the number of hours worked; the total pay period earnings; the specific sums withheld and the purpose of each deduction; and the net pay for each period." In short, the contractor was accused of keeping the farmworkers in the dark about exactly how much they were owed.

One individual, operating in both the Rio Grande and Pecos river valleys, ran afoul of the DOL in both places and managed to compile 90 violations in about a five-year period. His rap sheet portrays a kind of catch-me-if-you-can, one-jump-ahead-of-the-law *modus operandi*, supported by the DOL's willingness to negotiate and accept fines for a previous citation paid on installment while simultaneously slapping him with yet

Tools of the Trade: Plastic buckets carried chile to the table.

another violation. In fact, some of his fines were reduced through the appeal process, a common practice of the government agency and one also taken advantage of by other employers who, like the roving chile contractor, were often still paying off (or ignoring paying at all) a previous offense when another bureaucratically worded notice of violation was delivered. The contractors' record of full compliance with other laws was also very spotty. For instance, the Internal Revenue Service determined that only 20 contractors on a 1991 list of 193 who were registered between the Rio Grande Valley of south Texas and southern New Mexico paid federal income tax, Medicare, and Social Security taxes.

A study prepared by Pamela J. Reynolds of the Community Services Bureau, a New Mexico state agency, in 1985, when OSHA field sanitation standards did not exist, found that a majority of 33 farms checked lacked bathrooms or handwashing facilities. Out of a total of 73 New Mexico state OSHA inspections between 1987 and 1992, after the field sanitation standards were adopted, only a few farms were found to be in full compliance with the law. Infractions ranged from no bathrooms to not supplying individual cups for drinking water. Many employers were repeat offenders, for which they were collectively fined a grand total of about $2,400—about the cost of growing an acre or two of chile. Whether through malice or simple confusion, some contractors continued to disobey the law. They did not have to worry about an OSHA safety inspector breathing down their necks, because the bureau had no office in the chile belt and only periodically dispatched an employee from Santa Fe for field duty. Since the DOL had authority not only to revoke licenses but also to jail offenders, critics wondered why it allowed what they claimed was a systematic law-

breaking operation to thrive. In addition, the agency had the power—though it never used it—to impound illegally produced "hot goods," in this instance literally and figuratively—chile.

From the perspective of more than a few employers, the DOL was nitpicking over conditions hard to meet in the circumstances of farm labor. The issue of labor law violations reached critical mass in 1990 and was the heated topic of two meetings in Las Cruces and El Paso that year. Workers and UTAF activists repeated their grievances. Farmers were upset at DOL investigations occurring in the middle of the chile harvest. Dino Cervantes decried a DOL bus roadblock that resulted in one labor shortage in a ripening field, preventing the delivery of the crop to the processor. If there were contractors disobeying the law, added Cervantes, they should be put out of business promptly without victimizing the farmer.

Angry contractors showed up at both meetings. Alberto Cigarroa denounced what he said were attempts to paint the crew leaders as outlaws. Pedro Valdez of Sunland Park claimed that workers were not making minimum wage because the farmers refused to pay more money. The growers, continued the contractor, were themselves "cheated" by chile processors who did not set weigh scales properly.

It was in this atmosphere that El Paso contractor John Gasper was hauled into court repeatedly by TRLA. Claiming he was under siege, Gasper held meetings with Deming chile farmers, Border Foods, and the Farm Bureau and convinced them to fork over thousands of dollars for his defense. In the eyes of Gasper, his hassles originated from his refusal to join in UTAF's early organizing efforts because he was more interested in earning a decent income to support his family. It was a blatant case of "reverse discrimination" he later said, brought about by the union's strategy to "knock that Anglo out" so that the remainder of the contractors would "buckle under us." The labor contractor likewise voiced resentment against DOL officers he said singled him out while ignoring other contractors' violations. Gasper's lawyers then went on the offensive, filing bankruptcy protection for him and appealing the decision to a circuit court in Louisiana. Gasper, in one bankruptcy petition later withdrawn, stated a 1991 income of $6,200 per month and expenditures that year of $30,000 for home furniture. "Financial ruin may be in the eyes of the beholder," said TRLA attorney Nancy Simmons.

Vega vs. Gasper gave the beleaguered contractor headaches, but his problems were only beginning. In a class action case filed in 1991, *Reséndez vs. Gasper*, plaintiffs sought damages for what they listed as a wholesale violation of federal law, including minimum wage, payroll records, nonreporting of taxes, and retaliation.

The suit arose from an incident on November 7, 1991, in a Deming chile field, when several workers got into a dispute with Gasper, claiming that he had brought them to a field full of rotting, white "ghost" chiles. "It would have been impossible to pick more than one bucket of chile per hour," charged a plaintiff. "I have been a chile picker for over 10 years," stated José Contreras Molina in an affidavit. "I know what kind of chiles are good and bad and I also know how well the harvest will be. I realized, as well as my coworkers, that this was a bad field." The dissidents demanded to be taken back to El Paso but Gasper refused. Some workers alleged that "El Johnny," as Gasper was nicknamed, physically struck other pickers and his bus drivers forced people to work. The refuseniks walked at least nine miles, in two groups, to Deming. One of the

workers called Olga Pedroza at CLC, who contacted lawyer Carlos Ogden in Deming to arrange a taxi ride back to El Paso.

Gasper's attorneys responded that the complaint was a "union conspiracy," that their client offered to raise the price per bucket, was rebuffed, and promised to transport the workers back to El Paso at the end of the picking day. Gasper was incensed that lawyer Carlos Ogden was the same attorney who had assisted him with getting amnesty for former illegals. A year later, on November 17, 1992, a bus owned by John Gasper was cruising down Interstate 10 in El Paso after completing a day of red chile picking on a farm run by Martin Sweetser in Deming. As the bus approached the Sunland Park overpass, the light turned red, and the driver attempted to stop, pumping what he quickly discovered were nonworking brakes. The bus hit the front of a 1991 Geo Prizm driven by 18-year-old Lisa Marie Hernández, and it narrowly missed flipping over the guardrail onto the humming traffic below, throwing workers from their seats, injuring 13 (including nine taken to the hospital), and scattering red chiles on the ground.

TRLA attorneys filed suit against both Gasper and Sweetser, seeking to collect more than $500,000 in damages for medical and emotional compensation and for not paying the minimum wage or keeping accurate payroll records. In their affidavits, plaintiffs described a difficult enough time in the fields even before the crash. For example, the declaration of 63-year-old Antonio Hernández Soria noted that the chile they were picking was spicy and many workers were sneezing. Of the collision, farmworker Manuel Sánchez Cortez said: "I tried to hold onto the seat, but fell out when the bus flipped, hurt my calf and head and my elbow. I still have a headache, my neck hurts, and my elbow and calf still hurt." The driver was recorded in the *El Paso Herald Post* as saying "I had complained to Mr. Gasper about the brakes, and they said they were going to get them fixed." Gasper in turn charged the young man with taking the bus without his permission. "Don't touch the bus," he claimed he told the young man.

At the time of the disaster, Gasper was not licensed to operate as a farm labor contractor, his authorization finally having been pulled by the U.S. Department of Labor a couple of months earlier. It had taken 13 years of mounting citations for the DOL to act. According to a 1991 statement by DOL regional administrator Bill Belt, the agency had assessed more than $8,500 in fines against the El Paso crew leader, citing him in six separate cases for not having safe transportation, lacking adequate insurance coverage, employing undocumented workers, hiring unregistered farm labor contractor assistants, keeping incomplete or inaccurate records, and not posting the legal terms of employment. And all of this was long before the November 1992 wreck.

Although Gasper had won delays or victories in several cases (a judge ordered TRLA to pay attorney fees to Gasper for improperly using information from bankruptcy court in legal proceedings against the contractor and TRLA appealed), by 1993 he was clearly a man under strain. His law firm in the Meléndez case had severed ties. Bills piled up. He blamed his misfortunes on the machinations of TRLA and UTAF, emphasizing that the El Paso legal services branch was "like a snake, they're like a leech, if you beat them they get furious." A perplexed Gasper could not understand the charges levied against him as "an abuser of Mexicans." He had spent $11,000 from his own pocket, he said, to win amnesty for 156 workers, had always made up the difference to equal minimum wage

if an old worker could not pick piece rate, for a while was the only contractor paying into unemployment insurance, and all his children were "half-Mexican and half-Italian." What was more, he was a single parent trying to raise seven daughters. "I don't know what's on their pea-pickin' minds, but it grinds," complained Gasper. According to the former labor contractor, he had spent more than $100,000 in 10 years defending himself, lost two houses, had his name soiled by bad press, and even been "left out to hang" by the Farm Bureau, which stopped their financial aid.

Characterizing TRLA's charges as "bullshit," Gasper added that "it cost me thousands to prove these people are assholes." The end result, sighed Gasper, was that he had "beat all the battles and lost the war." "They broke my ass," he concluded, "you gotta have money to fight these people. I'll be out on the goddamn street homeless. They ain't gonna stop until they put me in jail . . . I don't believe what's happened. I should be on *60 Minutes*."

But Gasper had Mark Schneider, the quick-spoken TRLA lawyer in El Paso, steaming mad. According to Schneider, Gasper had "cooked the books," maintaining two sets of records for the same payroll, and having had no bank accounts to account for his finances. The TRLA attorney characterized Gasper's stance as an example of "cry-babyism by people who are violating the law." Schneider's goal was to "try to put him in jail as an example." In the final analysis, Schneider did not entirely lay the blame for labor law-breaking on the purported connivance of Gasper or fellow *contratistas*, since in every "load there were people not getting minimum wage."

The real problem, in his mind, was that processors were not paying farmers enough and were giving incentives for cost-cutting measures and low bidding by the contractors for each job.

This led to a squeeze on profit margins that inevitably fell on the backs of workers. It was as if the chile production system was designed to relegate people to poverty. "It's an incredible system," opined Schneider, "and I think when people eat chile and salsa around the country, you know word is gonna' get out that chile just doesn't have this exotic, sexy taste of the Southwest and mariachis and Mexican beer, it's really flavored with the workers' suffering . . ."

Political strife led to a shake-up in the El Paso TRLA office in the summer of 1993, culminating in Schneider's removal from the Gasper case, and the embattled contractor's luck improved when the farmworker legal group offered to settle three lawsuits filed against him. With the lawsuits behind him, Gasper went on his own offensive, seeking to recover money he claimed processors owed him for back harvests and legal fees. Then when the New Mexico Farm Bureau hailed an October 1994 decision in the Fifth U.S. Court of Appeals that threw out Judge Bunton's ruling in the *Gasper vs. Vega* case holding Gasper liable for payment of travel time to and from the chile fields, instead of bringing out the champagne glasses Gasper questioned the reason for celebration. A letter from El Paso Farm Bureau attorney Scott A. Agthe thanked Gasper for his "cooperation and assistance in overturning Judge Bunton's erroneous decision," but reminded him that since he had been released from further liabilities as a result of his out-of-court settlements, Agthe's firm would no longer represent him. "I won for the farmers . . . and I got payed [sic] back by ruining me," fulminated Gasper. From then on, John Gasper stayed out of the chile rows.

In the fields, very high transportation insurance costs levied on contractors drove many buses from the highways. Chile pickers paid $3 to $5 in gas money to hitch rides in converted minibuses, vans, trucks, and cars—yet another deduction from a shrinking paycheck. UTAF demanded the elimination of the labor contract system and its replacement with direct contracts between growers and workers.

Farm Bureau Vice-President Bob Porter, for one, was not thrilled with the legal hullabaloo, regardless of occasional, important victories like the one gained in the Fifth Court of Appeals. He lashed out against TRLA and CLC, criticizing the two agencies for sending vague letters to farmers filled with "unsubstantiated allegations" and "threats" only to follow up with offers to settle out of court. In spite of Porter's invective, Farm Bureau members attempted to reach at least a modicum of understanding with the legal services groups. Eddy County members invited CLC attorney Pedroza to a meeting in Carlsbad, New Mexico, to speak on labor law. It was a short-lived truce, however.

In July 1993, Pedroza filed a lawsuit against the Workers' Compensation Administration of New Mexico on the grounds that not requiring mandatory inclusion of farmworkers under workers' compensation constituted discrimination and a violation of the equal protection clause of the U.S. Constitution affecting a whole class of people, who in this case were Mexican-born laborers. The Farm Bureau blasted the suit, asserting that most farmers already had private liability insurance covering workers in the event of an accident. The CLC retorted that such insurance required a lawsuit to prove employer culpability, whereas workers' compensation was a no-fault, easier-to-obtain solution. Later, the CLC's suit was thrown out of court on the grounds that the farmworker legal advocates could not show that the New Mexico State Legislature intentionally discriminated against

Mexicans when it excluded agricultural laborers from workers' compensation

It was not the best of times for the once-bustling Las Cruces legal activist center. Like other legal services providers, CLC fell prey to Newt Gingrich's 1995 Contract with America. By 1996 the office suffered a one-third budget cut and was restricted from pursuing class-action lawsuits. Attorney Pedroza watched her staff disappear into thin air and, with them, the ability to proactively pursue cases. Hampered by the budgetary and legal constraints, she was reduced to handling a few walk-in cases. "What I don't do is go down to the bridge [El Paso], because I can pick up 30 cases," she lamented.

For former 1993 workers' compensation case plaintiff Macedonia Luna, it was a simple matter of justice denied. Injured in a 1992 fall in an onion field, he was having trouble picking chile and paying the bills. His experiences certainly were not unique in the chile or other agricultural industries: it was one of the country's most dangerous occupations. This fact was hard for urban folk, who sometimes held an idyllic impression of country life, to comprehend. But the work of getting food to the nation's population was a risky job that involved cuts from tools, scrapes with machinery, bouts with the weather and insects, and the hazards of chemical pesticides.

Notes

1. John Gasper, interview by author, El Paso, TX, September 1993.

2. Voluntary Petition for Bankruptcy (Chapter 13), 17 April 1992, U.S. Bankruptcy Court, Western District of Texas; Meléndez, et al. vs. Martin Sweetser and John Gasper, United States District Court, Las Cruces, NM.

3. Martin Sánchez and Mark Schneider, Texas Rural Legal Aid, interviews by author, El Paso, TX, September 1992 and June 1993.

4. Amy Boardman, "The New Mexico Chile Fields War," *Texas Lawyer*, 3 June 1991, 1, 24.

5. Ismael Camacho, interviews by author, Las Cruces, NM, September 1986 and May 1992.

6. Olga Pedroza, interviews by author, Las Cruces, NM, 1991-93.

7. Donna Snyder, Centro Legal Campesino, interview by author, Las Cruces, NM, August 1993.

8. *New Mexico Farm and Ranch*, October 1968, 8; December 1968, 8-10; May 1971, 15; December 1971, NMFLB Resolutions.

9. Erik Ness, interview by author, Las Cruces, NM, September 1986

10. Joel Cruz and Joe Romero, Centro Legal Campesino, interviews by author, Las Cruces, NM, December 1985 and September 1986; *Los Angeles Times*, 18 November 1985. Ruth Marcus, "Pending Nominations Have Legal Services at Crossroads," *Washington Post*, reprint in *Albuquerque Journal*, 1 September 1989.

11. Orlando Cervantes, interview by author, Vado, NM, September 1986.

12. Dr. Clyde Eastman, NMSU, interviews by author, Las Cruces and Albuquerque, NM, July-August 1993.

13. Camarina Ballarso, interview by author, Las Cruces, NM, February 1993.

14. Court decisions, e.g., Hodgson v. Okada, 472 F.2d 965 (10th Cir. 1973), cited in Memorandum of Opinion and Order Jesús Antúnez et al. vs. G&C Farms Inc., Gary Riggs and Demetrio Alaniz, U.S. District Court for the District of New Mexico, Howard C. Bratton, Judge.

15. Debra Smith, telephone conversation with author, September 1986.

16. Kent Paterson, "Farmworkers," *Coatimundi*, Summer 1987, 20.

17. Carlos Marentes, interviews by author, El Paso, TX, December 1985 and September 1986; Rhodes/Galarza Step Narrative, R. Anaya, Compliance Officer, U.S. Department of Labor, Wage and Hour Division, El Paso, TX, 18 November 1983.

18. Nora Lozoya, USDOL Dallas office, telephone conversation with author, September 1986; Carlos Marentes, letter to Joseph A. Wysong, Asst. Area Director, U.S. Department of Labor, Wage and Hour Division, El Paso, TX, 5 October 1989.

19. Hernández et al. vs. James Franzoy, Gabriel Galarza and Zeferino Sánchez Rodríguez, U.S. District Court Western District of Texas, El Paso Division, 1985.

20. Barbara Urrutia, interview by author, El Paso, TX, December 1985.

21. Zeferino Sánchez Rodríguez, interview by author, El Paso, TX, December 1985.

22. Ricardo Anaya, interview by author, El Paso, TX, September 1986.

23. "Assessments in Farm Labor Strike Forces," USDOL document released to author under Freedom of Information Act, 11 December 1990; Diana Peterson, USDOL-Dallas public relations, telephone conversation with author, November 1990; Bill Diven, "Feds Investigating Driver of Accident Vehicle," *Albuquerque Journal*, 7 December 1990; USDOL violation notices, penalty assessments, and payback schedules for 21 labor contractors in Texas and New Mexico, documents released to author under FOIA, 1994.

24. Pamela J. Reynolds, *Farmworker Field Sanitation Study*, Community Services Bureau, State of New Mexico, 15 November 1985.

25. New Mexico State OSHA, New Mexico Environment Department, records of inspections, 1987-92; Karen Wade, NM State OSHA, interview by author, Santa Fe, NM, May 1993; Dennis Ozment, Internal Revenue Service presentation, New Mexico Chile Conference, Las Cruces, NM, February 1993; Lynda McDevitt, IRS, letter to author, 21 September 1993.

26. "Minutes of the November 15, 1990, Meeting of the West Texas-New Mexico Migrant Coordinating Committee"; annual public meeting minutes, 13 December 1990, El Paso, TX; USDOL documents released to author under FOIA.

27. Reséndez vs. John W. Gasper, U.S. District Court for the District of New Mexico, Las Cruces, NM, 1991; Meléndez et al. vs. Martin Sweetser and John W. Gasper, U.S. District Court for the District of New Mexico, Las Cruces, NM, 1992; *El Paso Herald Post*, 19 November 1992; *El Paso Times*, 19 November 1992.

28. John Gasper, telephone conversation with author, October 1994.

29. "New Mexico Farmers Score Major Victory in Labor Arena," NMFLB press release, 26 October 1994.

30. Scott A. Agthe, letter to John Gasper, 28 October 1994.

31. John W. Gasper, letter to author, 31 October 1994.

32. Bob Porter, presentation, New Mexico Chile Conference, Las Cruces, NM, February 1993.

33. Erik Ness, "Eddy County hears from Legal Services attorneys at a packed meeting," *New Mexico Farm and Ranch*, January 1993.

34. *The Courier* (Hatch, NM), 5 August 1993.

35. Macedonia Luna, interview by author, Anthony, NM, September 1993.

36. *Agriculture at Risk: A Report to the Nation*, 3d ed. (Iowa City: National Coalition for Agricultural Safety and Health, 1989), 1-5.

37. Olga Pedroza, interview by author, Las Cruces, NM, August 1998.

Peppery Paradoxes

16

Pesticide Black Market ▪ DDT Mystery ▪ Hell's Angels Crop Dusters ▪ Eco-Nazis ▪ Invasion of the Pepper Weevil

For decades, Fred Harris played a big role in the success of southern New Mexico agriculture. The proprietor of Farmer's Market and Supply in Hatch, a business he took over from the late Clayborn Wayne in 1983, Harris sold and applied fertilizers and pesticides. A frank man, he did not come across as a knee-jerk defender of agricultural chemicals, and in fact he had more than his share of troubles with the pesticides that did not always work the way the manufacturer intended.

In his time, he had a $35,000 lawsuit filed against him because a farmer claimed that Harris's insecticide did not kill lettuce worms; he had been contacted by a lawyer for a Derry grower who was forced to plow up three acres of chile supposedly damaged by a faulty Farmer's Market pesticide application; and he had been questioned by the New Mexico Department of Agriculture for dumping old pesticide barrels at the Hatch airport, an action Harris said was the fault of a crop-dusting partner who did not make

him privy to his plans. Nevertheless, like the true-blue loyalist to his profession he was, Harris was needled by dyed-in-the-wool environmentalists and others who wanted right-to-know provisions put on the books. And while conceding that the "César Chávezes of the world have done a lot of good," he thought farmworker campaigns to ban or restrict pesticides were overblown. Personal experience taught him better, he said.

Long before he spent his days assisting customers over the phone or from behind the austere counter at his downtown Hatch storefront, Harris was a field man, an individual who is the eyes of the crop duster from the ground, guiding the chemical-carrying pilot to the target below. He did this day in and day out, checking the plane's coordinates from behind a stream of parathion and never getting sick. One day his firm sprayed a field with parathion about 100 yards from where a group of field laborers was toiling. "All of a sudden the people got so sick they couldn't see straight, when the fact of the matter was that every one of them—we proved it—was drunk, had come back to work so stinking drunk that they couldn't see straight, and they were vomiting because of the fact that they were carrying a great big hangover."

Harris, nevertheless, was getting out of the application end of the business because insurance rates were skyrocketing, partly because of farmer lawsuits against pest-control specialists for damaging crops or for not alleviating a problem as promised, a situation Harris explained was sometimes actually due to the chemical itself and not the user. It was better to sell the formulations and let others take the liability risks, he concluded.

Harris was not alone in his troubles. In 1986 Pecos Valley chile growers damaged their crop with the herbicide Dual, sparking lawsuits. Counterparts in the Mesilla Valley reported no such troubles, but the pesticide manufacturer made further usage contingent upon farmers' signing a waiver of liability. The Hatch pesticide dealer felt pressured on other fronts as well. The mid-1980s was a time of sharp national debate over the continued use of large amounts of agricultural chemicals on the nation's food supply, and the reverberations of this policy conflict reached into the chile-growing valleys of south-ern New Mexico. Pesticides were a charged, emotional issue, with concerns centering around possible groundwater contamination, bee kills, contamination of foods, and worker exposure.

Battle lines were drawn. On one side were groups like the Farm Bureau and the National Agricultural Chemicals Association, which defended pesticides as vital for the productivity of American agriculture. On the other were environmentalists and farm labor organizations calling for stricter controls or phaseouts of substances whose long-term ecological and health effects were still not known in many cases. Doña Ana farmworker María Martínez exemplified the worker side of the issue. A former domestic worker from Torreón, Coahuila, Mexico, Martínez snuck across the border in 1985 and gravitated to the chile and onion fields, one of the few occupations open to her, she believed, because of her lack of schooling. For a time, she was pulled off buses by *migra* agents, trekked the mountains of Cristo Rey, and lived in the Las Uvas fields before settling in at a small Doña Ana apartment where warmly colored pictures and a stereo enlivened the interior. Once, remembered Martínez, she was working in a Doña Ana lettuce field with 30 to 35 other people when a spraying rig moved through the rows, spreading an insecticide.

"We all began to feel sick, the grasshoppers started to die. We told the contractor, 'Can't we stop for a half hour or an hour?'" said Martínez. "But he didn't want to pay us for that hour. We needed [the money], we continued working. I vomited—the men can take it better than the women. I felt sick, but we didn't stop." Besides, Martínez, like others, was "accustomed" to the use of chemicals, particularly in lettuce but also in chile. Another time Martínez was in a Rincon sweet potato field when an overflying plane dumped chemicals near the workers. "It was falling on us," she described. In neither case did Martínez see a doctor, first because she had no money and second because she was afraid of losing work.

Incidents like the ones reported by Martínez are not supposed to happen. The Environmental Protection Agency (EPA) labels each chemical, spelling out under which conditions it should be used. But the regulations become useless when they are ignored or when users go so far as to experiment with chemicals not approved by the authorities. From time to time, enforcement officials have investigated the goings on of the pesticide black market. For example, in 1989 the New Mexico Department of Agriculture put a stop-sale, use, or removal order on 750 pounds of granular carbofuran owned by a Roswell farmer. According to the NMDA report to the EPA, the insecticide was part of a batch distributed to Pecos Valley farmers by an unlicensed applicator.

The year 1984 in particular was a busy one for authorities. It picked up steam in April, when the U.S. Customs Service in Albuquerque detained a package mailed from France to New Mexico Vintners, a remote vineyard in the dry country near Elephant Butte Reservoir. Upon inspection, the parcel was found to contain Simazine, a herbicide not registered for use in the United States. One package was leaking. Alerted to the contraband by the EPA, NMDA inspector Gary Laswell embarked on a weeks-long paper chase to determine who owned the vineyard and who sent the illicit package.

Not getting very far, he drove up to the vineyard with U.S. Customs inspector Jim Hughes. The pair encountered Roger Morel, to whom the package had been addressed, and Patrice Cheurelin, the son of the vineyard's owner. Both denied knowing about the package and signed sworn affidavits to the EPA to that effect. In his report, Laswell surmised that Jacques Cheurelin, the owner, had most likely mailed the herbicide to New Mexico.

Around the same time that Laswell and Hughes were tracking down the Simazine senders, another NMDA inspector, Vince Peña, received a report that an illegal chemical was being used on chile crops near Deming. Peña's probe paid off a year later when farmer Darrell McCauley and applicator By-Ag Air Inc. admitted using Thimet, a pesticide used in the past on cotton but not registered for chile peppers. NMDA suspended By-Ag's license for three months and McCauley, a former Young Farmer of the Year, was handed a warning letter and ordered to accept temporary FDA monitoring of his crop. The 1985 crop was tested, no residues of Thimet were discovered and McCauley was given official permission to ship the chiles to market.

In September 1984, a story broke in the *El Paso Herald Post* about recent, alleged use of the banned pesticide DDT on an Anderson family chile farm in Hatch under contract to Old El Paso. Reporter Susan Benesch "lifted" pod samples from the field and from the Hatch airport and had them tested by University of Texas at

El Paso professor Howard Applegate, who announced that high levels of DDT and a breakdown product, DDE, showed up in the samples. Concerned by the report, Old El Paso and the farmer asked NMDA to conduct their own investigation. The agency complied but did not find DDT residues in its own samples. NMDA blithely concluded that Benesch had served as "an unwilling dupe" in the farmworkers' union publicity campaign. But rains had washed the chile field between the time of Benesch's samplings and NMDA's and unnamed scientists quoted in her story—supported by Applegate later on—postulated that heavy rains could have washed away the DDT. Applegate himself had no immediate explanation for the discrepancy between the samples tested by himself and NMDA.

Several federal and state agencies joined together in the DDT hunt. Traces of the chemical were detected by NMDA in southern Otero County, quite a distance from Hatch, and the Texas Department of Agriculture reported there was some evidence of possible recent DDT applications around Dell City near the Texas-New Mexico border. The DDT mystery was never resolved and higher-than-expected levels of the chemical in soil and animals cropped up in the Southwest well into the 1990s. Observers offered several explanations. Some suspected that migratory birds returning from Latin America, where the product was still employed, were bringing residues with them back to the north where it had been outlawed. Others theorized that DDT took much longer to break down in the environment than originally believed. And some held that perhaps DDT was being smuggled in from Mexico, though this could not be confirmed.

Notwithstanding periodic illegal uses, routine troubles arose from airborne pesticide drift.

Experts pointed out that even under the best of conditions, chemicals strayed from their targets. This phenomenon drew greater attention as different crops requiring different pesticides were planted near each other, as more field hands arrived in agriculture, and as urbanization spread to country fields. In 1986-87 California officials destroyed some of that state's chile because it contained a chemical used to defoliate nearby cotton fields that did not have a parallel approval for chile. A New Mexico chile processor worried that similar drift-induced residues might cause its product to be confiscated in California, too. Meetings were held between the NMDA and chile growers, but it was decided to permit the use of defoliants near chile fields anyway.

Sometimes, apparent carelessness was the reason for drift, as NMDA reports to the EPA between 1983 and 1989 indicated. Marc Osman, the proprietor of Rio Ag Inc., a Mesilla Valley aerial applicator, was a familiar face to the NMDA. In the spring of 1986, Osman's pesticide-laden plane sputtered and crashed near Mesquite while carrying a load of Guthion. The pilot was lucky, escaping the fate of 33-year-old James Strickland, killed 26 years earlier just to the south in Berino when his onion-spraying aircraft hit telephone wires, caught fire, and exploded, frying the unfortunate crop duster. A recovered Osman took to the skies again, and in September was defoliating cotton near La Union. This prompted a call to the NMDA by local resident Ruth Herrera, who complained of a strong smell. Vince Peña checked this out and exonerated the applicator, finding "no violations on Mr. Osman's part, and he was not careless or negligent. The chemical has a strong odor and is obnoxious to some people. Mr. Peña's conclusion was that farming and country living are not always compatible," said the NMDA report.

But trouble continued to dog Osman. In 1987 Rio Ag had pesticide drift on two men working on Josie Bazán's Anthony property and applied too much Nudrin to Carl Nakayama's onions, causing the vegetables to turn brown. Up the valley in Radium Springs, Rio Ag's over-flights of John Peterson's house culminated in a confrontation in which Peterson waved a shot-gun at a company plane. "The pilots around here are like the Hell's Angels," later remarked Peterson, an ex-pilot himself.

Another southern New Mexico aerial appli-cator wracked up a record equal to Rio Ag's. A year after confessing to applying an unregistered chemical on McCauley's chile, By-Ag was in the Mesilla Valley substituting for the grounded Osman following his crash. One day the princi-pal of the La Union elementary school, which was still in session, contacted the NMDA to protest the spraying of a nearby field during school hours. At least three other complaints of By-Ag's practices were made by Deming resi-dents, who said planes flew close to their homes. But By-Ag's crowning violation was yet to come.

In the summer of 1989, U.S. Department of Labor inspectors Ricardo Anaya and Clay Gibson were checking the labor situation in a field near Vado. Suddenly a By-Ag plane flew overhead and sprayed the two men and a crew of farmworkers with pesticide. No serious illnesses were reported, but Gibson and Anaya filed a complaint. Subsequent NMDA enforcement action resulted in the suspension of By-Ag owner Albert Yates's license for six months.

If the antics of Rio Ag and By-Ag caused consternation in rural quarters, misuse and mis-applications of pesticides in New Mexico chile fields still had not reached the degree found in other sections of the country. Not that every-thing was always fine, but on a comparative basis,

fewer chemicals were needed for chile. For instance, in 1983 about 32 percent of planted chile acreage used insecticides as compared to 55 percent for cotton and 86 percent for alfalfa hay. Ironically, chile was applied as an insecticide for other crops in Africa. New Mexico farmers seemed unaware of this use.

Agricultural poisons and then chemicals had always been an element in the chile grower's plan. In the early days, tobacco was mixed with soap for a sudsy, aphid-eradicating solution. Calcium arsenate was tried on weevils. Then chemicals like DDT and toxaphene were har-nessed. The organophosphates and carbamates followed. Farmers counted on substances such as parathion and carbofuran to kill thrips and nematodes, Treflar to control weeds, Ethephon to hasten the ripening of chile to red, and Copper Kocide to eliminate fungus. "I wouldn't let my bird dog in the field," cautioned Dr. Emory Shannon to a group of growers in 1992, while giving a talk on the fungicide.

The chemicals varied in toxic strength from high to low, with the potential for adverse health effects ranging from short-term acute symptoms of dizziness and headaches to possible cancer from long-term exposure in the case of parathion. Some, like carbofuran or nitrate-based fertilizers, were a groundwater contaminant in other states and in parts of New Mexico.

The realization that chemicals beneficial to food production might also be polluting the water supply of future generations stirred the EPA into mandating state groundwater protec-tion policies. The Farm Bureau jumped on board and announced its willingness to cooper-ate with the NMDA and other authorities in keeping the water tables clean and healthy. The New Mexico Environment Department, funded by an EPA grant, began investigating water quality in the Rio Grande and Pecos valleys. Wells and drainage canals were sampled, and the initial reports were encouraging. Up to this point, New Mexico had apparently escaped the severe pesticide-induced poisoning of groundwater experienced by other states, but Environment Department field staffer Kitty Richards was cautious in her optimism.

A consumer movement on pesticides also emerged in the 1980s, sparking ample controversy over food safety. To some extent, the specific concern with chile was unaddressed. A very limited pesticide sampling program was undertaken in New Mexico, and the number of samples was too small to get an accurate picture. But lest people think they were ingesting unsafe New Mexican-grown chile, it should be noted again that fewer chemicals had been used on this crop in the past than on others and there were no reports of large-scale consumer poisonings such as occurred on the West Coast in 1985 when hundreds fell ill after eating watermelons tainted with aldicarb.

At the greatest risk were those who applied the chemicals and especially the farmworkers who labored in the fields after they had been treated. Officials at the New Mexico Occupational Health and Safety Bureau and La Clínica de Familia, a federally funded farmworker health clinic located a stone's throw from the massive Stahmann Farm pecan orchards in the Mesilla Valley, reported that their staff had witnessed or heard about worker exposures, but nobody really knew the true nature of the problem in New Mexico. That was because New Mexico, unlike some other states, did not require physicians to report incidences of pesticide poisoning. Also contributing to the information gap were two other factors. First, many doctors were not trained to distinguish pesticide-related symptoms from the general symptoms they resembled. Second, farmworkers were reluctant to report exposures.

"What we're recognizing is low-dose exposure. People are working in the fields and getting it on their hands," said Dr. Frank Crespin, the former medical director of La Clínica. "The problem is there—it's just real hard to sort out. Nobody knows the long-term effects."

A few workers had accounts to share. El Paso farmworker Pedro Melero was picking red chile at a farm owned by Mesilla Valley farmer Ignacio Bustamante in October of 1987 when he developed rashes and became ill. Melero suffered burns on his feet and difficulties with his circulatory system. He initially sought treatment from a Juárez doctor and tried to get compensation from Bustamante, who refused. The chile farmer admitted using a chemical on the farm (he could not remember which one) but insisted that Melero was already sick before the alleged exposure occurred. The 56-year-old Melero, claiming he was unable to work due to the injury, attempted to find a lawyer since he could not file for automatic workers' compensation because farmworkers were not covered under New Mexico law.

Another El Paso picker, Pedro Gonzales, reported direct exposure from pesticide drift. In the fall of 1989, Gonzales was employed by John Gasper in the Deming chile harvest. One day he and several coworkers were overcome by fumes from a nearby crop duster. "I was vomiting and feeling dizzy but didn't say anything," Gonzales said, adding that he and his companions neglected medical attention for fear of losing their jobs. Cases like Melero's and Gonzales's prompted calls for tougher enforcement of pesticide usage. Critics charged that the NMDA, the agency charged with enforcing EPA pesticide law, had a

The Pesticide Controversy: Farmworkers at a 1994 pesticide-awareness training in Hatch, New Mexico.

conflict of interest resulting from its promoting pesticide use while at the same time being responsible for going after lawbreakers. The department had six inspectors to cover the entire state, and in 1987 it left one position open, reporting a budget surplus to EPA, from which it received most of its pesticide program funding.

"More people have to be used to monitor the use of pesticides in New Mexico and the general condition of agriculture in rural communities," asserted UTAF's Carlos Marentes. "There are a lot of problems—health problems—due to the lack of enforcement of laws and regulations in New Mexico." A 1988 report by the Renew America Project, a Washington, DC-based environmental group, gave New Mexico a

failing grade for its pesticide protection programs. The state did not require physician reporting, did not require farmers to post warning signs in sprayed fields, and did not have farmworker training or right-to-know provisions like neighboring Texas.

NMDA personnel tended to shrug their shoulders at the criticism and pointed out that much of the misuse actually occurred in urban settings where careless homeowners and unlicensed, fly-by-night pest exterminators proliferated. NMDA pesticide enforcement chief Barry Patterson acknowledged frustration over the legal inability of his department to levy civil fines against pesticide law violators (they had to be brought before backlogged courts), and he planned to request from the New Mexico State Legislature the authority to do so. As for farmworker protection, Patterson was waiting for the EPA to act. The federal agency was in the process of issuing updated national standards, which were expected to extend reentry times (the amount of time after an application before it is presumed safe to enter a treated field) on a number of chemicals, require field posting, and provide more training and protective gear for applicators.

The EPA's rulemaking involved an oft-criticized, 13-year odyssey that began in the latter half of the Carter Administration and ended just before George Bush was voted out of office. In 1985 the agency experimented with what it called "negotiated rulemaking," a consensus-building approach that invited the national Farm Bureau, the chemical industry, and labor advocates to forge common ground. Less than a year later, farmworker representatives led by the UFW and the Farm Labor Organizing Committee stalked out of the meetings, accusing the EPA of not seriously considering their demands for a ban on the most dangerous chemicals.

The EPA moved ahead on its own, but the pace of reform stalled because of staff turnover, limited resources to handle the hundreds of comments pouring in to Washington, and the entanglement of George Bush's and Dan Quayle's White House in determining whether the new rules were burdensome to industry. New standards were finally issued in 1992, but analysts such as former Texas Department of Agriculture pesticide official Ellen Widess wondered how effective they would be in the absence of vastly increased funding for enforcement purposes.

In the interim, farm laborers in New Mexico and elsewhere suffered pesticide exposures. Thousands of cases were medically documented

in California alone between 1982 and 1987, mainly in grape pickers. By the EPA's own estimates, 300,000 farmworkers a year were exposed to pesticides. How many of these cases could have been averted had the EPA moved sooner is something that will never be known. Gradually the tide shifted toward less pesticide use—at least in spirit. The EPA cancelled some products (new ones came on the market), tighter restrictions were slapped on others, and biological controls were researched at NMSU and other schools. A state-funded New Mexico Organics Commodity Commission was created in 1991, stamping the official seal of approval on the concept of pesticide-free produce. Commercial chile growers were slow to make the change as going organic would necessitate an expensive transition, but a few tested the waters. In 1993 the Biad Chile Company announced a 60-acre organic chile farm in Hidalgo County.

The new buzzword in pest elimination was Integrated Pest Management, a broadly interpreted methodology that combined sensible growing practices and natural predator controls with judicious pesticide usage. In New Mexico, the participation of NMSU in such projects represented a subtle yet significant shift from just a few years before, when, beset by philosophical disputes, an Integrated Pest Management task force set up by then-Governor Toney Anaya failed to move forward.

All was not smooth sailing. The new measures served to renew and widen debates over the efficacy of chemical versus nonchemical controls. And old hands in the pest control business worried that overzealous federal measures would strip the chile farmer and others of tried-and-true weapons in their ongoing battle against pestilence. In December of 1991 NMDA pesticide chief Barry Patterson warned farmers at the New Mexico Farm and Livestock Bureau convention of dangers emanating from know-nothing bureaucrats in the EPA. The agency had been filled with eastern university, liberal arts graduates, typically women, unversed in the needs of agriculture. There were "eco-Nazis" among them, he declared, bent on dictating agriculture's policies. The most dangerous man in America today, said Patterson, was "Henry Habicht III," a prototype EPA deputy administrator caricatured in a drawing handed out by Patterson as being an impatient, fist-pounding, desk-bound autocrat sporting a Hitleresque mustache. If current EPA policy trends continued, forewarned the NMDA official, the agricultural industry would pack up and go to Mexico, where there was less control on pesticides.

Ironically, it was a Mexican connection that put pest management strategies in the chile fields to a test in the early 1990s—the pepper weevil. In reality, the pepper weevil was an old pest in chile, neither Mexican nor North American properly speaking. It was reported decades ago in California and as far back as the 1920s in New Mexico. But the Land of Enchantment's chile fields had been free of the weevil scourge in recent memory, enjoying a respite from the periodic infestations suffered elsewhere. A tiny, long-beaked creature which, if magnified in 3-D, would make a great rival for Godzilla in any grade-B flick, the pepper-loving weevil had been on an eating binge in Mexico and up for snacks in Florida, Texas, and other locales. The insect was indiscriminate in its chile preferences. Jalapeños, serranos, bells, and any other capsicum in its path were fair game for tasting, their half-eaten pods left in field rows.

In August 1992, a field man for a chile processing company was checking things out in the mid-Mesilla Valley when he stumbled upon a weevil-infested plant. He immediately contacted the NMDA, and staff were dispatched to comb pepper land for the incorrigible weevil. The miniature monsters popped up in Doña Ana, Luna, and Chávez counties—the heart of the empire. Alarm bells went off and several hundred acres were sprayed. The season passed and no further serious outbreaks were logged. NMDA ordered an early plow-down of picked chile fields so that weevil larvae could not survive in the debris, while farmers crossed their fingers and held their breaths, happy that a cold New Mexican winter would finish off any surviving warm-weather-loving weevils.

In the midst of the uncertainty, the top weevil expert in the United States, Dr. David Riley of the Texas A&M Agricultural Experiment Station in Weslaco, arrived in chile country. He told eager listeners at the 1993 Chile Conference that cultural controls were key to stopping or limiting outbreaks. This meant not planting other weevil-attracting plants like nightshade next to chile, quickly getting rid of plant stalks or leftover residues after harvest, and closely monitoring the fields for signs of the pest. If all else failed, chemicals were the final solution, but only at a certain time when the adult weevils were on the outside of the plant. Riley's words were hardly off his lips when New Mexico experienced another weevil problem, this time months before the 1993 harvest.

The hardy creatures, hitchhiking on winter chile imports from Mexico, were turning up in great quantities in the New Mexico stores by the spring. NMDA inspectors were stretched thin, examining produce outlets, supermarkets, and warehouse distributors in Albuquerque, Roswell, Las Cruces, Truth or Consequences, and other cities. When the tell-tale sign of adult weevils or larvae was detected—BB-sized holes in the pod or brownish caps—owners were told to destroy the lot or send it back to the shipper.

Personnel at an El Paso inspection station admitted to frequently observing weevils, but they were powerless to act. That left action up to the states. The NMDA approached the USDA to see if the feds could stop the weevil at the border. Farmers were worried. But the answer was no. The weevil was classified a "cosmopolitan pest," long-established in the United States, and the USDA had no legal authority to quarantine the insect at the border. Hoping to resolve the issue, the NMDA wrote a letter to Mike Espy, Clinton's new Secretary of Agriculture. In June 1993, the NMDA hosted a weevil-scouting school to train the participants in field identification of the bugs. The New Mexico Chile Commission donated the funds for weevil traps. If hot spots were pinpointed, a chemical arsenal awaited. Guthion, Asana, Lannate, and other potent insecticides were recommended as the final—or at least the seasonal—solution.

On July 21, 1993, just days before the first green chile pickings, the bad news arrived. The NMDA announced that three weevil infested fields had been located in the southern Mesilla Valley. Days later, more were added to the list, including two in Deming. In mid-August the Department quarantined the entire Mesilla Valley and part of Luna County. Farmers plagued by weevils were ordered to plow up or spray over the field. Growers were worried, not having experienced an outbreak of this kind in their lifetimes.

"You go to fight this critter and there's no guarantee you're gonna win," said Chile Commission chair Don Hackey, who cautioned that multiple chemical treatments would reduce profits. Experts calculated that each spraying

cost $30-50 per acre, with up to 10 applications possible a season. A $500 per acre weevil bill might wipe out the incentive to plant. Moreover, the ecological consequences of repeated sprayings could result in the disappearance of beneficial insects. "It's like a coyote and rabbit situation," analogized Hackey. "You have a lot of rabbits. The coyote population builds up, builds up, until the rabbit population crashes, and then the coyote population dies off. It's the same in the insect world." Several weeks into the harvest, at least one grower noticed secondary pests like aphids cropping up in the chile. A new question then surfaced: how to control the aphids, chemically or otherwise?

For a couple of seasons, the weevil infestations slacked off. But by 1997, fields were once again being lost to the persistent pest. U.S. Customs inspectors kept spotting weevils on the ever-increasing chile shipments from Mexico, but no action was taken to stop them. NMDA downplayed the infestations and there was no public talk of federal or state regulation to stop the imports. To do otherwise would impair a growing, multimillion-dollar business gliding along with the blessings of the North American Free Trade Agreement (NAFTA).

The weevil infestations posed a grave threat to the New Mexico chile industry. Heretofore, not as many pesticides were required on chile as on other crops, though problems occurred on occasion with those that were employed. A weevil infestation promised to change this picture. The weevil, if out of hand, could well "devastate a crop," as NMDA's Dr. Carol Sutherland concisely put it.

Growers had the choice of heavy spraying or watching their investment munched away in the fields. Yet pesticides were more costly and an added hazard to the applicator and those working in the fields. In short, New Mexico chile growers were faced with similar circumstances confronted by Mexican farmers to the south. They were now in a quandary, up against the probability of more weevil outbreaks and chemical spraying, which in turn would kill beneficial insects and open up a whole new Pandora's box. And it happened at the very time the chile business had reached the pinnacle of its success.

Notes

1. Fred Harris, interview by author, Hatch, NM, December 1985.

2. *New Mexico Department of Agriculture Biennial Report, July 1, 1986-June 30, 1988*, 24-25.

3. Information on pesticide violation cases from documents obtained from the U.S. Environmental Protection Agency through the Freedom of Information Act by the author and the New Mexico Public Interest Research Group in 1988. 4th Quarterly Report, NMDA Bureau of Pesticide Management to U.S. EPA, 18 October 1985, 9; 1st Quarterly Report, NMDA Bureau of Pesticide Management to U.S. Environmental Protection Agency, 26 January 1984, 4.

4. María Martínez, interview by author, Doña Ana, NM, June 1993.

5. NMDA Bureau of Pesticide Management, Case No. 89-24, 1989.

6. Complaint Information Form, Robert Murphy, U.S. EPA, to Gary Lasswell, NMDA, 10 April 1984; NMDA Inspection Report, Gary Lasswell, 8 May 1984, 1-3; Roger Morel and Patrice Cheurelin, affidavits to U.S. EPA, Engle/Truth or Consequences, NM, 8 May 1984.

7. 4th Quarterly Report, NMDA Bureau of Pesticide Management to U.S. EPA, 23 October 1984, 6; 4th Quarterly Report, NMDA Bureau of Pesticide Management to U.S. EPA, 18 October 1985, 3.

8. *El Paso Herald Post*, 6 September 1984.

9. 4th Quarterly Report, NMDA Bureau of Pesticide Management to U.S. EPA, 23 October 1984, 9.

10. Howard Applegate, telephone conversation with author, December 1992.

11. Kent Paterson, "New Mexico Farmworkers," *Coatimundi*, Summer 1987.

12. Charles Sánchez and Tom O'Brien, U.S. Fish and Wildlife Service, interviews by author, Albuquerque, NM, 1987-88; Associated Press wire story, 24 July 1992.

13. *New Mexico Department of Agriculture Biennial Report 1986-88*, Las Cruces, NM.

14. 3rd Quarterly Report, NMDA Bureau of Pesticide Management to U.S. EPA, 6 August 1986, 8.

15. *New Mexico Farm and Ranch*, June 1960, 8.

16. 4th Quarterly Report, NMDA Bureau of Pesticide Management to U.S. EPA, 31 October 1986, 11; 3rd Quarterly Report, NMDA Bureau of Pesticide Management to U.S. EPA, 1987, 5-6.

17. John Peterson, telephone conversation with author, April 1990.

18. 3rd Quarterly Report, NMDA Bureau of Pesticide Management to U.S. EPA, 6 August 1986, 5; 1st Quarterly Report, NMDA Bureau of Pesticide Management to U.S. EPA, 1986, 4-5.

19. Joe Wysong, U.S. Department of Labor, telephone conversation with author, May 1990.

20. Barry Patterson, NMDA, interview with author, Las Cruces, NM, April 1990.

21. NMSU Cooperative Extension Service, *Pesticide Use in New Mexico Major Crops in 1983*, 6, 20.

22. *New Mexico Farm and Ranch*, August 1970.

23. *New Mexico Extension News*, June 1926, 3; *13th Annual Report of the Cooperative Extension Work in Agriculture and Home Economics*, 30 June 1927, W. L. Elser, Director, Gov. Richard C. Dillon papers, NMSRCA; *17th Annual Report of the Cooperative Extension Work in Agriculture and Home Economics*, 30 June 1931, W. L. Elser, Director, Gov. Seligman Papers, NMSRCA; Leslie Clayshulte, presentation, *Proceedings of the Fifth Annual Fruit and Vegetable Short Course*, New Mexico College of Agriculture and Mechanic Arts, State College, NM, 16-17 January 1958.

24. U.S. Environmental Protection Agency, Pesticide Fact Sheet, Ethephon, 29 September 1988; W. Powell Anderson, "Chemical Weed Control in Chile Peppers," presentation to 1985 New Mexico Chile Conference, Las Cruces, NM; Stephen H. Thomas, *Results of Nematicide Tests in Chile Peppers, Las Cruces, New Mexico, 1986, 1988, 1989*, Dept. of Entomology, Plant Pathology and Weed Science, NMSU; Dr. Emroy Shannon, presentation, 1992 Chile Conference, Las Cruces, NM, February 1992.

25. Dr. Marion Moses, testimony before Senate Rules Committee, Sacramento, CA, 21 February 1990; Dr. Marion Moses, "Cancer in Humans and Potential Occupational and Environmental Exposure to Pesticides," *AAOHN Journal*, March 1989, 131-36.

26. "Chemical Watch," *Pesticides and You* (National Coalition Against the Misuse of Pesticides), March 1991, 5.

27. Bob Porter, NMFLB, interview by author, Las Cruces, NM, April 1990.

28. Kitty Richards, New Mexico Environment Department, interview by author, Las Cruces, NM, April 1993.

29. K. Paterson, op. cit.

30. For example, New Mexico Environment Department, NMDA, and the City of Albuquerque planned four chile samples for residue testing in FY 92. Memorandum of Meeting, New Mexico Pesticide Memorandum of Understanding, 30 July 1991.

31. Dr. Frank Crespin, telephone conversation with author, May 1990.

32. Pedro Melero, interview by author, El Paso, TX, April 1990.

33. Ignacio Bustamante, telephone conversation with author, May 1990.

34. Pedro Gonzales, interview by author, El Paso, TX, April 1990.

35. Van Kozak, EPA, to Lonnie Matthews, NMDA, 29 January 1988, re: FIFRA FY-1987 Final Evaluation New Mexico Department of Agriculture, EPA evaluation, 26-28 October 1987.

36. Carlos Marentes, interview by author, El Paso, TX, April 1990.

37. Nancy Nickell and Scott Ridley, *Reducing Pesticide Contamination: The State of the States 1988 Focus Paper* (Washington, DC: Renew America Project, 1988), 2, 10, 13, 16, 24, 26.

38. Barry Patterson, interviews by author, Albuquerque, NM, June 1988; Las Cruces, NM, April 1990.

39. Kent Paterson, "Pesticides in New Mexico," radio series broadcast on KUNM-FM, Albuquerque, NM, February 1986.

40. Associated Press wire story, 13 August 1992.

41. *In These Times*, 16-22 January 1991.

42. Jay Friedman, New Mexico Organic Commodities Commission, telephone conversation with author, February 1991.

43. Vince Hernández, Biad Chili Co., interview by author, Albuquerque, NM, December 1993.

44. Author's interviews with Dr. Ron Bhada, Mike English, and other members of the NMSU "E-Team," Las Cruces, NM, April 1990.

45. Sam Hitt, former Anaya task force member, telephone conversation with author, November 1987.

46. Barry Patterson, presentation to the New Mexico Farm and Livestock Bureau meeting, Albuquerque, NM, December 1991.

47. *New Mexico Extension News*, October 1929, 2.

48. David G. Riley, *The Pepper Weevil and Its Management*, Texas Agricultural Experiment Station, L 5069, n.d.

49. Marjorie Lewis, NMDA, presentation to the 1993 Chile Conference, Las Cruces, NM, February 1993.

50. Dr. David Riley, presentation to the 1993 Chile Conference and interview by author, Las Cruces, NM, February 1993.

51. Dr. Carol Sutherland, NMDA, telephone conversations with author, June-July 1993.

52. Fred Gjerk, assistant director NMDA, telephone conversation with author, July 1993.

53. Don Hackey, interview by author, Rincon, NM, August 1993.

54. Author's telephone conversations with growers and U.S. Customs personnel and with NMDA spokeswoman Lana Dixon and NMSU Doña Ana County Extension Agent Javier Vargas, October 1997.

Free Trade, Round One

17

Chile Inspectors ▪ The Pepper Professor ▪ Illegal Pesticide Residues ▪ Weevil's Wrath

Held up by wooden supports, the sagging Bridge of the Americas in El Paso hosts many of the 2,000 commerce-laden trucks that cross the frontier every day. Big rigs, pickups, and vans rumble across the concrete-banked Rio Grande, lugging between the two nations the stuff of trade that greases the economic wheels—auto parts, toxic waste, clothing, food, and floral arrangements. At this crossing, and at the others of the "Paso del Norte," a tradition of commerce that began on the ancient Indian trade routes and the Camino Real between colonial Chihuahua and Santa Fe is pursued with vigor.

A bevy of uniformed inspectors rushes around the waiting trucks, checking and ripping up crates, opening boxes, and sampling peppers for pesticide residues. Amid the hustle and bustle, a van piled high with bleached steer skulls heads for the novelty market. One of the most popular commodities here is the chile pepper in all its manifestations: fat, plump poblanos, juicy little jalapeños, sleek long greens, sunny yellow hots, and others. Vicente Muñoz, an employee of a Mexican food broker, waits patiently with coworkers while a USDA inspector lifts a sample of long green chiles and takes them inside the building where the FDA officer might send the peppers to a laboratory for pesticide testing. Muñoz has been through this routine many times and is nonchalant about the wait: "The Department of Agriculture and the Food and Drug Administration and those from Customs inspect us, we pay [the tariff] and we're done."

Every day, Muñoz ships chiles from all parts of Mexico, handling the cream of the regional harvests trucked in at various times from Colima, Nayarit, the Bajío, Sonora, Sinaloa, and Chihuahua, whose bounty of jalapeños, serranos, and yellow hots he regards as the best. Demand for the product has grown, he asserts, and business is especially good during the New Mexican off-season when the Chile Capital's fields are hibernating for the winter.

> *"I think everybody is going with chile. Everybody is trying to do his best for himself."*
>
> —GILBERT DE LA ROSA, MEXICAN CHILE FARMER

As the hot food market exploded in the United States, Mexican chiles graced U.S. tables. Processors experimented with them, supermarket shoppers nabbed them from produce bins, and distributors introduced them canned, bottled, or fresh. One big company, La Costeña, mounted a major television advertising campaign directed at the Spanish-speaking population in the United States. Playing on the cultural sensitivities of the immigrant sector, La Costeña employed the kind of dramatic theme music heard in Mexican soap operas. The ads featured a man and a woman, sultry Mexican actress Laura León, to sell chiles. To appeal to the Anglo segment, the company exported milder concoctions of its sauces, a successful strategy brainstormed by Dr. Fabián García and later adopted by others, including the transnational Del Monte.

Figures compiled by two Mexican researchers, J. A. Laborde and E. Rendón-Poblete, showed a steady increase in exports to the United States between 1978 and 1987. And from 1989 to 1991 Mexican chile sent to the United States soared in value from almost $25 million to about $39 million. In the Delicias district of Chihuahua alone, thousands of hectares were cultivated to satisfy the appetites of U.S. consumers. Seasonal pickers traveled from as far as Oaxaca and Zacatecas to be paid 7 to 10 cents a kilo for chile packed by companies such as Herdez, Walker Foods, Pace, and La Victoria.

Close to the border, Juárez area growers reaped the advantage of having New Mexico State University at their doorstep. They attended NMSU meetings, purchased NMSU-produced seed stock, and received advice on growing techniques. In a sense the business was the completion of a circle that began when chile seed was transported up the Rio Grande from the Mexican interior. Centuries later, hybrid forms of that seed were returned to Mexico to be grown and then finally sent back to the States as ripe fruit. The New Mexican long green chile even found a market among Mexican buyers.

True, Mexican chiles had long been exported in dried forms to the United States, supplying the bulk of the U.S. market in the early part of the century, and companies like Pace, Anderson-Clayton, and Del Monte counted decades of buying from growers in places like the Bajío and Veracruz. But in the early 1990s, something different was in the air, a perceptible sense of excitement, trepidation, and questioning about the industry's future, an uneasy mood brought about by the prospect of a North American Free Trade Agreement (NAFTA) between Mexico and the United States, a pact that vowed to eliminate all trade and investment barriers to chile and all other commodities. An El Paso artist, Gregory J. Cook, captured the mood by painting and displaying a series of biting social commentaries on NAFTA at El Paso

City Hall. Appropriately enough, he used Taco Bell hot sauce to sketch the cartoons.

Getting a jump start on NAFTA, U.S. investors planted new chile lands around La Colonia Victoria south of Columbus, New Mexico. In coastal Sonora, a group of Mexican growers contemplated increasing their output for the U.S. market, figuring that NAFTA would give them "more guarantees, more security, and less U.S. government taxes," as farmer Rodolfo Garza of the Hermosillo region said.

On the other side of the Sierra Madres, in the dry, vast desert country between Ciudad Juárez and Chihuahua, Mexican communal farmers seized on the pepper as one possible solution to the turbulent changes sweeping their nation's agricultural system. One hundred miles south of Ciudad Juárez, huge cornfields rise surprisingly from the gray landscape of the Chihuahuan desert, giving sustenance to the *ejidos*, or collective farms, of the Villa Ahumada region. At the Álamos de Peña *ejido*, one man says there is little credit for the *campesinos* and not enough work to sustain them, impelling some like himself to seek work in the United States.

Several miles away at the Ejido Benito Juárez, men gather in a square-like meeting ground in front of the steel-coated buildings. The *ejido* members have mixed opinions about free trade. "We're hoping that through free trade or through some businessman in the United States, they'd be interested in helping us here in the countryside," ventured Ramón Herrera Mendoza. "We have the water and the land, and if we were provided with the technology, these lands could be farmed to their maximum."

In front of a well-shaded house, Professor Eleodoro León Orcepa, an *ejido* advisor from the Escuela Superior de Agricultura Hermanos Escobar in Ciudad Juárez, proudly displayed to North American visitors a handful of chiles grown on the *ejido* without pesticides, in contrast to many other farms in Mexico. A *norteño conjunto* band belted out an accordion riff and a drum roll as his big hands grabbed a cayenne, then a New Mexican, and then a yellow hot like a triumphant fisherman showing off a regal trout. "We have hardworking people and we feel very proud of this, and we think we could produce anything. It's only a question of what do you want," offers Orcepa.

Ejido Benito Juárez's chile acreage in 1992 was small—14 or 16 hectares—and was intended mainly for the national market, but people here knew of the chile bonanza on the other side of the river and scoped out the possibilities, all with an eye toward staying on their land. One prominent Mesilla Valley grower approached the *ejido* that summer to strike up a deal for his processing operation, and the Mexican farmers wanted U.S. contracts "to give people the means to work where they're from, so they don't have to go to another country," explained Orcepa.

On both sides of the Río Bravo, chile country in the 1990s was abuzz with talk of free trade. Del Monte Foods of Mexico, a leading lobbyist for NAFTA, was brash about the possibilities. Company executive Mario Tello, apparently unmindful of the New Mexican chile industry, claimed his country's peppers "don't compete with any U.S. agro-industrial products." On the other hand, some New Mexican farmers viewed the cross-border chile exporters with a twinge of nervousness. NAFTA allowed a five- to ten-year reduction in tariffs and duties, delivering a decade-long breathing spell for growers and processors in the two nations, though strangely enough, the phase-ins were scheduled for all the growing seasons except the peak of the New Mexican season, which was

NAFTA's Port Chile: Mexican chile imports at Columbus, New Mexico, 1998.

slated for an immediate duty elimination as of NAFTA's implementation in January 1994.

Once the "trade barriers" were down, NAFTA chile headed north in increasing volume through New Mexico's two principal ports of entry: Columbus and Santa Teresa. From 1994 to 1998, shipments through Columbus alone increased from one million kilos to 34 million kilos. Huge semitrailer loads, each bearing 38,000 pounds or more of pods, crossed the border for processing plants in the southern New Mexico chile belt. By the end of the decade, trucks with Mexican license plates were visible outside chile plants in the Hatch and Mesilla valleys, unloading Mexican red chile purchased for as cheap as eight cents a pound.

In Albuquerque to the north, rumors abounded in the summer of 1997 that the bargain-rate sacks of green chile selling at the beginning of the season under the name of "Hatch Chile" for as low as $6 per gunnysack were really Mexican-grown chile. With workers in the Chihuahua growing area earning between $7 and $20 per day, small growers like Raúl Medina wondered how they could possibly compete at a time when the U.S. minimum wage had just risen to $5.15 per hour. However, bigger farmers saw an opportunity. In contrast to previous years when Mexican chile was imported by wholesale brokers or corporate processing companies, a few New Mexican growers directly contracted the new business.

Given the structure of the market, those that could expect to prosper in the future needed to wear several hats and to have one foot in Mexico and the other in the United States. The modern chile farmer would have to be simultaneously a grower, contractor, middleman, and primary processor, like it or not.

In a competitive environment, some claimed that even a couple of cents difference in tariffs could determine business. Hatch Valley farmer Ángel Baquera, encountering both tight fresh and dried chile markets, claimed he had been priced out of the San Antonio jalapeño business by Mexican peppers that were sold for as much as 12¢ cheaper per pound.

In theory, U.S. processors were generally the most supportive of the pact, for they stood to gain from the best of both worlds. An elimination of trade barriers would allow them to import tariff-free chile from Mexico and then reexport it as an ingredient in salsa or processed food. As Amigos' Foods Arnold Orquiz sized it up, it was a relationship already well in place, but free trade promised fewer brakes on capital. He negotiated with an international broker to process and export chile rellenos and burritos, made with Mexican chile from Sinaloa or Chihuahua, to Mexico for the "ready-to-eat" market. "What we're trying to do after we stuff 'em and process 'em, [is] sell 'em back to Mexico to keep the money coming and going instead of just going or just coming."

Free trade ushered in a complex set of new questions about the nature of U.S.-Mexico trade, while leaving old ones unanswered. Built on an evolving agricultural relationship between Mexico and the United States, the treaty had within its thousands of pages hopes for new opportunities and forebodings of new pitfalls. On the skeptical side, some U.S. farm-

ers voiced fears that NAFTA would threaten their business because of cheaper labor expenses in Mexico. New Mexico cayenne chile farmer Dino Cervantes figured that producers in Mexico paid half as much in harvest labor costs as producers in the United States. David Runsten, a free trade researcher for the California Institute of Rural Studies, estimated in 1991 that farmworkers in central Mexico, where many vegetables for the U.S. market are grown, earned from 65 to 85¢ an hour, a rate equivalent to 1960 wages in the United States.

In essence, however, what U.S. growers were really faced with was not the prospect of competing with the Mexicans per se, many of whom ran small farms that paled in technological comparison, but with U.S.-based corporations and farmers who were gradually assuming increased control over Mexican agricultural production. The leading names of international agribusiness—Del Monte, Pet, Campbell's, and Green Giant, among others—were already well entrenched in Mexico, contracting and processing foods in *agro-maquilas* established in Mexican cities.

Yet the New Mexico chile industry had many hands to play. For instance, chile crop yields were often half in Mexico what they were in the U.S. Southwest. Moreover, in Mexico chile wilt outbreaks and pepper weevil infestations posed a threat to the business, the latter problem resulting in crop losses of 30 percent in certain years. Where the weevil was genuinely out of hand, entire harvests could be written off as lost. Additionally, fuel, fertilizer, and transportation costs added to the overall expense, and Mexican agricultural research trailed the programs at NMSU and Texas A&M.

A few U.S. processors with experience in Mexico cited previous problems with contract fulfillment when Mexican farmers, suddenly able to get a higher price for chile on their own national spot market, pulled out of a negotiated deal. Moreover, there was no nationwide system of standards or classification for chile in Mexico. Would-be investors sometimes walked away disappointed, as happened to the Las Cruces company that found it could not purchase 15 or 20 tons of destemmed chile at a profitable rate.

The entire Mexican contracting system was light years behind New Mexico's, a fact that gave processors pause in their expansion plans. Perhaps most significantly, Mexican chile producers were not dependent on the demands of the U.S. contract or fresh markets, having at their own disposal a huge customer base in large, burgeoning centers such as Mexico City and Puebla. Like ancient lorries bearing tribute to Aztec emperors, truckloads overflowing with poblanos, jalapeños, serranos, güeritos, and virtually every other type of pepper arrived daily at the mad bustle of Mexico City's Central de Abastos, or wholesale food market, where they sold one recent summer for anywhere from 20¢ to $1.35 per kilo. When prices in the U.S. market dipped, which was frequent by the end of the century, Mexican growers could simply turn to their own domestic market, where they sometimes earned more money than was possible in the United States. Still, the shattering of internal Mexican markets in the wake of the post-Salinas peso devaluation tempted Mexican exporters, despite higher costs for imported manufacturing materials, to hustle a greater share of their business north, west, and east of the border.

One famous Mexican canner, La Xalapeña, was the quintessential national enterprise. Founded in the city of Jalapa, Veracruz, in 1880, the company claimed to have coined the term "jalapeño," since the pepper became known for the town in which the chile was processed, though it was actually shipped in to the coffee-producing region from other Mexican states. At home, La Xalapeña was locked into competition with big firms like La Costeña, not unlike the Pace-Old El Paso rivalry in the United States. But economic and cultural trends abroad changed the company's outlook and style. In the late 1900s, the creation of the nacho in the United States drew the cannery's attention to a new market. "Before, exports to the U.S. were directed at 10 or 12 million Mexicans living in the U.S.," said Antonio Ballesteros, sales manager for the firm. "But now, the American himself is beginning to consume [chile]." La Xalapeña, a company name practically synonymous with Mexican culture, gradually became absorbed into the global marketplace. Overseas, customers included the British, Japanese, and Filipinos.

With Mexican producers looking offshore, was NAFTA, then, an immediate threat to the very existence of the New Mexico chile business? From a processor's perspective, Border Foods' Martin Steinman weighed the differences in producing chile in Mexico and the United States. He noted that wages were low, but that inputs—chemicals, energy, machinery, and transportation—were costlier south of the border. "Perhaps there might be an advantage, although a small advantage, in the actual production of the crop, but in order to get that crop here to the U.S., I think we have the advantage."

Then there was the matter of New Mexicans' (and a growing legion of visitors') diehard loyalty to their own homespun, sumptuous green chile. The fresh green market was bursting at the seams. More people moved into or visited New Mexico, and tourists were known to stuff a bag of frozen pods in their luggage for the journey back to bland-land. In addition, if NMSU researchers were successful, new forms of packaging could help open larger markets thousands of miles away from the freshly picked peppers. Other factors connected to the question of quality crop growing gave the New Mexicans a jump on the gun.

A big unresolved issue in the NAFTA challenge was pesticide usage. Some growers in Mexico were caught up in a vicious battle against the pepper weevil and other insects, employing chemicals to make a last-ditch effort to rescue their crops. Largely untrained, many were reliant on word of mouth or chemical company salesmen for pest-control information, a system that did not always bode well for the best health or environmental outcomes. In a rehash of the old "Circle of Poison," there were instances in which chemicals not approved for chile in the United States—but nevertheless developed and promoted by U.S. companies —were applied on Mexican chile ultimately sold across the tollgates of the Río Bravo.

USDA Port Inspector William Coppenbarger inspects Mexican-grown jalapeños, Columbus, New Mexico, 1998.

FDA spot samples were taken of jalapeños, chilacas, árbol, pasilla, guajillo, and other varieties, a peppery basket of plenty flowing across the border. This was the job of Jack Grady, a husky FDA consumer-safety inspector for the ports of Columbus, New Mexico, and El Paso and Presidio, Texas. On a typical day, Grady sat in his office at the Bridge of the Americas customs station, handling inquiries and walk-ins, stamping and filing a stack of official border entry forms, and inspect-

ing cans of jalapeños for signs of microbiological contamination. If a fresh pepper sample pulled by a USDA employee at the terminal outside his quarters was selected for testing, Grady's office then sent it to a government laboratory in Dallas and had 24 hours to get the results back to the broker or the product was allowed to enter the United States. If the sample was in violation of allowable EPA pesticide residue limits, the FDA was supposed to destroy the chiles or send them back to Mexico, practices another government official at the site said he had witnessed. A common method of destruction was to throw the chiles in a dumpster and pour Clorox over them.

In repeated reports between the 1970s and 1990s, the U.S. General Accounting Office (GAO) criticized the FDA for only checking about one to two percent of all imported produce. But Grady was a man self-conscious about his job. A hiring freeze was in effect and he'd been assigned the task of checking three ports almost 300 miles apart. When a staff person from a congressional member's office visited and suggested that he inspect Columbus, New Mexico, more regularly, he pointed out to her that there was only a dirt road going directly between El Paso and Columbus, forcing a drive on the highway through Deming and then south to Columbus—a full day's trip. "Then she said, 'well, we'll pave the road,' " added Grady. Not that the GAO's or the congressional staffers' concerns were off the mark—it was just a question of who would pay for health and safety matters arising from the two countries' burgeoning trade.

The U.S. government had been aware of the pesticide residue problems in Mexican chile for years, refusing entry, for example, to peppers in 1977. Yet the violations continued to mount. FDA records from two ports of entry in Texas between 1986 and 1993 showed residue violations on approximately 14.5 percent of 875 samples of serranos, long greens, jalapeños, and pasillas, a figure more than double the average for other Mexican produce, about three to seven times higher than for imported produce from other nations, and 14 times higher than for U.S. produce. The numbers were far higher than

FDA personnel claimed was the average for imported produce in testimony before Congress in 1991. Other samples were close to being illegal, "but no cigar," according to Darrell Brown, the head of the FDA lab in Dallas. Many contained from five to nine chemicals, some of which, like DDT, had long ago been outlawed in the United States.

Ten of the substances, including Azodrin, Cholorthalonil, and cypermethrin, did not have EPA-approved tolerances for chile. The situation got so bad that in 1992, the governments of Mexico and the United States entered into an agreement whereby any shipper of poblano or serrano chiles—the two chiles with the worst residue violations—would first have to put shipment samples through an independent laboratory for testing before being allowed entry into the United States.

Occasionally, FDA personnel were forced to play a cat-and-mouse game with previously detained shippers who tried to conceal their identities by using other names. "Most of the times we catch them, sometimes we don't," said Dallas FDA industrial chemist Billy McGill. Eduardo Díaz, a chemist for Pace Foods, noticed that tested Mexican jalapeños at the company lab in South Texas exceeded FDA pesticide guidelines. In 1991, Díaz was terminated from his position, alleging in a subsequent Texas lawsuit that Pace sacked him in a move to quash hassles over the use of chiles with pesticide residues. Pace official Rod Sands disputed Díaz's story and declared that the San Antonio salsa maker had higher quality standards than FDA.

An obvious question hovering above the whole controversy was whether imported, pesticide-laced Mexican chile products were safe to eat. Unfortunately, science had no definitive answer even 50 years after the chemical revolution burst on the world agricultural scene. A debate raged in the United States that pitted some scientists, environmentalists, and consumer advocates against other scientists, the American Farm Bureau Federation, and chemical companies. Seemingly in the middle was a waffling EPA, responsible for testing and for setting safety-level tolerances, but often the object of criticism from one side or another. Critics of the regulatory system, like the Natural Resources Defense Council, pointed to the unknown synergistic effects of ingesting foods that had multiple chemicals acting together that could enhance their potency, or the disproportionate impact pesticides might have on the still-developing bodies of young children.

George Corcoran, the chairman of the Department of Pharmacology and Toxicology at the University of New Mexico, scanned some of the illegal residue sample numbers and said that they were of potential concern, but that enormous quantities would probably have to be consumed in order to be hazardous. The greatest risk, he added, was faced by those "who apply the pesticide and work directly with pesticides, where a large overexposure to pesticide is possible."

As the pesticide-food safety debate unfolded in the United States, agricultural chemicals, many of U.S. manufacture, were being employed in Mexico. And as in the north, it was pesticide and agricultural workers who encountered the worst immediate risks. In May 1991, explosions rocked the Agricultura Nacional de Veracruz plant in Córdoba, Mexico, which made a parathion-containing product called Dragon, a popular pest killer that three years later could be still found stacked in bags for public viewing on a street in a neighboring town in the state of Puebla. The accident released a toxic cloud that resulted in 500 people falling ill and the evacuation of 1,600. Years later, hundreds complained of symptoms, the contaminated site remained in the town, and compensation was moving at a snail's pace.

A sampling of additional mass poisoning cases in Mexico stretches from the Tamaulipas cotton fields in the 1960s to the San Quintín tomato export farms of Baja California in the 1980s and the Nayarit and Jalisco tobacco plots of the 1990s, where Huichol Indians picked tobacco for the U.S. and Mexican markets under a cloud of 2-4-D, paraquat, DDT, and other pest-killers. The government of Mexico, under environmentalist pressure and anxious to get NAFTA past a wary U.S. Congress, announced in 1993 that henceforth it would require any shipper of export crops, peppers at the top of the list, to first hire an agronomist for chemical consultation. Plans to open FDA-approved labs in Mexico for residue analysis were also announced. How small, cash-strapped Mexican chile farmers would afford these professional services was anyone's guess.

Without a doubt, the pesticide issue hung over NAFTA like a lead weight dangling on a string. On a deeper level, however, it signified the two distinct agricultural states of development: On the one side, there was the United States with its high-tech farm machinery, world-class research institutions, futuristic yields, and relatively stricter (though many would still argue, inadequate) controls on pesticides. On the other, there was Mexico with its uneven degrees of efficiency ranging from state-of-the-art irrigation systems on one farm to burro-drawn plows on another, underfunded agricultural research, less well-developed transport systems, and thinly enforced environmental laws. "We're more than 20 years behind in technology," summed up

Roberto Flores, a student at the agricultural college in Juárez.

Certainly, it will only be a matter of time before Mexico catches up to U.S. agriculture, especially if a new infusion of foreign capital intensifies the move toward export-oriented agriculture. As the surge of chile imports in the mid to late 1990s showed, free trade would surely encourage the harvesting of more Mexican acres for the U.S. market.

Notes

1. Vicente Muñoz, interview by author, El Paso, TX, April 1993.

2. La Costeña commercial, KLUZ television, Albuquerque, NM, 29 August 1994.

3. *El Paso Herald Post*, 8 October 1993.

4. J. A. Laborde and E. Rendón-Poblete, "Tomatoes and Peppers in Mexico: Commercial Production and Research Challenges," *Tomato and Pepper Production in the Tropics* (Taipei, Taiwan: Asian Vegetable Research and Development Center, 1989), 527; J. A. Laborde Cancino and Octavio Paz Campodonico, *Presente y pasado del chile en México* (México, D.F.: Instituto Nacional de Investigaciones Agrícolas, 1984).

5. NAFTA Agriculture Fact Sheets: Commodities, USDA Economic Research Service, 1993.

6. César Hernández, Delicias delegate to Sindicato Nacional de Trabajadores Obreros Asalariados del Campo, interview by author, Ejido Benito Juárez, Chihuahua, Mexico, September 1992.

7. Gilbert De La Rosa, telephone conversation with author, June 1993.

8. *Albuquerque Journal*, 29 November 1992.

9. Rodolfo Garza, interview by author, Las Cruces, NM, February 1993.

10. Ramón Herrera Mendoza, interview by author, Ejido Benito Juárez, Chihuahua, Mexico, September 1992.

11. Eleodoro León Orcepa, presentation, Ejido Benito Juárez, Chihuahua, Mexico, September 1992.

12. Laura Carlsen, "New Products, New Markets," *Business Mexico*, July 1991, 28-29.

13. Author's interviews and telephone conversations with U.S. Customs and USDA personnel, Santa Teresa and Columbus, NM, October 1997 and October 1998; telephone conversation with Deming grower Cass Keeler, October 1997.

14. Angel Baquera, interview by author, Arrey, NM, August 1994.

15. Arnold Orquiz, interview by author, Deming, NM, July 1992.

16. North American Free Trade Agreement Information Sheet, U.S. International Trade Commission, 27 November 1991.

17. Claire Poole, "Please pass the hot stuff," *Forbes*, 27 April 1992; *El Paso Herald Post*, 8 October 1993.

18. *Albuquerque Journal*, 22 November 1992.

19. José Reyes, Mexican attorney and trade consultant, presentation, Governor's Rural Economic Development Conference, Grants, NM, October 1993.

20. Stephen Lande and Nellis Crigler, "Food for Thought," *Business Mexico*, May 1994, 10.

21. Author's price surveys of supermarkets and popular markets, Mexico, D.F., and Puebla, Mexico, July 1994.

22. Antonio Ballesteros, interview by author, Xalapa, Veracruz, Mexico, December 1995.

23. Frances Moore Lappe and Joseph Collins with Cary Fowler, *Food First: Beyond Myth and Scarcity* (New York: Bantam, 1977, 1978), 329-30.

24. Dino Cervantes, testimony to the U.S. Commission on Agricultural Workers, Las Cruces, NM, 23 October 1991, 223. FOIA document released to author.

25. David Runsten, California Institute of Rural Studies, testimony to the U.S. Commission on Agricultural Workers, Las Cruces, NM, 23 October 1991, 28-29. FOIA document released to author.

26. Roger Burbach and Patricia Flynn, *Agribusiness in the Americas* (New York: Monthly Review Press, 1980), 165, 184, 254, 256, 257, 263.

27. Peter Baird and Ed McCaughan, *México-Estados Unidos: relaciones económicas y lucha de clases* (México, D.F.: Ediciones Era, S.A., 1982), 299-330.

28. *Albuquerque Journal*, 16 May 1993.

29. Dr. David Riley, Texas A&M, telephone conversation with author, June 1993.

30. Author's interviews with chile sellers in Mexico, D.F., and Puebla, Mexico, July 1994.

31. Martin Steinman, interview by author, Albuquerque, NM, April 1993.

32. Jack Grady, interview by author, El Paso, TX, April 1993.

33. See, for example: "Better Regulation of Pesticide Exports and Pesticide Residues in Imported Food is Essential," U.S. General Accounting Office CED 79.43, 24 June 1979; "Food Safety and Quality: Five Countries' Efforts to Meet U.S. Requirements on Imported Produce," U.S. General Accounting Office/RCED 9055, March 1990.

34. *El Financiero*, 28 November 1995.

35. Iván Restrepo with Susana Franco, *Naturaleza muerta: Los plaguicidas en México* (México, D.F.: Ediciones Océano, 1988), 135.

36. Food and Drug Administration, sampling results for the ports of El Paso, TX, Laredo, TX, and Columbus, NM, computer printout, late 1986 to early 1993. Records obtained by the author under the Freedom of Information Act.

37. Darrell Brown, FDA, telephone conversation with author, June 1993.

38. Billy McGill, telephone conversation with author, April 1993; Jim Lahar, FDA, telephone conversation with author, April 1993.

39. *Santa Fe Reporter*, 8-14 September 1993.

40. Jennifer Curtis, Natural Resources Defense Council, telephone conversation with author, June 1993.

41. Prof. George Corcoran, interview by author, Albuquerque, NM, May 1993.

42. Susana Franco and María Eugenia Acosta, Mexican Action Network on Pesticides and Alternatives, interviews by author, Mexico, D.F., July 1994.

43. *Albuquerque Journal*, 5 May 1991; *Mother Jones*, December 1986; *Unomasuno* (México, D.F.), 12 June 1989; Marcos López Torres, *Envenenamiento* (Ciudad Juárez, México: Escuela Superior de Agricultura Hermanos Escobar, 1991), 111-13.

44. Patricia Díaz Romo, interview by author, Mexico, D.F., July 1994. Díaz spent several years researching pesticide usage in Nayarit and Jalisco and produced the film *Huichols and Pesticides*.

45. Susana Valadez, Huichol Center for Cultural Survival and Traditional Arts, and Miguel Carrillo Gonzales, Huichol community leader, interviews by author, Albuquerque, NM, September 1994.

46. M. Pullano, FDA special assistant for international regulatory issues, telephone conversation with author, August 1993.

47. Jesús Silva, spokesman for Embassy of Mexico, telephone conversation with author, Washington, DC, August 1993.

48. Roberto Rivera Flores, interview by author, Ejido Benito Juárez, Chihuahua, Mexico, September 1992.

Free Trade, Round Two

18

LABOR'S CROSS-BORDER LEGACY

Gloves off for Farmers and Labor ▪ Return of the Bracero? ▪ The Dino and Dolores Debate ▪
Bridge Blockades and Tractorcades

Provoked in part by the NAFTA negotiations, a 1991 showdown between labor and management occurred in chile country, taking place this time not in the fields but on the campus of NMSU. Farm labor advocates and employer representatives revisited an old, acrimonious debate on the issues—labor shortages, housing, mechanization, minimum wages, international competition, and even a quasi-return to the bracero program abolished by Congress back in 1965.

The meeting had a bit of déjà vu, recalling a 1950 conference in El Paso when the Farm Bureau lined up against Catholic activists, the National Farm Labor Union, and the NAACP. The 1991 rematch was a federal hearing arranged by New Mexico's senior Republican Senator Pete Domenici. Convened by the U.S. Commission on Agricultural Workers, a body set up by Congress in 1986 to review the immigration law's impact on the availability of agri-

cultural labor, the purpose of the event was to gather testimony on how the new law had affected growers and workers.

But as is the case in politics, policy cannot be separated from economics, particularly when old, set ground rules are about to be thrown out the window because of proposals like NAFTA. So instead of focusing on the actual numbers of people available to bring in the yearly chile crop, the witnesses tackled just about every conceivable question related to New Mexico chile. Farmworker advocates arrived at the meeting armed with statistics showing below poverty-level earnings and episodes of law-breaking in the fields and made a plea for justice. Their spokespersons were attorneys Olga Pedroza and Mark Schneider, UTAF coordinator Carlos Marentes, Bishop Ramírez of Las Cruces, and the Farmworker Project's Rubén Núñez.

On the opposing side, the chile farmers were supported by NMDA officials and represented by

> *"If the price of the chile crop doesn't go up . . . the bankers are going to exercise a judgment against the producers and want to take their land."*
>
> —MANUEL HERNÁNDEZ VILLA, MEXICAN FARMER

NMFLB leader Bob Porter, Chile Commission head Don Hackey, Andy Núñez, and Dino Cervantes. Collectively or individually they proposed a new bracero program, raised the issue of federal subsidies for housing and transportation in order to compete with Mexico, and dropped the threat of mechanization as a solution to the labor "problem." The underlying issue prompting the hearing was an alleged worker shortage caused by the departure of ex-undocumenteds from the chile fields, now unshackled from the constraints of their illegal status and able to move about freely in the job market.

In one form or another, southern New Mexico growers had complained about labor shortages dating back to World War I—if not earlier. For a time, locally recruited laborers satisfied the needs of agriculture, but commercial growth demanded a bigger workforce. Farmers relied on an imported labor force, initially Depression-era migrants from the Ozark country ejected from their land by the dust-blowing winds. A number of African-American cotton pickers rounded out the ranks. The reception the migrants received was not always warm. A Las Cruces newspaper, *The Rio Grande Farmer*, editorialized against the "unwelcome immigrants" who were "living in filthy surroundings in the outskirts of our towns" and who supposedly managed to "multiply like rabbits in the hills." On the other side of the Organ Mountains, in the Roswell area, officials reacted sternly to protests organized by the Agricultural Workers Industrial Union. A 1933 march was suppressed, and chief organizer Harry Rauert eventually was arrested on "vagrancy" charges.

During the early part of the Second World War, the Dust Bowl migrants were replaced by German and Italian prisoners of war. After 1943 came the braceros, Mexican contract guest workers who were housed on farmers' properties or in the former POW camps. At cotton's peak in the 1950s, 24,000 Mexican braceros were officially reported as working in New Mexico. They not only worked cotton but harvested apples in the Mimbres Valley, tomatoes near Deming, and other vegetable crops statewide.

Almost from its inception, the bracero program was wracked by controversy. Growers were irked by the paperwork requirements worked out by the governments of Mexico and the United States. At one point they pushed for an expedited system whereby the brown-skinned Mexicans would be given a "white card" to enter the land of the red, white, and blue.

Disagreements over wages and working conditions mounted. Disturbed by reports of a deadly encephalitis outbreak in Doña Ana

County unconnected to the bracero agreement, the Mexican government imposed a 10-day ban on braceros in Doña Ana County in 1958. On the day the prohibition was removed, five braceros were injured north of Doña Ana when the sidewalling of a Harvey Farms truck broke and sent them tumbling onto the ground. Later, two Mexican farmworkers were killed near Tularosa while en route to Colorado after a fire broke out on their bus and they jumped out before the vehicle had fully stopped. Such incidents caused the Mexican government to demand better insurance and higher pay for the braceros contracted to New Mexico, one of the lowest wage-paying states in the nation. In 1961 Mexico City threatened to withhold the labor force unless New Mexican farmers paid a new wage rate set by the U.S. Department of Labor, which itself warned of a revocation of the state's right to have braceros.

Led by the Farm Bureau, growers sued the USDOL, contending that its wage surveys did not take into account housing and transportation as part of the overall wage. NMSU Professor George Dawson, funded by a Farm Bureau grant, surveyed 325 farms to show the Labor Department that New Mexico farmers were providing higher pay in the form of transportation and housing (amenities offered by growers in other states, too). The study convinced DOL to lower the pay scale for workers.

Despite the conflicts, more than a few farmers and workers looked back favorably on the bracero program. On paper, at least, braceros were guaranteed a minimum wage, employer-provided housing, transportation, medical care, and a form of workers' compensation. Other than the minimum wage and loosely enforced transportation standards, nothing of the kind was generally offered to the chile pickers of the space

age. And even the minimum wage, as court cases and surveys indicated, was not always paid. That was how far things had come in a quarter century. In the pre-Chávez years, the rumblings of unionization and the demise of the guest worker system emanated from California, where the AFL-CIO's Agricultural Worker Organizing Committee (AWOC) was demanding an end to the bracero program as an impediment to organizing. Professor Dawson warned New Mexico farmers of shifting political winds, calling AWOC's campaign a "systematically, carefully laid out plan to create confusion, unrest and trouble for farmers in securing labor for their fields." Bad press, he continued, was painting a false picture of deplorable farm working conditions which, if true, would mean that "agriculture is in for a major revolution."

Finally, the bracero issue was settled in 1964 when Washington cancelled the program. Twenty-five years later it was back on the growers' agenda. The modern labor shortage issue first came to widespread public notice in 1985 when Deming growers and Border Foods met with the New Mexico Dept. of Labor to discuss government aid in recruiting to alleviate what they said was a shortage of pickers. Look for local help, they were told. Growers' fears of a dawning mass labor shortfall were heard in the next year in the national debate over the Immigration Reform and Control Act (IRCA). In the farmers' estimation, the law would not only block new job-seekers but eliminate old ones as well, who would seize the opportunity of their newly legal status to find higher paying jobs in the cities.

"[Mexican workers] are absolutely vital in this 2,000 mile stretch of border between here and California," asserted the Farm Bureau's Erik Ness. "The labor is not available in the United

States." In this stance, the Farm Bureau found a friend in New Mexico Senator Pete Domenici. The Republican solon stood before Congress and warned of a threat that the immigration law would pose to New Mexico growers, who predicted the drying up of a plentiful labor pool. Domenici also opposed legalizing the illegals. Congress approved the Replacement Agricultural Workers (RAW) provision as part of IRCA in 1986, permitting the secretaries of agriculture and labor, in the event of a domestic worker shortage, to authorize the entrance of upwards of 500,000 foreign guest workers.

The stage had been set for a modern bracero program. Then in what was almost a self-fulfilling prophecy, some chile farmers declared a labor shortfall during the 1989 harvest, a year when UTAF members at the Santa Fe Bridge refused to ride out with low-paying contractors.

The Farm Bureau laid the blame at the feet of the border-tightening and amnesty-granting provisions of IRCA. "The U.S. government is single-handedly ruining a partnership that has been going on for 100 years between the two countries," charged Erik Ness. Reports surfaced of chiles rotting in the field, and the New Mexico Department of Agriculture estimated a loss of $2.4 million to farmers and an unknown amount to processors because of downtime.

"In some cases the farmers and processors lost them [chile crops] because they weren't able to harvest them," said Farm Bureau Vice-President Bob Porter. "It wasn't huge amounts except to the individual grower, and if it's his, it's a huge amount." Senator Domenici appointed a committee of farmers—with no worker representation—to consider solutions to the alleged problem. NMFLB gave thumbs down to an existing foreign guest worker program, H2A, because according to Porter, the law's housing stipulations

were cost-prohibitive to New Mexico farmers, who would be forced to shell out $1,300 per worker in housing upgrades even before the harvest season began.

In 1990 the Domenici-appointed committee requested that the USDOL and the USDA study the possibility of invoking the Replacement Agricultural Workers section of IRCA. UTAF and unemployed farmworkers in El Paso ridiculed the notion of a worker shortage. "It's hard to realize that people are blind to see there are plenty of workers willing and available to harvest the crops," responded Sandy New. "And why they want to bring in workers from another country is absurd, other than [that] bringing in workers from another country is to keep wages down and exploit the workers. How long can we put up with things like this?"

In late 1990 New Mexico chile farmers were denied a RAW force as Washington declared that no labor shortage existed. Nationwide, it was a time of high farmworker unemployment, boosted by California drought, Texas freezes, and a new influx of undocumenteds. By all accounts, there was no lack of workers, but many had a new-found freedom to be choosy about for whom they worked and had gained greater ability to move between fields.

In 1993, NMSU sociologist Clyde Eastman released a study on 119 amnesty beneficiaries, concluding that most did not flee the fields once they were legalized. "But what the act has done in this area, to everyone's surprise, is legalize probably an excess of farmworkers," said Eastman.

However, NAFTA gave the labor shortage question a new shot in the arm, and it resurfaced at the October 1991 U.S. Commission on Agricultural Workers hearing. Farmer Dino Cervantes conceded there was not so much a shortage of willing workers as, in his view, a

Free Trade on Fire: UTAF and the Democratic Peasant Front of Chihuahua blockade an international bridge between Ciudad Juárez, Mexico, and El Paso, Texas, 1993.

downturn in productivity. Bob Porter, on the other hand, minced no words: "We believe our area is in need of a guest worker program for Mexican nationals, whereby farmworkers are allowed to enter the U.S. on a seasonal basis and then return to their homes in Mexico at the end of the contract period. This proposal could be modeled somewhat on the bracero program of the 1940s and 1950s. Such a program would not replace American workers and could become a valuable tool in the implementation of a free trade zone between our nations."

In a rapid question-and-answer, tit-for-tat exchange, Cervantes got into a round with

Dolores Huerta, the UFW's gutsy vice-president and the only labor representative on the Commission. The two had learned agriculture from different sides of the fence. Cervantes, the son of chile farmer Orlando Cervantes, had worked for the big meatpacker Hormel in the heat of the 1985-86 strike that tore apart the little town of Austin, Minnesota, returning to a New Mexico chile industry beginning to see strife of its own. Huerta, a New Mexico native, had walked countless picket lines with César Chávez in California, built the union from scratch, and nearly lost her life once to the club of a San Francisco policeman. Their words neatly summed up the ongoing divide between farmers and farmworkers and tied together the burning issues hanging over the chile industry. Their exchange transpired in part as follows:

Huerta: In part of your written statement and also your spoken statement, you said that workers in the United States must realize their conditions are as good or better than any country in the world. They must justify that condition by increased productivity and reduction of drug abuse and alcoholism, et cetera. Now, how would you compare the farmworkers in the United States with other United States workers?

Cervantes: The farmworker is . . . in the eyes of most U.S. workers, probably a depressed individual. They are paid a little bit less. But in the eyes of the world economy, they would probably be considered very above-average.

Huerta: Well, I think the only problem is that if you have a U.S. worker that lives in the United States, he doesn't have the same type of living as, say, a worker in Honduras, or some of these other places that you have mentioned, even Mexico. I am sure that the food, housing, and clothing is cheaper in these other third-world countries than in the United States of America. So I think it's a very big burden to say to the farmworker in the United States, you should be happy that you are here in the United States. Let me give you a job. Look at what these other workers are getting. He's living here in the United States. He or she has to compete at the gas station with another worker that is getting a better wage than he is, probably getting more benefits than that worker is.

Cervantes: Unfortunately, you're putting a scope around the United States that doesn't exist anymore. We live in a world economy today where we have to compete against those other workers. If you took the relative living expenses of Mexican harvesters and the ones here, they wouldn't come anywhere close to the difference in wages. Mexican harvesters live under—I was at one of our farms this year, and it sickens me, maybe some people should go down there. There were 30 people under two pieces of plywood that was hung from trees.

Huerta: You're making my point. You are saying that the United States worker should be happy that you are working here, because look at those workers down there. I am saying that the United States worker is living in the United States. They are paying U.S. rents. They're paying U.S. prices for gasoline. They are paying U.S. prices for groceries.

Cervantes: But the whole point is that they are living. A lot of those people in Mexico, I wouldn't consider that a life if you're living under a piece of plywood and you're having to cook on an open fire.

Huerta: Well, I think it's unfair to U.S. workers to say that you have to compete with that worker over there.

Cervantes: But that's a fact of life. They do have to compete. We go to processors and they say they can get produce from Mexico and they can get produce from me. They don't say, well, we want your workers to be treated better. They don't tell me that.

Huerta: Well, I was going to say, that's a feudalistic mentality for you to say to the workers, "you should be happy because we are giving you a job."

Cervantes: I am not saying we are happy. In fact, I am very sympathetic to the worker. I advocate that everybody have a Cadillac and live in the Taj Mahal. I would like to see our workers stable. But the reality of it is, where does that come from? That's one of the problems. I talked about the government subsidy. You want to take it from the farmer, and what I am telling you is, the farmer is dry. You have got to look elsewhere.

The union leader and the chile grower bantered a while longer, disputing government subsidies, free market economics, and world trade, and leaving the hearing as far apart as they entered. In retrospect, the farmers lost a round that day. Neither subsidies for housing and transportation nor guest workers were immediately forthcoming. A year later, the Commission issued its long-awaited report to Congress and recommended against a sudden activation of the RAW program, concluding that there was no worker shortage, but it tossed a bone in growers' direction by urging Congress to reexamine the strict H2A regulations governing housing and employment accommodations. Broadly speaking, pesticides, immigration, production costs, and labor were all pieces of a larger economic puzzle spotlighted by the NAFTA debate. And the free trade furor could not be understood without looking at the bigger world picture, which was punctuated by parallel talks for a General Agreement on Tariffs and Trade and by emergent trading blocs in Europe and the Far East. The internationalization of chile, a phenomenon present ever since birds carried seeds from their South American birthplace to spots across the Americas and that then continued with Christopher Columbus's voyages, was an accomplished fact, and one that extended far beyond U.S.-Mexico relations. Tabasco peppers hailed from Honduras and Colombia, curry powders from India, and hot red peppers from China. In fact, the U.S. government pursued an active policy of boosting this trade, exemplified by the U.S. Agency for International Development's assistance to paprika growers in the African nation of Zimbabwe in the 1990s.

For UTAF, free trade and its talk of new braceros and mechanization was a bosses' ploy, conceived, negotiated, and paid for by multinational corporations and their friends in high places, a weapon to pit poorly paid workers in one country against more poorly paid workers in another, all the while wrapping themselves up in the rhetorical blanket of competitive production and pricing.

Indeed, three firms with interests in the salsa or canned chile business—Borden, Hormel, and Bruce Foods—sat on one or another of the NAFTA negotiating committees in 1991. UTAF had other reasons for opposing free trade, based on the group's international posture. NAFTA emerged at the same time as the administration of President Carlos Salinas de Gortari was steamrolling legislation through the Mexican Congress to divide the titles of the *ejidos* among individual members and permit their sale.

UTAF feared these lands would wind up in the hands of wealthy investors or foreign corporations, accelerating a process already well underway for decades as companies like Beatrice, Green Giant, Campbell, Ralston-Purina, Anderson-Clayton, and Del Monte and individuals like "onion king" Othal Brand, the flamboyant mayor of McAllen, Texas, and one-time archenemy of the Texas Farmworkers Union, grew crops, contracted with local farmers, or established "agro-maquilas" that shipped finished foods to the United States.

Since free trade would allow cheaply produced U.S. corn into Mexico and possibly overwhelm the technologically poorer Mexican *campesino* who cultivated corn as a cash staple, UTAF worried that members who resided on the *ejidos* and picked chile seasonally in New Mexico might end their days as a dispossessed agricultural proletariat, joining the ranks of homeless chile pickers in south El Paso and elsewhere.

"Free trade is going to push workers off their land," predicted Sandy New. "They're not going to be able to compete with the small crops—beans, corn. It'll displace a lot of workers who, of course, will come north. It's going to be a field day for the growers."

A major crisis pervaded the Mexican countryside in the 1990s, previewing the disastrous consequences of NAFTA in the eyes of critics. Apples from the United States and South America outsold Chihuahuan apples. North American dairy products weaned consumer tastes away from locally produced goods. International competition sent cotton growers back to the drawing board. Chile prices fell.

Amid the restructuring, growers' debts in Mexico mushroomed, with the 1994 peso devaluation sending interest rates to the moon and doubling or tripling loan portfolios many found impossible to pay. At the same time that chile prices fell, foreclosures on land loomed. Pest infestations added to the toll. Harvested chile acreage in the state of Chihuahua decreased from 13,438 hectares in 1992-93 to 8,628 in 1993-94.

The economic catastrophe was compounded by a devastating drought, northern Mexico's worst in decades. The land, even in the once-bountiful Delicias Irrigation District, simply shriveled up as teasing rain clouds appeared above praying growers only to dissipate without delivering the coveted gift. Lands went fallow and cattle succumbed to thirst. It was a good time for the flocks of vultures circling overhead.

"Our producers are now in a crisis," said Manuel Hernández Villa of Delicias. "If the price of the chile crop doesn't go up, the farmers aren't going to be able to pay the bankers and the bankers are going to exercise a judgment against the producers and want to take their land."

A massive exodus from the land was certainly possible, leaving the *campesinos* with the prospect of becoming *maquiladora* workers or the latest illegals—at the very same moment President Clinton acted on an old idea of the Reagan administration to seal off the border. The truth of the matter was that many had no place to go.

One peasant activist, a young man from the town of Cuauhtemoc, had crossed over before, working in the cities of Albuquerque, Pueblo, Greeley, and Casper. In Hatch, he had set his feet between the chile rows and his hands on the chile bucket, feeling "marginalized" in the process. "You feel strange, there's nothing like the mother country. I've worked in the U.S. with the illusion of bringing ourselves up a little economically. But nobody wants to leave their land. One leaves because of the necessity. Here we have our customs, our family, our culture. We don't want to leave behind all that." For him, and others, there was a special bond to the *tierra*, that earthly sliver of "ancestral inheritances that parents and grandparents, those that fell in the Revolution, left for us. All for us."

The Mexican farmer, hailing from a revolutionary tradition whose embers still smoldered in the barely suppressed fires, did not take economic threats lying down. While the Zapatistas of Chiapas were preparing their New Year's Day armed uprising on the other side of the country, in the state of Chihuahua, toll booths on federal highways were occupied in 1993 to the reported delight of overcharged drivers. A protest encampment was set up on the Juárez side of the Bridge of the Americas and a tractor set ablaze in protest. In the Plaza of Chihuahua City, feet away from the spot where Padre Miguel Hidalgo was executed by the Spaniards, a ring of old tractors was parked in a semicircle, configured in a symbolic show of self defense. A group of men—

chile farmers, cotton, corn and bean growers, and small dairymen—protested for months. Some were ex-braceros, including a tiny, smiling man holding an old, perfectly preserved plastic bracero card and chatting with another bracero veteran, invoking memories of cotton-picking days in the Pecos Valley of New Mexico.

The protests spread, spearheaded by the Frente Democrático Campesino (Democratic Peasant Front) and El Barzón, the latter a group made up of formerly prosperous farmers who were suddenly being pushed into destitution. The demonstrations, frequently led by horsemen, highlighted the unrest gripping the countryside.

When former President Bush and President Carlos Salinas de Gortari clasped hands to dive into the free trade waters together, UTAF and Mexican allies reached out to form cross-border alliances of their own. In May of 1991, UTAF and the Frente Democrático Campesino of Chihuahua blocked a lane of traffic on the Santa Fe Bridge in joint opposition to NAFTA. Other bridge protests ensued, arm in arm with garment workers and teamsters. In April of 1992 the union signed a "Protocolo sin Fronteras," or "Protocol without Borders," with two Mexican opposition leaders, Jaime García Chávez of the Democratic Convergence and Cuauhtemoc Cárdenas of the Democratic Party of the Revolution, the 1988 presidential candidate who many believed was cheated out of the office through a massive vote fraud engineered by the PRI party machine. On the noisy heights of the Santa Fe Bridge stood Carlos Marentes, the son of a Juárez factory worker, and Cárdenas, the son of Lázaro Cárdenas, one of Mexico's most revered presidents, signing a joint document that upheld the rights of all workers to "be treated as human beings with the same rights and aspira-

tions, independent of their national or racial origin or religious belief or political preference."

UTAF's free trade activism extended beyond simple opposition to what the labor group regarded as a bad treaty. A member of the national Rural Coalition, UTAF saw a need to build long-term relationships between Mexican and U.S. agricultural communities. The idea was to not only form a joint political force, but to launch cooperative trading ventures between the Mexican *ejidos* and small U.S. farmers—sort of a grassroots trade pact consummated on the farms of rural North America instead of the corridors of power in Mexico City and Washington, D.C.

UTAF and the Rural Coalition hosted an unusual encounter along the border in September of 1992. They assembled an eclectic mix of guests, bringing together Native American activists, antinuclear dumping organizers, small Midwestern farmers, African-American cooperative members from the Deep South, California migrant organizers, writers, Catholic seminarians, and Mexican campesinos.

On the final day, the conference attendees strode up the pathways of the Santa Fe Bridge and walked among the weekend shoppers. A pair of Oaxacan *indígena* women begged for dollars above the boldly painted strands of political graffiti. Gazing into the gray summer mist of El Paso-Ciudad Juárez, Hubert Sapp, an organizer of southern African-American farmers and a Rural Coalition leader, voiced the sentiments of many of those standing with him that day:

"We think that the formal signing of the treaty [NAFTA] is merely a detail. The relationships between the two countries are something that've been in progress for a long period of time. And just as the trade agreement represents the coming together of the wealth and the powerful of both countries, to their own benefit, we the people of these two countries and people from rural communities can figure out ways of coming together ourselves for each other and promoting mutually beneficial trade."

Sapp finished speaking, the reporters turned off their camera lights and closed up their notebooks, and the crowd dispersed, returning the bridge to its chile picker caretakers who guarded it each night, near the spot where hundreds of years ago Oñate's caravan carried the seeds of the future New Mexico chile empire up the Camino Real from Chihuahua. It was significant that in 1992, the 500th anniversary of the adventure of a Venetian sailor that propelled the chile pepper into a worldwide journey of its own, matters of international trade had once again taken center stage, forcing a second look at far-from resolved questions of product exchange and economic equality, labor rights and immigrant guarantees.

And it was perhaps noteworthy that at least one impetus for this reexamination in one part of the globe came from the struggle of thousands of Mexican chile pickers, vital participants in a one-time "mom-and-pop" industry, as grower Orlando Cervantes once called it, now transformed into a global enterprise managed by large corporations with headquarters worlds removed from the chile fields.

In truth, these were all issues defining the tortured saga of U.S.-Mexico relations, present to one extent or another in the chile pepper industry. After all, it was chile seeds from the indigenous Mexican heartland that were sown in the hinterlands of the Rio Grande Valley centuries ago; it was an obscure pepper, the Tabasco, obtained in a U.S. military strike against Mexico, that first whetted commercial appetites outside chile country; it was a Mexican student, Fabián García, who rescued the disease-worn New Mexican chile industry and embarked it on a commercial bonanza; and it was Mexican women and men, in their thousands, who tended and picked the crop for its final trip to the dinner plate.

Chile was *the* hot commodity in a world truly without borders.

Notes

1. *New Mexico Agriculture*, September 1950.

2. Sigurd Johnson, "Migratory-Casual Workers in New Mexico," Press Bulletin 870, Department of Agricultural Economics, New Mexico Agricultural Experiment Station, State College, NM/Division of Social Research, WPA, Washington, DC, 21 March 1939, 4-5.

3. *Rio Grande Farmer*, 16 August 1934.

4. *Roswell Morning Dispatch*, 21 June and 1 July 1933.

5. Hatch Valley Friends of the Library, *History of the Hatch Valley* (Hatch, NM: n.p., 1989); *For a Better World*, New Mexico Extension Service Annual Report, 1947.

6. *Farm Placement Program Report 1958-63*, New Mexico State Employment Service; *New Mexico Farm and Ranch*, September 1965, 10-12.

7. *New Mexico Farm and Livestock Bureau News*, May 1947.

8. *Las Cruces Sun-News*, 2, 3, 4, 5, 9, 15, 23 September 1958.

9. *New Mexico Farm and Ranch*, July 1961, 13-23.

10. *New Mexico Farm and Ranch*, January 1960, 17.

11. Phillip J. Leyendecker, *Annual Report to the President 1960-61*, NMSU, College of Agriculture and Home Economics, 6.

12. George Dawson, "Meeting Labor Requirements for Vegetable Production and Harvest," *Proceedings of the 5th Annual Fruit and Vegetable Short Course*, 19-20 January 1961, Cooperative Extension Service, NMSU, 41-49.

13. Standard Work Contract as Amended (bracero), Jesús María Holguín, El Paso, TX, 29 September 1953.

14. *Albuquerque Tribune*, 22 April 1986; Martin Steinman, telephone conversation with author, September 1986.

15. Erik Ness, interview by author, Las Cruces, NM, September 1986.

16. *Congressional Digest*, March 1986, 83.

17. Carlos Marentes, telephone conversation with author, September 1989.

18. Fred Gjerk, NMDA, testimony, U.S. Commission on Agricultural Workers, Las Cruces, NM, 23 October 1991.

19. Bob Porter, interview by author, Las Cruces, NM, April 1990.

20. *Albuquerque Journal*, 19 February 1990; *Albuquerque Journal*, 15 April 1990.

21. Sandy New, telephone conversation with author, October 1991.

22. *Albuquerque Journal*, 11 November 1990.

23. *Albuquerque Journal*, 1 August 1993.

24. Dino Cervantes and Dolores Huerta, U.S. Commission on Agricultural Workers hearing, Las Cruces, NM, 23 October 1991, *Appendix II Hearings and Workshops before the Commission on Agricultural Workers 1989-93 to Accompany the Report of the Commission*, 816-17.

25. Luis Valdez, "Tribute: Dolores Huerta," *Image*, 12 August 1990, 9-11.

26. U.S. Commission on Agricultural Workers, *Report of the Commission on Agricultural Workers Executive Summary*, November 1992, 1-13.

27. Joe Parker, telephone conversation with author, March 1993.

28. Office of the U.S. Trade Representative, membership lists of NAFTA agricultural commodity negotiators, September 1991.

29. *Albuquerque Journal*, 8 November 1991.

30. Roger Burbach and Patricia Flynn, *Agribusiness in the Americas* (New York: Monthly Review Press, 1980), 165, 184, 254, 256, 257, 263; Othal Brand, testimony to the U.S. Commission on Agricultural Workers, Weslaco, TX, 17 January 1991, *Appendix II Hearings and Workshops before the Commission on Agricultural Workers 1989-93 to Accompany the Report of the Commission*, 571.

31. Sandy New, interview by author, El Paso, Texas, July 1991.

32. Secretaría de Agricultura, Ganadería y Desarrollo Rural, Unidad Planeación, México, Chihuahua agricultural statistics for 1992-93 and 1993-94.

33. Democratic Peasant Front and El Barzón members, interviews by author, Chihuahua, México, August 1994, October 1995, and June 1996.

34. Octavio Legaretta, SAGAR Chihuahua delegate, interview by author, Chihuahua, Mexico, June 1996.

35. Manuel Hernández Villa, interview by author, Cuauhtemoc, Chihuahua, October 1993.

36. Democratic Peasant Front member, interview by author, Cuauhtemoc, Chihuahua, October 1993.

37. Hubert Sapp, speech given at the Santa Fe Bridge, El Paso, TX/Ciudad Juárez, Mexico, September 1992.

Conclusion

19

Surely, Don Juan de Oñate could not have imagined the legacies of the chile seeds his charges planted in New Mexico centuries ago. At the end of the twentieth century chile was virtually inescapable. Upon deplaning in the Albuquerque airport, visitors to the gift shops were immediately struck by the turquoise-colored bottles of salsa, the neatly wrapped packages of pods, and the strands of short $20 *ristras*. Once quoted to oldtimers, the *ristra* prices jolted memories of the five-foot long strings sold for a fraction of the price.

For the tourist to the Land of Enchantment, the plunge into the chile culture was just beginning. Billboards on the highway north to Santa Fe directed guests to dining experiences where chile and margaritas spiced the atmosphere. Below the hundreds of balloons launched from the Kodak Albuquerque International Balloon Festival, whose crafts included a high-flying model of the chile-profiting Norwest Bank's

Miss Piggy, burrito dealers sold out the store to global visitors and introduced New Mexico chile to yet another new crowd. All the while, a soccer team, the "Chiles," played for the benefit of the sports-minded.

On all fronts, the pod's image graced the face of T-shirts, jewelry, postcards, drawings, and trinkets of all kinds. Across New Mexico, from the streets of the Duke City to the dry gulches of Hidalgo County, entrepreneurs leaped aboard the processing bandwagon, daring to challenge the "big boys" of chile capital with new frozen, dried, and powdered products. Undoubtedly, this activity could not possibly have done without an honored and permanent home for chile memorabilia. Over at NMSU a chile museum was planned, thus elevating the pepper to the status of a historic artifact as well as a modern miracle, right alongside the Mimbres pot, the adobe block, the Remington rifle, the Harvey dining car, and the first atomic bomb.

Still, New Mexico was only the base of the chile trail that had long outgrown Oñate's path. Diners, attracted by the heat and sensation, mulled over pepper pods and salsa spoonfuls in London, Amsterdam, and Tokyo. On television, the news reports carried stories of the capsicum as a possible medicine for asthma and allergies. In South Carolina researchers announced a new, explosive cayenne of their own. In the halls of the U.S. Congress, chile heads revived an old bill sponsored by former New Mexico Representative Manuel Luján to once and for all designate the pepper as "America's Official Food."

International food processors, joined by powerful new players like Mexican-owned Mission Foods and Heinz, flooded the market with steamy new wares. Donning their battle gear, Hormel, Taco Bell, and Frito Lay all enlisted in the latest Mexican foods blitzkrieg against old standard bearers like Pet/Old El Paso. Price wars, coupon campaigns, and Superbowl Sunday salsa promotions were par for the course, marshalling in a renewed round of glitzy contests to see which company would stumble and drop its chiles the fastest.

Image enhancement was also the order of the day. Taking a cue from the most sophisticated product marketeers of the day, Taco Bell flashed a high profile on the tube, scheming to flood shopping malls, theaters, airports, schools, and stores with mini taco stands where a customer could always find a dab of hot sauce to make it through the day.

Company leaders compared their marketing war plan to that of the Disney Company, wishing to become for fast food what Disney became for entertainment. "Our overall strategic intent is to be the dominant food leader in the 1990s," ballyhooed Taco Bell executive Don Pierce. "I suggest you all boycott Taco Bell," fired back Pet's Miles Marsh. In a fittingly symbolic act, Taco Bell moved part of its corporate offices from economically declining California to financially trendy New Mexico, locating them on a Rio Rancho bluff perched above the Middle Rio Grande Valley where small chile farming was becoming a disappearing tradition, and not far from the gargantuan computer chip factory run by Intel Corp., which obligingly opened its own cafeteria serving up chile from the Southern Rio Grande Valley.

The slogan "Green Chile, High-Tech and Adobes" was a step closer to reality for former New Mexico Economic Development Department Secretary William García, who had resigned his state planning post for a high-level public relations job at Intel.

Such was the fate of the spicy staple that was once a family treasure of rural, native New Mexicans and a common bond linking together isolated villagers toughing it out in a beautiful but often bitter land where a few dollars from chile pods might just make the winter a little more bearable. On the northern roads to Taos, millions of decibels from the thud and tinsel of the world's capitals and within earshot of the mysterious humming sound bugging locals, the survivors of the great northern New Mexican chile story handpicked their own pods, haggled at roadside stands, and strung together *ristras*. For 70-year-old Paul Romero of Velarde it was approaching the end of an era. After calculating the amount of personal labor devoted to his crop, he concluded that "it's not worth it." Less expensively produced chile from the south made commercial growing in the north a risky endeavor: "You're not getting a good price for it over here. And like I say, commercial chile comes from Las Cruces, and they just murder you over here." Romero, however, vowed he would continue to grow chile for home consumption "just to keep up the culture."

Hundreds of miles down the Rio Grande, in the middle of the boom district, small farmer Raúl Medina voiced remarkably similar complaints. Rival growers were unloading big quantities of green chile on the supermarkets for between 3¢ and 7¢ a pound, and the chains in turn were selling 35-pound burlap sacks for $8 or $9, sometimes for as low as $5. That put Medina in the touchy position of explaining to customers why he thought his sacks were a bargain.

"And I say, I really can't afford to go down . . . I don't think I'm trying to cheat anyone just because I have, say, a 45-pound bag of chile and I'm trying to make 12 bucks out here. We have to try to get a little better price on our crop," he said.

Still farther south, on the old El Camino Real in Mexico between Chihuahua City and New Mexico, the chile trail blazed by Oñate, Carlos Carvajal halted his battered, chipped pick-up and wondered whether he and his partners could find a direct market in the United States for their jalapeños. Middlemen, he explained, were earning several times the price they paid for the crop to farmers like himself. "They're fucking us," he moaned.

The boom definitely had its down side, and overproduction of red chile especially marked the harvests of some years. Barns were stuffed with red chile no one would buy. Processors' "pipelines" were full. Prices plummeted. Old lands reeked of the wilt, and there were plots in the Hatch Valley farmers swore would no longer grow chile.

In productive fields the crop smiled to the sun, but it stiffened as scouts scoured the buds for signs of the notorious pepper weevil, the bane of the industry and sure-fire spoil sport of the party. June Rutherford, whose father Joseph Franzoi helped begin the Hatch chile phenomenon decades earlier, spoke out. "It's going out of bounds," she judged, "people need to cut down and let the industry rest a little."

Few would soon forget the hellish season of 1995, when every conceivable plague seemed to be unleashed at once. Windstorms knocked down young plants, leaving behind moonscape-like blots. Grasshoppers and flea beetles arrived to feast. A plant virus known as curly-top conjured up stands of yellowish, stunted plants from the Rio Grande Valley to Deming. Old-timers, some with better than a half-century in the trade, considered it the worst year ever in their memory.

Vesting their faith in the miracles of science, growers tried newer seed types that promised to reverse stagnating yields and increase profits. Like a fickle and preoccupied Romeo bored with the same old conquests, the land wanted something new and exciting. Whereas Fabián García's No. 9 had given way to Roy Harper's No. 6 and No. 6 had surrendered to Roy Nakayama's No. 6-4, newer suitors called Ortega, Alpha, Sonora, and Joe E. Parker came knocking on the door.

A handful of growers, taking a different approach, contemplated expensive drip irrigation systems to control water allocations and also experimented with organic farming techniques.

Over time, longtime farmers like Rutherford had watched the business transformed from a couple thousand to tens of thousands of acres, and they experienced the competition increase along with the yield. They had also witnessed the bottom fall out of the barrel. New Mexico chile acreage fell from 34,500 acres in the peak year of 1992 to 16,200 in 1999. And, like four years earlier, natural disasters swept the fields. U.S. Secretary of Agriculture Dan Glickman declared 14 chile-growing counties disaster areas, and chile farmers later became eligible for federal crop insurance payments. The Century of Chile was over.

For farmworkers, the downturn translated into frozen wages, fewer hours of work, and more out-of-pocket expenses to obtain a ride from El Paso to the southern New Mexican farms. Piece rates for green chile stagnated in the mid to late 1990s, averaging around 70¢ a bucket for the first picking. Some workers reported piece rates for buckets of cayenne and jalapeño, two varieties that faced extensive NAFTA competition, actually dropping during the decade.

Processors cut their own assembly-line costs and simultaneously raised those of the harvesters by being more picky about which chile was delivered. Demands for destemmed chile in the field were more frequent, though the extra work was not met with an equivalent raise in the piece rate. Field workers were forced to be more discriminating about the size or color of the chile they grabbed, thus slowing down the pace of work in the field and the number of *fichas* earned by day's end.

A 1994 survey of 148 El Paso-based chile pickers found 86 percent of them making less than $6,500 per year; nearly half, 44 percent, had household incomes below $3,500. "I haven't progressed in 10 years," groaned one sombrero-wearing man standing underneath the floodlit glare of the "Bermuda Triangle" at the Santa Fe Bridge. Nationwide, it was a time of declining pay for farmworkers. Surveys by agricultural economists and the USDA claimed wage drops ranging from 7 to 20 percent in the period from about 1980 to 1996.

Yet there were always those at the bridge for whom the nightly chatter about the best fields and pickings were but the faint echoes of unrecognized glory days. Guadalupe Gonzales hobbled on a crippled ankle to and from his cardboard hovel near the railroad tracks. A Durango native like so many others in the southwestern farm labor force, he had sweated for 28 years in the fields and factories of El Norte. Put out to pasture like a used-up draft horse and receiving no income, he was having trouble, just like Gloria Escovedo, in getting his injuries treated. He demanded to know how he might get his social security. "It's my money, I haven't worked all these years for nothing," he angrily blurted out, turning his back to the black patches of the night.

Former bracero Miguel Originales, after being injured by a tractor in a 1995 accident in a New Mexico chile field, was another individual forced into involuntary, unpaid retirement. For all his years of toil, the $400-plus-a-month Social Security disability check he received— his sole source of income—was jeopardized with a cutoff threat in early 1997 when the U.S. Congress contemplated terminating the benefits for legal immigrants. Shaking his head in bewilderment, Originales said he did not know what he would do in the absence of a pension or workers' compensation—benefits still denied to New Mexico's farmworkers after a U.S. District Judge finally ruled against the Centro Legal Campesino's 1993 suit seeking inclusion of farmworkers in the program.

On a vacant El Paso lot, reportedly once used by drug traffickers for midnight drops, and ironically across the street from the Border Patrol's detention center, Sin Fronteras/UTAF finally opened their long-awaited farmworker center in early 1995. Named the "Border Agricultural

Workers Center" and built in a Mayan architectural style, the facility offered medical screenings, social service agency referrals, and nightly lodging for up to 150 workers. "It took a lot of struggle to open the building," commented Carlos Marentes, standing in front of the new building one evening. The Center, which featured an indigenous Mexican theme and artwork, provided a warm shelter for dozens of chile pickers, making it the first project of its kind ever in the region dedicated to the needs of the seasonal laborers. It was no accident, said Marentes, musing over the architecture, that the center's entrance faced south to Mexico, a stone's throw across the train tracks and river.

Marentes recalled how one city official wisecracked to the farm labor leader, "It's hard for us to imagine you running this center. When we think of you, we think of blocking bridges, protests, and work stoppages." "What's wrong with that?" replied Marentes. "The only way to get something is by struggling." But the 10-year effort to construct the center,

Early to Rise, Early to Pick: El Paso farmworkers on the early morning streets, 1998.

which was marked by innumerable delays, did not come without a political cost. Energies which could have been spent on field organizing were expended on countless hours of political battles

with El Paso bureaucrats. In addition, the farmworker center issue aggravated internal conflicts within Sin Fronteras/UTAF, contributing to a falling-out between Marentes and several longtime members of the board and staff. The split became public in early 1995 when some farmworkers walked out of a board meeting, chanting support for Marentes.

Through it all, thousands of chile pickers maintained their customary rituals between the months of late July and December. In the morning, they were up at the crack of dawn, rustling the leaves of another Doña Ana or Luna County field, in view of the Florida Mountains and the peaks of the Three Sisters, less than an hour from the Mexico of Oñate and the Aztec chile seeds he decided were important to take to the new colony of the north. In an old land where borders were a recent, historic phenomenon of national governments, Doña Lincha and her farmworker cohorts from the 1986 amnesty generation could now work freely and speak without fear of deportation.

After nearly a century of border crossings, El Paso remained an important farm labor recruiting center, not only for the Southwest but for other parts of the United States as well. Nationally connected contractors shipped workers as far east as Pennsylvania and New Jersey, where the Mexicanos replaced Puerto Rican field hands and other nationalities in crops such as mushrooms, tobacco, and fruit.

On the surrounding highways leading into and out of the Paso del Norte, the farmworker housing crisis continued unabated. Typical of the southern New Mexico of the day, those workers who could saved up money for that small plot of land in Trailerville. Sometimes, the dwellings were warmed with faulty propane tanks, and in the Deming area one farmworker was asphyxiated from one of the heaters in a shack, never again to see the sun as it climbed above the giant chile fields. Over in Hatch the main Rio Grande bridge

was fenced off and the farmworkers thrust on a new odyssey for cover. The trailer war moved south from Salem, over to the colonia of "El Milagro," and into the village of Hatch itself. Doña Ana County Commissioner Ken Miyagishima, apparently irked by the trailer proliferation, organized a network of spies to report new illegal hook-ups in the county. Zoning laws targeting trailers unsightly in the eyes of some prompted the city of Hatch to issue eviction notices affecting about 100 farmworkers. In 1994, 13 people joined with Centro Legal Campesino and sued the city for allegedly violating the residents' equal rights under the Fair Housing law.

Reviewing records of Hatch Village Council meetings, then-CLC attorney Donna Snyder uncovered evidence of blatant racism directed against the Mexican farmworkers, with some Hatch residents referring to fieldworkers in derogatory language and complaining there were "too many Mexicans" in town. Soon enough, the issue attracted national attention, leading the United States Department of Justice to file its own suit against Hatch. "From 1986, the Village of Hatch, through its Mayor and Board of Trustees, has engaged in a course of municipal action intended to prevent permanent resident aliens of Mexican national origin from living in the village," accused the DOJ. "This course of action has been carried out, among other ways, through the use of zoning and land use policies which have effectively removed mobile homes as a source of affordable housing for such persons."

In 1995, the DOJ and Southern New Mexico Legal Services combined the federal and state suits into one case before the United States District Court in Las Cruces. The next year, Hatch settled. Village officials agreed to monetary awards for the plaintiffs and promised to improve housing opportunities. *Colonias*, which first appeared in Hatch and other parts of Doña Ana County, emerged in the Pecos River Valley and Luna County. After several years it became clear that the unincorporated communities were not going away, and they were in fact being transformed into the newest towns to arise in New Mexico.

The Colonias Development Council, a new grassroots organization formed from the seminal campaigns of the Las Cruces Roman Catholic Diocese, made its presence felt in the region's politics after 1994. State and federal politicians dutifully toured places such as Colonia Vado, located south of Las Cruces, meeting with the residents and learning firsthand about the infrastructure needs. Belatedly, federal funds shepherded by Senators Domenici and Bingaman were spent to build wastewater treatment facilities and upgrade some roads. But experts considered the monies only a drop in the proverbial chile bucket, and the need for a community health and educational infrastructure remained pressing. In this spirit, a physicians' task force called for primary clinics in places like Deming and Roswell. A mobile health clinic carrying doctors and nurses traversed the chile belt, serving hard-to-reach patients. "We need doctors, nurses," pleaded Michael Quintana, migrant coordinator for La Clínica de Familia.

In Deming, the scene was strikingly reminiscent of the one in Hatch at the peak of the chile boom in the old capsicum capital: Instead of the Pic Quick, workers gathered at the Snappy Mart store for employment. Bodies crowded whatever lodgings could hold them—campers, motels, and boarding houses. At one house in Deming's downtown, up to 20 workers slept on cots, paying $20 a week for the space, netting the landlord over $1,600 per month. Nearby, 45 or more chile workers shared small upstairs rooms and downstairs bunk beds in a cramped but cozy guesthouse that the proprietor compared to a "European hostel." Between dinner and bedtime, several minimum-wage earning renters explained why they had come, complaining about the lower salaries and high cost of living in Mexico. Honing his laundry and cooking skills, one man admitted to being a little worried about his family. "I send them a little bit of money to keep them going," he asserted, parroting the motives and promises made by thousands before him who crossed the border.

Despite farmworkers' vital role in the Luna County economy, anti-immigrant sentiments surfaced in Deming. Some locals were miffed at the workers' presence, and the city council considered an anti-loitering ordinance. Former patients and staff of the Mimbres Memorial Hospital complained of discriminatory treatment accorded Mexican nationals. One distraught young woman, María Ortega, charged a hospital staff person with initially turning away her sick 10-month-old baby one morning in 1995 because of worries that the mother could not pay the bill. Three days later, Ortega's little Abner was dead of Reyes syndrome.

Alarmed state, federal, and congressional representatives gathered at a Deming meeting in which farmworkers were noticeably absent and vowed to supply more shelter. The old tent city idea was brought up as a temporary measure but eventually not acted upon. Years passed without relief. "We have a housing problem," admitted Mayor Baca in the latest exercise in crisis management. As in Hatch, little foresight had gone along with the chile boom. Fifty years earlier, New Mexico A&M economist P. W. Cockerill advocated stabilizing New Mexico's farm labor force, saying that the "extent to which housing is available is also an important factor on the success of this venture."

"The Bermuda Triangle," El Paso, Texas: At the dawn of the 21st century, homeless farmworkers were common on the streets of the border city.

Decades had gone by since Cockerill's observation and the housing stock was still minimal. But then there were some who had a house but no job. In a small Anthony home, former Old El Paso worker Valentín Parra and his wife wondered what do to with their lives. In 1992 he was electrocuted by an unprotected cable while on a painting assignment. Almost pronounced dead, he recovered but was unable to return to work, suffering from loss of strength and psychological difficulties. His workers' compensation was running out and he didn't know where a substitute income would come from. "He worked 8, 10, 15 hours a day, he put in his 8 hours at work and came home and did the yard work," said his wife, Esperanza Parra. "We lived on a little farm and he raised nuts, and now he doesn't work . . . in a half hour he gets tired."

Esperanza's friend Diana Sosa, who called to break the bad news of Valentín's near-fatal electrical encounter to his wife, recalled other people who had been injured processing chile, sometimes left without either their physical stamina or an adequate pension to enjoy their golden years.

Back on the farm, a few chile-picking machines clanked the sound of mechanization.

World economic developments intensified grower fears of losing out to cheaper competition and spurred efforts to mechanize the harvest. A Nebraska mechanical harvesting company called on farmers to put technology in place of people. "We have also seen conditions where the labor refuses to pick a field because they do not believe there is enough harvest to provide a decent wage. As these labor problems escalate, there appears to be a primary solution to this problem and that is mechanization," stated the authors.

Those words made horse sense to Farm Bureau Vice President Bob Porter, speaking from the podium at the 1993 chile conference in Las Cruces. Outside were a handful of mechanical harvesters on display. Almost shouting hallelujah, Porter declared, "We need to mechanize as fast as we can to eliminate the need for hand labor, so it's nice to see those machines outside."

Mechanization, though, was a long-range proposition. A Las Cruces company selling mechanical red harvesters claimed that a farmer could save $28,000 for every 100 acres of red chile. But at a going price of more than $100,000 per machine, farmers were not busting down the doors to the store, especially since human labor harvest costs were still low. By the 1990s, mechanical thinners had reduced some work. There were a few machines for red chile and jalapeños but none in use for the cayenne or standard New Mexican variety that still defied the forces of technology and required multiple pickings. As processor Don Biad acknowledged, human hands in the chile fields were still a necessity.

But what if, in the not-too-distant future, plant breeders or geneticists designed a made-for-the-machine green chile? What did it mean for the chile picker? What did it mean for the grower? Certainly, a portion of the workers could find jobs on the machine assembly, as Cosimati's machine demonstrated that one still needed a crew, however reduced, to sort the plants on the conveyor belt. Others would find work on the remaining hand-picked farms, or in the processing industry. But it's hard to imagine what might happen to thousands in towns with high unemployment like El Paso and Deming, or in Doña Ana County. Would Salem wind up a rural ghetto in the Hatch Valley? Would more homeless ex-farmworkers crowd El Paso street corners? Would families finally established in the Mesilla Valley be forced to migrate to areas where other crops had not been mechanized and compelled to compete with locals? What would happen to the María Martínezes and the Lorenza Primeros, pickers with little formal education who had made a career of chile?

And what would happen to the growers, especially those with smaller acreage not economically feasible for the large-scale pickings needed to make the machines cost effective? Would they be able to rent machines? If not, would they be able to compete with machine-picked chile? Would they quit growing chile? Would some be corralled into other occupations, perhaps joining María Martínez and Lorenza Primero on the unemployment or career training line?

All these were serious questions, requiring planning and foresight, little of which was evident in the New Mexico of the 1990s. In the foreground lay the issue of mechanization's social cost, charged on credit and accrued with long-term interest over decades as thousands of human beings were drawn to the New Mexico chile fields year after year, eventually given legal status to stay, and sold plots to erect their trailer homes. Lourna Bourg of the Southern Mutual Help Association, a group that worked with displaced Louisiana sugar cane harvesters, noted that environmental impact statements were required of large-scale developments, and "we sure as heck should be able to do economic impacts."

Other crops had been partially or completely mechanized in the past—sugar beets, tomatoes, cotton, and Louisiana sugar cane. There were both positive and negative outcomes. While relieving to the human body, mechanization had also introduced a whole new set of social problems. On a historical level, crop mechanization temporarily left hundreds of thousands of Mexican braceros with little work and inspired the creation of the low-wage maquiladoras along the U.S.-Mexico border, an industry which in turn created new dilemmas of pollution, family breakdown, and job dislocation far from the transferred factory site.

But in the bigger picture, machine harvesting never really eliminated stoop labor on the farm. While one crop used machine power another took people power. So for the foreseeable future at least, there would be field workers toiling away at dawn's break on the farms of the Rio Grande, Pecos, Mimbres, and Animas valleys. And solutions to the problems they faced demanded action in southern New Mexico and west Texas.

Back in 1992, three Roman Catholic leaders, El Paso Bishop Raymundo Peña, Las Cruces Bishop Ricardo Ramírez, and Juárez Bishop Juan Sandoval Iñigues, came together to issue their statement on the chile industry, suggesting a few pennies' increase for each bottle of salsa to alleviate low-wage problems. They added, "everyone in the food chain bears responsibility. That includes the growers, contractors, processors, marketers, as well as the consumers. . . ."

In that same quincentennial year, a film entitled *Green Gold: From the Maya to the Moon* celebrating the Columbian exchange—or pillage, depending on one's viewpoint—was released, featuring the chile pepper as one of the miracle plants appropriated by the Old World.

A half millennium later, New Mexico chile was indeed gold for some, but barely a copper penny for others. So as the New Mexico chile industry approached the twenty-first century, it was strapped with a historical legacy that would tailor whatever space-age suit its commanders had in mind, with one foot stepping out to the twenty-first century, the other stuck in the nineteenth century. Such was the backdrop to another season in chile country. Below the Florida Mountains in the undeclared chile capital of Luna County, the irrigation pumps sucking deep into the desert ground nourished the rows of budding young chiles, while over in the Rio Grande Valley the canals were burst open and filled with the once frosty magic waters of the distant Rio Arriba mountains.

Farmers in Artesia, in Socorro, in the Española Valley, in Deming, in Hatch, and in Las Cruces wondered what plague of nature—wilt, weevil, or water—was in store for them this year. In the border cities and far over to the west and east coasts, the food processors prepared for another year, unloading their crates and mash barrels, tuning up their transport trucks, reviewing the applications of job seekers, and cranking up the roasters and eye-stinging assembly lines.

And at the foot of the Santa Fe Bridge, in the middle of that international collision zone known as El Paso-Ciudad Juárez, someone belted out a few lyrics to the women and men headed for the hot, muddy fields of the Chile Empire.

Notes

1. *Agricultural Research*, U.S. Department of Agriculture, February 1993.

2. *Advertising Age*, 8 February 1993, 3.

3. *St. Louis Business Journal*, 5 April 1993.

4. *Restaurant Business*, 10 August 1993.

5. Ray Montgomery, Poor Folks Corporation, interview by author, Albuquerque, NM, February 1995.

6. Leaflet distributed at anti-Proposition 187 rally, Albuquerque, NM, February 1995.

7. *New Mexico Progress* (Sunwest Bank), June 1993.

8. Paul Romero, interview by author, Santa Fe, NM, September 1993.

9. Raúl Medina, interview by author, Garfield, NM, September 1992.

10. Carlos Carvajal, interview by author, Chihuahua, Mexico, October 1993.

11. June Rutherford, interview by author, Hatch, NM, September 1993.

12. *Albuquerque Journal*, 4 September and 23 October 1999.

13. *New Mexico Agricultural Statistics*, USDA/NMDA, Las Cruces, NM, 1992, 1993, 1994, 1995, 1996, 1999; author's interviews with farmers and county extension agents, Luna and Doña Ana counties, August 1994 and August 1995.

14. Tierra Del Sol Housing Corporation (Las Cruces, NM), *Farm Labor Housing Survey*, 1995.

15. Guadalupe Gonzales and chile pickers, interviews by author, El Paso, TX, August 1994.

16. Miguel Originales, interview by author, El Paso, TX, February 1997.

17. Carlos Marentes, interview by author, El Paso, TX, March 1995.

18. *El Paso Herald Post*, 27 March 1995.

19. *The Courier*, 10 August 1995.

20. Donna Snyder, telephone conversations with author, July 1995 and October 1997; United States of America vs. Village of Hatch, New Mexico, CIV 95 0636 HB, June 16, 1995, U.S. District Court for the District of New Mexico.

21. *Crosswinds* (Albuquerque, NM), July 1997.

22. *Las Cruces Bulletin*, 10 August 1995.

23. *Las Cruces Sun-News*, 11 March 1995; 15 June 1995.

24. "North American Free Trade Agreement (NAFTA) and Border Health: Preparing For the Impact on New Mexicans," The New Mexico Border Health Council, position paper, June 1993.

25. *The Courier*, 26 May 1994; Michael Quintana, telephone conversation with author, August 1993.

26. *The Courier*, 28 October 1993.

27. *Deming Headlight*, 12 October 1993.

28. Author's interviews with chile pickers, Deming, NM, November 1993.

29. *Albuquerque Journal*, 18 February 1996.

30. Sam Baca, interview by author, Deming, NM, November 1993.

31. Valentín Parra, Esperanza Parra, and Diana Sosa, interviews by author, Anthony, NM, September 1993.

32. P. W. Cockerill, *Labor Needs for Seasonal Operations on New Mexico Farms, Bulletin #299*, New Mexico Agricultural Experiment Station, January 1943, 12-13.

33. Red Hot Chile Pickers (Chappell, Nebraska), "Crisis in the Chile Fields," leaflet, 2 February 1993.

34. Lorna Bourg, telephone conversation with author, July 1992.

35. Dennis Nodin Valdés, University of Minnesota, interview by author, Albuquerque, NM, August 1993. Valdés is one of the foremost scholars on the history of U.S. agricultural labor.

36. Catholic Bishop's statement, Office of the Social Ministry, Las Cruces Diocese, Las Cruces, NM, 1992.

Index